RED FLAG IN JAPAN

RED FLAG
IN JAPAN

INTERNATIONAL COMMUNISM
IN ACTION 1919-1951

Rodger Swearingen
and
Paul Langer

GREENWOOD PRESS, PUBLISHERS
WESTPORT, CONNECTICUT

Acknowledgments

W<small>E</small> should first like to thank Dr. William B. Pettus without whose encouragement and kindness the writers would not have found the strength for this undertaking.

For their contributions and assistance over a period of years, we are indebted to General David P. Barrows, former President of the University of California, to Dr. Clyde Kluckhohn, Director of the Russian Research Center, Harvard University, to Dr. Hugh Borton, Acting Director of the East Asian Institute, Columbia University, to Dean T. E. Strevey, Dr. Ross N. Berkes, and Dr. Theodore H. Chen of the University of Southern California, and to William L. Holland, Secretary General of the Institute of Pacific Relations.

During more than five years of intensive research at various libraries and document centers in the United States and Japan, the writers were treated with the greatest consideration and were given all possible assistance. We are particularly grateful to Dr. Edwin G. Beal, Chief of the Japanese Section of The Library of Congress and to his assistants, Mr. Andrew Y. Kuroda and Mrs. Lillian K. Takeshita. To Dr. Nobutaka Ike, Curator of the Japanese and Korean Collections at the Hoover Institute and Library, Stanford, California, we owe a similar debt of gratitude.

To list all those who assisted us in various capacities both in this country and abroad would be an impossible task. Nevertheless, without in any sense minimizing our debt to others not mentioned here, we should like to include a special word of appreciation for Mrs. Olga H. Gankin, Assistant to the Director, Hoover Institute and Library, for Dr. Raymond Firth of the University of London, for Mrs. Evelyn Colbert of the U.S. Department of State, for Dr. Kazuo Kawai, formerly Professor at Stanford University, for Messrs. H. Yamakawa, M. Sano, S. Nabeyama, S. Mitamura, and J. Kazama, former leaders of the Japanese Communist Party, and for Mr. M. Ogawa of the *Nippon Times* and Mr. N. Yoshioka of the Far Eastern Affairs Research Association (*Kyokuto Jijo Kenkyukai*), whose continued interest and efforts on our behalf have been invaluable.

Dr. Edwin O. Reischauer, Dr. Merle Fainsod, and Dr. Toshio Tsukahira of Harvard University, Dr. Hugh Borton and Sir George B. Sansom of Columbia University, and Dr. Allan B. Cole, formerly of Claremont Colleges, read all or part of the manuscript. Their sacrifice in time and energy and helpful suggestions are gratefully acknowledged, although the writers are, of course, solely responsible for any errors in fact or opinion that may remain.

Acknowledgments

In preparing the manuscript for publication, we were indeed fortunate to have had such competent and devoted editors. Miss Emily Brown, with the assistance of Miss Janet Lemon, helped us immensely with revisions and corrections of the first and second drafts. We cannot adequately express our appreciation for the continued, patient assistance of Miss Shirley Duncan, who, after offering a number of valuable suggestions with respect to organization and style, edited and typed the entire manuscript in its final form.

Los Angeles
February 21, 1952

R. S.
P. L.

Contents

Introduction

ONE of the major themes of the history of our times is the impact of the technically more advanced civilization of the peoples of the Occident on the numerically greater peoples of the Eastern world. The billion and more people of Asia are reeling from the physical and spiritual blow of that impact. Their traditional civilizations have been shaken, in some places shattered, and the waves of the shock have carried back to the Western world.

Another great theme of contemporary history is the growing conflict between two contradictory forces which have emerged from Western society. Though antithetical, both are the product of common factors, such as the increasing complexity and integration of modern life and the rapidly improving means of communication. In some parts of the Western world the people have been developing greater and more perfect democratic controls over government and the other central organs of society; in other parts of the same Western world it has been instead the few who manipulate the machine of government who have been developing ever greater and more thorough controls over the details of the lives and the very thoughts of the citizens. The struggle between totalitarianism and the free societies has been shaping up for some time; the half-concealed, half-open war of the Communists upon the Western democracies represents merely the latest phase of this struggle within our own civilization.

In Asia these two great themes of modern times have tended to merge. Communism and democracy are both part of the same Western civilization which is having so violent an effect upon the East. They may be in conflict with each other, but this conflict, far from lessening the force of the Western impact on Asia, has made its effects all the more chaotic.

Marx believed that Communism would succeed first in the most advanced and most industrialized parts of the world. Paradoxically, it has won out only in the more backward areas. The strength of the Communists in any Western country tends to be in inverse ratio to that country's economic advancement. Wherever the urban industrial worker has had a voice in government, he has repudiated the proletarian role assigned him by the Communists. It was in the comparatively backward areas of Eastern Europe that Communism found its first stronghold, and from there its flow has been more toward the undeveloped areas of Asia than toward the industrial centers of Western Europe or America.

Asia has thus become the chief area of possible Communist expansion. To some degree already Westernized but for the most part not yet fully capable of maintaining the carefully balanced freedoms of democracy or of creating the mechanistic precision of totalitarianism, Asia is the great no-man's-land between the two Western ideologies. Short of all-out war, it is the great area for maneuver—for the winning of new converts and the discovery of new resources. So vast in population is this no-man's-land of Asia that the skirmishing there may well decide the battle between democracy and totalitarianism without its ever being fought.

In this great conflict within a conflict, Japan holds a very special place as the most thoroughly Westernized and most highly industrialized area in Asia. Though defeated and ravaged by war, Japan retains the only great concentration of industrial power and skills outside of Europe and North America. Strategically dominating the eastern edge of the great Eurasian land mass, equipped with an industrial plant which in the aggregate dwarfs that of the few other manufacturing centers of Asia, and possessing a population of eighty-four million highly industrious, skilled, and literate people, Japan still remains the strategic center of Eastern Asia. Its industrial capacity could spell the difference between success and failure for the economic hopes of Communists or liberals in that whole part of the globe. Japanese military power could be even more immediately decisive. At present it is nonexistent, but, if recreated with wholehearted determination—and any Communist regime in Japan would no doubt restore it as rapidly as possible—it could within two or three years profoundly alter the balance of power in the whole world.

But Japan's role in the ideological center of the struggle is perhaps even greater than in its more obvious military and economic aspects. As the Asian country which has experimented longest and most intensively with democracy, Japan represents a crucial test for the free societies of the West. If our system of popular control of government cannot succeed in Japan, where it has been given more trial than anywhere else in Asia, what likelihood is there that the other peoples of Asia will be willing to give it as much trial themselves?

For the Communists, Japan appears almost equally critical. Despite all the evidence to the contrary, the Communists seem to remain convinced that their doctrine must triumph through the urban proletariat. Nowhere in Asia is there any great body of urban industrial workers except in Japan. To doctrinaire Communists, therefore, it would seem to be the key country, not merely because of its industrial strength and potential military power, but even more because they feel that logically it above all other Asian countries should be Communist.

Thus, the course of Communism in Japan is in itself one of the most significant phases of the history of our times. It cannot be measured merely in terms of the few million individuals in Japan who have been attracted by the Communist dream or repelled by its realities. The fate of Communism in Japan will affect not only the future of this one important country but to an appreciable extent the future of all Asia and through Asia the whole world.

The story of Communism in Japan is important in another way. Communism is an admittedly conspiratorial creed. Its inner workings have always been carefully hidden from prying eyes. Its whole great home territory has been surrounded by an all but impenetrable wall. We know the thoughts of its leaders and their methods of action only in part, and what knowledge we have tends to be from fragmentary external evidence. But in Japan we find a relatively complete and intimate record of Communism. The whole history of the movement from its beginnings until now has been laid bare by a fortuitous combination of circumstances. Nowhere else in Asia, perhaps in the whole world, is the complete story of Communism so accessible as in Japan. Here we have a unique case study of international Communism—a case study which should throw light on Communist aims and intentions throughout the world.

In no nation can the Communist movement be said to be entirely typical of the movement as a whole, but Japan comes close to being a median land in this regard. Part of Asia, but at the same time the most Westernized land of the East, it combines in its Communist movement, as in other aspects of its life, elements characteristic of both Asia and Europe. The story of Communism in Japan is full of revealing parallels with the Communist movement in the Western world, while at the same time it affords special insight into the situation in the non-Communist areas of Asia.

Our full picture of Japanese Communism is in no small measure due to self-revelation. When General MacArthur released the Japanese Communists from prison in the autumn of 1945 and permitted them to resume their activities unmolested, the Communists reacted to their unexpected and unaccustomed freedom by issuing a flood of literature, which continued unabated until the worsening world situation and the growing militancy of the Japanese Communists forced General MacArthur to initiate controls over them in 1950. During these five years of uninhibited self-expression there appeared large numbers of reminiscences by former Communist leaders either still in active control of the party or in retirement as apostates, many official and unofficial party histories and records of conferences, and the usual plethora of polemic writings and political tracts. These are supplemented by the detailed records of the Japanese police and other governmental agencies, which kept close watch over the Japanese Communists until the defeat of Japan in 1945, and for the period since then by the records of the occupation authorities. In addition, there are many relevant Russian and Chinese sources. Together these add up to a remarkably complete account of the Japanese

Communists both from the outside and from the inside—from the point of view of the authorities and from the point of view of the Communists themselves.

It is most fortunate that two such competent scholars as the authors of this book have undertaken the gathering and study of these ample sources. This is a task of great importance, and they have shown themselves fully equal to it. They have performed a real service for those in our government whose duty it is to be informed on such matters and also for the private citizen, who should have a sounder understanding of the aims and procedures of the Communist movement.

The authors command the necessary languages for a study of this sort, including not only Japanese but also Chinese and Russian, and the translations they have included in this volume are their own; both authors have lived for a long time in Japan, where they had ample opportunity to observe the Japanese Communist party in action; and more recently they have had close contacts with research centers at Harvard and Columbia which are devoted to the scientific study of the Soviet Union and of Communism in general. This rich background has enabled them to marshal the vast body of factual material available to them in such a way as to present a picture of Japanese Communism which appears to be accurate both in general perspective and in detail.

The United States faces grave problems in the Far East. Perhaps the greatest problem of all, for it lies to some extent behind all the others, is our lack of sufficient knowledge of that area. Our difficulties in no small measure have stemmed from an absence of adequate studies of key aspects of the situation in Asia and from the even more distressing lack of persons competent to make such studies. This volume serves to fill the need in one crucial sector of the field and to indicate the rising level of American competence to study the problems of Asia. When volumes of this standard are commonplace and not exceptional, we shall be in a position to face our international problems with far more hope of success than we have today.

EDWIN O. REISCHAUER

Part I

COMMUNISM IN IMPERIAL JAPAN

CHAPTER I

The Setting

THE BIRTH of the Japanese Communist Party was a direct result of the Comintern's success in selecting, radicalizing, and reorienting a portion of the Japanese "social movement"; in a larger sense, the origin of the Communist movement in Japan may be traced back to the impact of the Russian Revolution upon socio-political forces generated by the Meiji Restoration.

About the middle of the nineteenth century Japan abandoned a policy of self-imposed seclusion in the face of Western insistence that she open her doors to foreign intercourse. Fifteen years later, the clan which had ruled the country for nearly three centuries turned over its authority to a new government, centering around the young Emperor Meiji and run by a team of spirited members of the warrior class. These military men were determined to create a nation strong enough to resist the advances of the Powers; hence, firmly in control of the government and granting the broad masses a minimum of political freedom, they embarked upon a course of vigorous Westernization.

Open to world trade and for the first time in centuries able to share in the intellectual life of all nations, Japan experienced a cultural and spiritual awakening. Many Japanese began to perceive—if only dimly at first—that the political institutions of Europe and America were the result of a long evolutionary process, that at the base of the much-admired scientific and technical progress were unfamiliar concepts of individual freedom and human rights. Eager to learn about the civilizations which had proved materially superior to that of feudal Japan, they began to sample a wide variety of Western writings and to examine the social and political philosophies which had made these civilizations possible. In answer to the continued demand for self-government, the ruling oligarchy in 1889 finally granted a constitution providing for a Diet chosen by a limited electorate.

As the Japanese studied the political philosophies of the West, they inevitably came in contact with the rising tide of socialist thought in Europe. Socialist ideas soon were flowing freely into Japan, where they met with sympathetic response among those who were then clamoring for freedom and justice. But, except for a short-lived attempt to establish a socialist party, the Japanese socialist movement as a political force remained largely in the realm of theory until the war with China toward the end of the century.

The Sino-Japanese War stimulated industrial expansion in Japan and swelled the ranks of labor. Factories multiplied, and profits increased sharply; but the growing army of industrial workers did not share in the fruits of the wartime boom. Long working hours, extremely low wages, and deplorable working conditions continued to characterize the Japanese labor scene. It is not surprising then that Japan's first labor union should have been formed about this time. Largely responsible for its subsequent growth was Sen Katayama, one of Japan's leading socialists who had just returned from a prolonged stay in the United States. *Labor World (Rodo Sekai)*, a small journal which Katayama founded in Tokyo, became the voice of socialism and exerted a marked influence on the workers of Japan. Who would not be moved by this familiar passage from its pages:

> The people are silent. I will be the advocate of this silence. I will speak for the dumb; I will speak for the despairing silent ones; I will interpret their stammerings; I will interpret the grumblings, murmurings, the tumults of the crowds, the complaints, the cries of men who have been so degraded by suffering and ignorance that they have no strength to voice their wrongs. I will be the word of the people. I will be the bleeding mouth from which the gag has been snatched. I will say everything.

As the twentieth century dawned, the prospects for the socialist labor movement in Japan appeared bright. Since the formation of the first union, three years earlier, there had been a steady increase in the number of labor organizations; minor successes had been scored through a series of strikes; and a general interest in social reform was in evidence. But in the spring of the year the Japanese Diet, composed almost exclusively of members of the wealthier class, passed a law declaring it a crime to agitate for higher wages or lower land rents and prohibiting workers and farmers from organizing.

With the opportunity for labor agitation gone, the political field seemed to offer the next best hope of improving the lot of the masses, and Japan's socialists were quick to see the possibilities. In the spring of 1901 Sen Katayama and Shusui Kotoku, another prominent socialist, organized the Social Democratic Party, the first genuinely socialist political organization in Japan. On the same day, Katayama was summoned to the Home Ministry and instructed to disband his group.

Prohibited from actively engaging in politics, the Japanese socialists turned their attention to "nonpolitical" work, the dissemination of socialist ideas. These were the fertile years for the "social movement." Socialism became the topic of discussion among liberal intellectuals and workers alike; Katayama and his associates toured the country holding meetings and speaking of peace and justice; idealistic young students like Kanson Arahata (later one of Japan's leading Marxists) pushed handcarts piled high with socialist literature into the most remote corners of Japan. Humanitarians and Marxists, to a large extent progressive liberals and very often Christians, the early Japanese socialists were bound together by common ideals of social justice and international brotherhood rather than by economic theory or political doctrine.

When war with Russia threatened in 1904, the Japanese socialists pledged to abide by the principles of peace and international coöperation. The opening of hostilities did not change this determination. Although harassed by the police, they continued to speak out fearlessly against war and imperialism. Even as Russian and Japanese forces clashed in Manchuria, Katayama appeared before the International Congress of Socialists in Amsterdam and startled the world by shaking hands with the Russian delegate.

During these war years the socialist movement in Japan grew increasingly radical and international in outlook. Appearance of the "Communist Manifesto" in the *Commoner's Paper (Heimin Shimbun)*, organ of the radical socialists under Kotoku and another important figure in the movement, Toshihiko Sakai, is indicative of this trend. This and other symptoms of a growing interest in revolutionary Marxism alarmed the government. Shortly thereafter, riots, resulting from public disappointment over the terms of the peace treaty with Russia, furnished the authorities with a convenient pretext for suppressing any and all socialist activity.

The formation of a more liberal cabinet a few months later somewhat eased the pressure and revived the latent desire of the socialists to work toward their goal through a political party. Early in 1906, the Japanese Socialist Party was established. It proclaimed its intention to strive for socialism but promised to remain within the limits of the law. A year later the Party was dissolved by the government when its leaders decided to abandon the principle of legality and came out in favor of a fundamental change in the existing order. Behind this decision was a clash of opinion between the faction led by Kotoku (by this time an anarchosyndicalist), who advocated "direct action," and Katayama's Marxian socialists, who stressed the necessity for political activity. The position of the "direct actionists" was strengthened by large-scale riots which occurred about this time at a copper mine north of Tokyo. These riots were apparently a spontaneous expression of dissatisfaction on the part of the workers; nevertheless, they had the effect of supporting the contention of the anarcho-syndicalists, who held that victory was possible through labor demonstrations alone. Since the socialists generally were assumed to have been behind the affair and because the authorities made no real distinction between the advocates of anarcho-syndicalism and of Marxian socialism, the incident served to increase the government's fear of the socialist movement.

Ruthless suppression of anything remotely connected with socialism followed. When, on June 22, 1908, the rival factions, in a display of unity, paraded together through Tokyo waving red flags and singing revolutionary songs, the police descended upon the group. During the ensuing riot, Sakai, Arahata, and other young socialist leaders were arrested. Ten of them—including Sakae Osugi and Hitoshi Yamakawa, who were later to become increasingly prominent in the social movement—were sent to prison in what has come to be known as the "Red Flag Incident." The announcement two years later that the anarchist Kotoku and eleven of his followers had been tried and executed for "having plotted the assassination of the Japanese Emperor" shocked the nation. The resulting popular resentment against radicals and increased police activity led to the virtual end of socialist activity in Japan for almost a decade.

Public distaste for socialism and mounting government pressure stemming from the Kotoku Incident not only precluded the continued existence of a Japanese socialist movement but rendered life itself unbearable for a socialist in Japan. Katayama fled to the United States. Others went to Europe or withdrew to their home villages. Pursued by the police, a few broke under the strain, went insane, or committed suicide. Many died in Japanese prisons. Some renounced their former beliefs. Of the prominent socialists, only Sakai, Osugi, Arahata, and Yamakawa remained in Japan and quietly continued to work on behalf of their cause.

The First World War brought to Japan an era of unprecedented prosperity. The major nations were at war, most of them actively; but Japan's contribution to the war effort consisted almost exclusively of providing supplies for her allies. Again, as in previous years, profits and prices rose; and wages failed to keep pace. By 1918 the discrepancy between war-inflated prices and inadequate wages had become so great as to make it all but impossible for the average worker to subsist. During August, in villages and cities throughout Japan, hungry crowds broke into stores and warehouses, set fire to newspaper offices, and wrecked business establishments. Government troops had to be called out to put down the widespread disturbances. Many civilians were killed and thousands were arrested before order could again be restored. Although the event appears to have been essentially an expression of public dissatisfaction which soon was to subside, Marxists in Japan, Russia, and the United States viewed these Rice Riots of 1918 as the glorious harbinger of socialist revolution.

CHAPTER II

Birth of the Party

TRADITIONAL Russian interest in Asia was not long in reappearing after the Communists seized power and established their Soviet Republic. For a short time it seemed as though the Bolsheviks, beset by serious economic and military difficulties, might be too busy at home to concern themselves actively with Communism in the East. Moreover, on the original timetable of world Communism, apparently Europe was placed ahead of Asia. Lenin had said:

> For the present, Communism can achieve success only in the West. The European imperialist powers enrich themselves by exploiting the colonial countries of the Orient. At the same time, however, they arm their Oriental subjects and give them military training. The West is digging its own grave in the East.[1]

If, initially, Europe had been assigned priority over Asia, it was in terms of strategy—not in terms of interest; for the Third International, or Comintern, formed by the Russian leaders in 1919 to further the cause of world revolution, took an international view of its ultimate objective: all areas of the globe, irrespective of their assessed immediate or potential value, were considered important to the success of the Communist plan for one world.

As early as November 1918, while Bolshevik activities in Europe held the attention of Paris, London, and Washington, the First Congress of Communist Organizations of the East was convened in Moscow. Participants, about forty in number, were drawn primarily from the Central Asian peoples on the periphery of Russia. A resolution adopted by the Congress provided for a Department of International Propaganda with twelve divisions, one of which was to be devoted solely to Japan.[2] The Communist program for Asia thus was launched four months before the First Congress of the Communist International. Although socialist groups in Japan had been invited to send representatives to the First Congress of Communist Organizations of the East, no Japanese delegates were present when the Congress opened, as the international situation had rendered impossible the trip from Tokyo to Moscow. Nevertheless, a message from Japan, addressed "To the Russian Comrades" and voicing opposition to Japanese intervention in Siberia, was read to the Congress by a Dutch delegate.[3]

Increasing Russian interest in Asia found expression at a Second

Congress of Communist Organizations of the East, which opened in Moscow on November 22, 1919 under the chairmanship of Stalin, Commissar of Nationalities. On the same day Lenin appeared before some eighty delegates with a stirring appeal to the peoples of the Orient:

> A majority of the Eastern peoples are in a worse situation than the most backward country in Europe—Russia. Yet we succeeded in uniting the Russian peasants and workers in the struggle against the remnants of feudalism and capitalism, and our struggle was made easy by the alliance of peasants and workers against capitalism and feudalism. And now, a liaison with the peoples of the East is of real importance . . .
>
> It is for you to discover the special types of contact between the advanced proletariat throughout the world and the toiling and exploited masses of the East . . .
>
> Owing to the existence of Communist organizations in the East, organizations which you represent here at this Congress, you possess contacts and are given a further opportunity to see to it that Communist propaganda is conducted in each country in a tongue which your people can understand.[4]

A summary of progress to date and the blueprint for Communist strategy in Asia were placed before the Second Congress of the Comintern in August 1920 by Gregory Zinoviev, its president:

> The Executive Committee of the Communist International concentrated its attention on the Parties of Europe and America. At the same time, however, it recognized that the Eastern question would assume great importance in the very near future. The Executive Committee organized two conferences which were attended by representatives of the revolutionary parties of China, Korea, Armenia, Persia, Turkey, India, and other countries of the Orient. As far as possible, the Executive Committee attempted to satisfy the spiritual needs of the revolutionary movement in the above countries. A large congress of peoples of the Near East—and, in so far as is possible, those of the Far East—has been called for August 15, 1920 at Baku, capital of Red Azerbaijan. The Executive Committee hopes that the delegates to the Second Congress will be able to be present at this conference . . .
>
> The Executive Committee is convinced that the forthcoming Baku Congress will have great historical significance. At the same time, the Committee realizes that its work on the Eastern question up to now has been far from adequate. The coming Congress of the Communist International must give precise directions to the Commu-

nists of the Eastern countries. The next Executive Committee shall determine the exact line of action for our partisans in these countries and render them all possible assistance in the approaching gigantic struggle.[5]

The Baku Congress of Nations of the Orient finally was convened in September 1920 after a series of frantic last-minute preparations. In terms of the Far East, its importance should not be overrated. Chief concern of the delegates was the matter of British imperialism in the Middle East. Nevertheless, the representatives of the Eastern nations, including Japan, were urged to rise and unite with the revolutionary workers of the West in a "holy war under the red banner of the Communist International".[6] Owing to the presence of Japanese troops in Siberia and to the confused situation then prevailing throughout much of European Russia, direct communication between Japan and Russia had become virtually impossible. Thus, only one Japanese, a certain Taro Yoshihara,* appeared at the Congress; and he had traveled on his own initiative from the United States.

That only one Japanese had been present at the Baku Congress should not be construed either as an absence of Japanese interest in revolutionary ideas or as a lack of response to Comintern overtures. On the contrary, the impact of the Russian Revolution had stirred the slumbering social movement in Japan, where widespread unemployment and unrest had followed in the wake of World War I as the unprecedented wartime prosperity came to an end toward the beginning of 1920. A major recession had developed, furthering the discontent and feeling of insecurity among the workers, who never really had shared in the short-lived boom. Looking toward the betterment of society, numerous associations, clubs, study groups, discussion societies, and militant trade-unions mushroomed during the period. Although they ranged in ideology from "moderate socialist" to "anarcho-syndicalist," the common denominator "socialist" was applied to all of them. These groups, which comprised the resurgent Japanese social movement, had crystallized into two major factions: the

---

*Also known as Gentaro Yoshiwara, he was elected an honorary member of the Presidium of the Baku Congress, together with several representatives of the western European Communist movement. Reportedly a member of the American Industrial Workers of the World (I. W. W.), Yoshihara made his appearance at several subsequent Communist conferences in the Far East. Called by some a Party traitor and by others a Comintern agent, he played a role in the Far Eastern Communist movement that is as yet difficult to evaluate. He was referred to in an official Japanese Communist Party publication in 1932, when his name appeared as that of a delegate to the Fourth [sic] Comintern Congress. His name and the text of his address, reported to have been made on the above occasion, have been deleted from the Party's postwar official history, which in all other respects seems identical with the original 1932 edition. Yoshihara was last reported in a Tokyo prison cell in 1937, drunk and boasting in English that he was a Comintern agent.

anarcho-syndicalists and the radical socialists. The former was led by the forceful Osugi; the latter, by the theorist, Yamakawa, and the more aggressive socialist leader, Sakai. Somewhere between the two factions stood Arahata.

In the summer of 1920 the leading figures in Japan's social movement put aside their ideological differences and agreed to coöperate in the creation of a Socialist League, an over-all organization which might prove more effective in the struggle for "democratic freedom." In the fall of the same year, Osugi secretly went to Shanghai where he participated in a Far Eastern Socialist Conference at which the Russian Comintern representative Gregory Voitinsky was reportedly present.[7] In view of the anarchist Osugi's outspoken criticism of the Bolshevik regime, it is not quite clear why the Comintern should have invited him rather than one of the leading socialists to attend the Shanghai Conference. In any case, before returning to Japan, he was offered, and accepted, Comintern funds for the publication of a radical paper after having agreed to take on a Bolshevik editor.[8]

With the appearance in Tokyo of this publication, *Labor Movement (Rodo Undo)*, early in 1921, a segment of the Japanese socialist movement entered a new stage—a stage marked by a more international and radical character and by increasingly close ties with Soviet Russia and with Communists in the United States. Largely responsible for this development was Eizo Kondo, one of the editors of the new paper and former member of the Japanese Communist group in New York.

Kondo, an adventurous youth, left Japan for the United States at the age of nineteen to learn something of the West. Perennially short of funds, he was obliged to work his way through school and subsequently toured the country arranging exhibits of Japanese color prints in the major cities of the United States. Still later, in New York, Kondo supported himself by running a one-man mail-order house devoted to Oriental art supplies. It was during World War I that he became acquainted with the Japanese socialist exile, Sen Katayama, who converted him to Marxism. Kondo and Katayama were among the first members of the Revolutionary Propaganda League, a secret, radical organization in New York and a forerunner of the American Communist Party.

The revolution in Russia and the Rice Riots in Japan deeply moved Japanese Marxists in the United States and apparently convinced Katayama and Kondo that the situation at home was ripe for the creation of a Communist Party. They agreed that Katayama would go to Russia to seek assistance among the Bolsheviks, while Kondo would return immediately to Japan to gather sympathizers and to organize them into a revolutionary force. Katayama left for Russia by way of Mexico, and Kondo sailed from San Francisco on the "Korea Maru" in May 1919.

Upon arriving in Japan he approached Katayama's old friends, subsequently became an active member of the Socialist League, and eventually was appointed by Osugi as his editorial chief in the first Comintern-sponsored publication in Japan.

While still on the staff of this anarchist paper, Kondo quietly began to advance his plans for the establishment of a Communist Party in Japan. By the spring of 1921 he had succeeded in interesting the recognized leaders of Japanese socialism—Sakai, Yamakawa, and Arahata—in his scheme. This small group of sympathizers agreed to send Kondo to China to seek more substantial Comintern support. Shortly thereafter he appeared in Shanghai.

A Comintern committee of twelve Chinese and Koreans, presided over by Pak Chin Shum, who had been sent from Moscow, listened to Kondo's report on the situation in Japan and made available to him a first installment of six thousand three hundred yen (about three thousand dollars)[9] for organizational expenses and propaganda work in Japan. On that occasion Kondo and another Japanese of his choice were invited to represent their nation at the Third Congress of the Comintern, scheduled to convene in Moscow in the summer of 1921.[10]

The truce between the Japanese socialists, whose radical wing gradually moved toward full acceptance and support of the Bolshevik stand, and the anarchists, was of only a temporary nature. Moreover, the Socialist League was suppressed by the government in the spring of 1921 before it had been able to consolidate its heterogeneous components. Even without police interference, it is improbable that the League could have survived the latent ideological conflict which had existed within the organization from the outset. Friction between anti-Bolshevik anarcho-syndicalists and pro-Bolshevik socialists increased gradually, leading to sharp exchanges of words in the columns of their respective publications and to an obstinate struggle for domination of Japan's growing trade-union movement.

When Kondo returned from Shanghai in the late spring, this schism had reached a critical stage; and the more radical socialists, who were awaiting his arrival, were ready to accept the necessity for a political party which would exclude the anarchists. The formation of this new party was slightly delayed by the untimely arrest of its would-be founder shortly after he had set foot on the soil of Japan. After a few weeks the Japanese authorities released Kondo for lack of evidence when he promised not to use for revolutionary purposes the unusually large amount of American currency he was carrying at the time of his detention.

In Moscow, as the Third Congress of the Comintern convened during the summer of 1921, Zinoviev stressed the importance of Japan to the world-wide revolutionary movement. The Russian emphasized: "It is essential that we should have better communications with Japan; we must secure a foothold in Japan."*

The Comintern's hopes for a Japanese Party appeared on the surface to have come a step closer to fulfillment in August 1921 with the formation of Kondo's Dawn People's (workers') Communist Party *(Gyomin Kyosanto)*.† Actually this small organization, despite its name and backing, failed to obtain Comintern recognition and never was regarded as a Communist Party in the Russian sense of the word. Kondo characterized his group as "an inevitable stage in the development of the revolutionary movement in Japan. Like a chaotic, formless nebula condensing into a star of definite shape, the Dawn People's Communist Party," he said, "was a product of the confused whirlpool of socialists, anarchists, and social democrats."[11] This description is not quite accurate for, in fact, none of Japan's leading socialists had participated in this association of enthusiastic students.

Probably upon the suggestion of Katayama, Chang T'ai-lei,‡ a Chinese member of the Third International, bearing funds and instructions, secretly visited Japan in the fall of 1921. In Tokyo he approached leaders of various radical groups (including the Dawn People's Communist Party) whom he urged to select promising young men for a Japanese delegation to a Far Eastern people's congress. The first delegate to leave Japan was Kyuichi Tokuda,§ a lawyer and one of Yamakawa's young disciples.

After a preliminary conference at Irkutsk, Siberia, toward the end of the year, the First Congress of the Toilers of the Far East opened in Moscow on January 21, 1922.[12] The purpose of the Congress was to devise ways and means of strengthening the Communist movement in Asia. Delegates included sympathizers from China, Korea, Mongolia, the Philippines, Java, America, and Japan. The Japanese delegation was a motley crowd; socialists and anarchists were present, as were Sen Katayama and Mosaburo Suzuki‖ and a number of others from the Japanese Communist group in the United States. Kiyoshi Takase spoke for the Dawn People's Communist Party, while the Wednesday Society

---

*Zinoviev, *Report on the Executive Committee of the Communist International for 1920-1921*. Moscow, [1922], p. 52. At this time Japan was still actively engaged in intervention in Siberia. The presence of Japanese troops in the area made travel between Japan and Russia difficult for Communist agents.

†Naimusho (Japanese Home Ministry), *Kyosanshugi undo gaikan* (Outline of the Communist Movement). Typewritten. [1934], chap. I, sec. 1. The name was derived from the *Gyomin-kai*, the Dawn People's Club, whose members formed the nucleus of the "Party."

‡In most Japanese works erroneously referred to as Chang T'ai-lo, he had been a young professor in Shanghai. He was among the founders of the Communist Party of China and had attended the Third Congress of the Comintern, held a few months before his arrival in Japan.

§Currently Secretary General of the Communist Party of Japan.

‖In the postwar period, one of the leaders of the Japanese Socialist Party.

(a group of politically inclined intellectuals led by Yamakawa and Arahata) was represented by Tokuda.[13]

By the end of the Congress there could no longer be any doubt that the Comintern was actively interested in Japan. In an appeal before the delegates Zinoviev stated:

> There is no issue without Japan; the Japanese proletariat holds in its hands the key to the solution of the Far Eastern question, and the presence at this Congress of the representatives of the Japanese workers is our only serious guarantee that we are at least starting on our way to a true solution of the problem.
>
> The only thing that really can solve the Far Eastern question is the defeat of the Japanese bourgeois and the final victory of the revolution in Japan . . . The greater then is the responsibility of the young Japanese proletariat.[14]

To the Japanese delegates the international atmosphere of the Russian capital must have seemed very different from the provincialism which characterized the home islands. Talk of the approach of world revolution filled the air. With funds and much enthusiasm, the Japanese revolutionists, seven in number,* set out on the long trip across the Siberian tundra, past Lake Baikal through the deserts of Mongolia, into North China and, finally, to Japan.†

When the group reached Tokyo, it found that the Dawn People's Communist Party had disappeared. Kondo and his followers had been arrested toward the end of 1921 for distributing subversive literature among troops in the Tokyo area. The item which brought the wrath of the police down upon the young radicals was a leaflet signed "Communist Party of Japan." Some sixty thousand of these "subversive" sheets had been printed and many of them distributed at dawn to homes in the Tokyo area where soldiers were being quartered during the Army maneuvers then in progress.[15]

This leaflet was considered by the authorities sufficient evidence to indict its authors on several counts. The text:

> Soldiers! Brethren!
> Do you know what is meant by loyalty to the Emperor and patriotism? It means being faithful to and being victimized by the ruling class that feeds on deceit and robbery. To fulfill your duty as a soldier is but to throw away your life for a capitalist state—for the state of an Iwasaki, a Mitsui, or a Yasuda [big family trusts], for a

---

*Several Japanese delegates remained in Moscow to enroll in the Communist University for the Toilers of the East.

†En route home, two of the Japanese delegates are reported to have suffered nervous breakdowns caused by fear for their own safety.

state of politicians in cahoots with the capitalists and riding on the people. . .
Wake up soldiers! Wake up brethren![16]

This incident spelled the end of the nineteen-member self-styled Communist group but by no means the end of radical activity.

Since their return to Japan, Tokuda and Takase had been meeting secretly with a number of socialist leaders to discuss with them the implementation of Comintern instructions for the formation of a "real" Communist Party in Japan. Arahata, Sakai, and Yamakawa, if reluctantly, agreed to sponsor such a party, and on July 5, 1922 the Communist Party of Japan was organized secretly in Tokyo "under the direct guidance and with the assistance of the Comintern."[17] This date is regarded officially as the birthday of the Party.[18]

CHAPTER III

Death and Resurrection

T HE First Communist Convention (Congress) in Japan was held at a private residence in Tokyo on July 15, 1922, ten days after the birth of the Party.[1] The Party's use of the term convention for this gathering is somewhat misleading. It should not be imagined that delegates arrived from all parts of Japan to select leaders and to discuss a platform. In the first place, the Party had been organized secretly; a number of its members were under constant police surveillance. Moreover, the Party itself, at this time, was merely a group of some forty radically inclined intellectuals. Little was accomplished at this session beyond the selection of a "Central Committee" of seven members, headed by Japan's veteran socialist, Sakai.*

At about this same time, Yamakawa published an article entitled "A Change of Direction in the Proletarian Movement," in a small socialist publication, *Vanguard (Zen-ei)*. This marked the beginning of a new trend in the history of the socialist movement in Japan. Since the turn of the century the Japanese socialist movement, characterized by a growing tendency toward theoretical discussion, gradually had drifted away from the masses. As a result, its program bore little direct relation to the political and economic development of the nation. Yamakawa's article pointed up the dangers of the "tragic spectacle" of a situation where those leaders capable of improving the lot of the masses were content to lose themselves in abstractions. The time had come, he pleaded, for the socialists of Japan to rejoin the masses they had left behind and to lead them toward a better future. Thus Yamakawa expressed what apparently had been in the minds of many of Japan's students and laborers, and they were quick to respond to the Party's call to action.

Sadachika Nabeyama, a young labor leader in Osaka, recalls that in the late summer of that first year the Party instructed its members to work toward the expansion of left-wing factions within the trade-unions.[2] In the fall of 1922, at Osaka, an attempt by trade-union leaders to bring all of their organizations under one roof was looked upon by the Communists as an opportunity to seize control of the labor movement. The Party achieved only a modicum of success, mostly negative, when the meeting broke up in a near riot between anarchist elements and the Communist-supported General Federation of Labor *(Sodomei)*. From this

*The other members of this first "Central Committee" were Yamakawa, Arahata, Takase, Hashiura, Yoshikawa, and Tokuda.

time on, anarchist strength within the ranks of labor steadily declined while Marxist influence increased.

The Communist Party of Japan made its debut on the international stage within six months after its birth. Several representatives of the newly formed organization were present when the Fourth Congress of the Comintern opened in Moscow during November 1922. Takase had left Japan secretly toward the end of September, bearing a letter from Sakai to Katayama, who had established permanent residence in the Russian capital. Takase's mission was to secure official recognition for the Party and to promote funds for propaganda and projected political action. At this Fourth Congress, the Japanese organization was officially recognized as the "Communist Party of Japan, Japanese Branch of the Comintern." Zinoviev reported to the delegates:

> The Executive Committee of the Communist International and its Presidium paid special care and attention to the younger parties which are making their first steps on the field of political mass action. With the assistance of the Executive Committee of the Communist International, organized Communist Parties and groups were established during these fifteen months in such countries as Japan, China, India, Turkey, Egypt, and Persia—countries wherein, at the time of the Third Congress, we had only a few loosely organized groups. Numerically, these parties are still very weak, but the nuclei have been formed...
>
> In Japan we have a small party which, with the help of the Executive Committee, has united with the best syndicalist elements. It is a young Party, but it is an important nucleus, and the Japanese Party should now issue a program.[3]

The Japanese Communist Party's relation to Moscow was now a matter of record, and the Japanese delegates left the Russian capital with a program drafted by the Comintern staff under the guidance of Nikolai Bukharin.

In Japan a number of conferences and special executive sessions were necessary to thrash out individual differences before members of the Party could agree upon a basic program. By the time the Second Convention (Congress) of the Communist Party of Japan was held at Ichikawa (near Tokyo) in February 1923,[4] new Party regulations had been drawn up; and, at a meeting in the Tokyo area a month later, Party members agreed upon the following demands: abolition of the monarchy, of the existing army, and of the secret and military police; confiscation of large estates as well as the property of religious organizations and of the Emperor, with redistribution to farmers; withdrawal of Japanese troops from China, Sakhalin, Korea, and Formosa; and diplomatic recognition of

Soviet Russia.[5] There was tacit agreement, however, that, so as not unnecessarily to endanger the lives of Party members, the demand for
abolition of the Emperor system should be handled with the greatest
discretion.

To furnish Moscow with an interim report and to seek additional in-
structions, Arahata, new Chairman of the Central Committee of the
Comintern's Branch in Japan, left in the early spring of 1923 for
Russia.[6]

Meanwhile, the Party began to develop a modest program of action.
The first step in this direction was the preparation of mimeographed
sheets, often translations from Russian originals, bearing crude reproduc-
tions of the hammer and sickle, the clenched fist, or the blazing torch.
More effective were domestic creations, appeals in simple and direct language, well adapted to the Japanese scene, designed to carry Communist
propaganda into the factory and farmhouse. One of these illegally dissemi-
nated leaflets contains a classic example of Marxist jargon with an Oriental touch:

> "The period of youth is the springtime of life," runs a well-known
> saying. But for the young worker can there be any such happy time?
> Let the worker, who is always squeezed, do the squeezing, just as the
> capitalist squeezes fish-oil. As long as the worker is silent, the capitalist
> is happy. . .
>
> Workers, fight! You have nothing to lose and a world to gain![7]

Despite such leaflets, the main focus of the Party's ideological offensive
was upon the weekly or biweekly magazine. It is almost impossible to
draw a clear line of demarcation between "legal" and "illegal" Japanese
publications which appeared by the dozens in the wake of World War I,
reflecting various degrees of sympathy for Marxist doctrine. After the
Dawn People's Communist Party Incident of 1921 and because of indications of Comintern activities in Japan the following year, censorship had
been tightened. Police measures shortened the life span of many a spirited
enterprise and, here and there, removed an editor from circulation. A few
publications which served as Communist propaganda vehicles and satisfied more than intellectual curiosity are worthy of note: *Labor News
(Rodo Shimbun), Peasants' Newspaper (Nomin Shimbun),* and *Vanguard.**

Seldom has a political party—Marxist or otherwise—counted among
its founders a larger share of intellectuals. To the young Japanese Party,
this abundant supply of professors and university students proved both

*Arahata, *Kyosanto wo meguru hitobito* (Men Around the Communist Party). Tokyo,
1950, p. 27. *Vanguard* merged in 1923 with *Studies in Socialism (Shakaishugi Kenkyu)*
and *Proletarian Classes (Musan Kaikyu)* and appeared for a short time under the new
name *Red Flag (Sekki)*, but a government order forced another change of name, this
time to *Class Struggle (Kaikyu-sen)*.

an asset and a liability. These intellectuals, who may account for the Party's inability to win early support among the masses, unquestionably contributed to success in the familiar field of education. The relatively liberal atmosphere of the period made it possible for students and their mentors to gather in discussion groups, despite occasional police interference. Nowhere were the young Communists more at home than here, and nowhere more effective! On the fifth anniversary of the Bolshevik revolution, November 7, 1922, some twenty of these intellectual circles were secretly drawn together to form the Student Federation. There is little doubt that Communists inspired this move. Soon, young men such as Yoshio Shiga, a brilliant student of political economy and an ardent Marxist, were in control of the most active chapters of the Federation— the New Man's Society of Tokyo Imperial University and the Cultural Association on the Waseda campus.*

A growing feeling of resentment against Waseda's ultraliberals led to the creation of an anti-Communist Military Studies Society, backed by nationalist elements among faculty and students. In May 1923 bloody clashes between members of the two opposing camps, at the inaugural meeting of the Society, gave rise to a demand for the resignation of certain faculty members suspected of Communist sympathies, among them Manabu Sano,† a professor of economics.

Sano was born in 1892 on the island of Kyushu. Sports apparently occupied so much of his time in high school that his studies suffered. Nevertheless, at Tokyo Imperial University he became one of the top men in his class. A law degree in 1917 gave no hint of the many hours he had spent over volumes of socialist literature. By that time he preferred Marxism to law, and his reputation among leftist elements had grown. During the next few years Sano was active in the New Man's Society and the Cultural Association, which were to produce an increasing number of young Marxists.

Sano, by the spring of 1923 a Party member, appeared unconcerned when the police began to investigate conditions at Waseda University. The presence of certain documents in his office, however, promised to become a serious problem. At the first opportunity he ⌐oved a copy of Party by-laws and the minutes of the First and Second Party Conventions and turned them over for safekeeping to a friend. That this friend—as

---

*Shiga, who today is one of the most important members of the Communist Party of Japan, reflects: "Of course, the movement was not exclusively an independent student affair; the Communist Party had participated enthusiastically." Tokuda and Shiga, *Gokuchu juhachi-nen,* pp. 113-114.

†On a few occasions when Sano is mentioned in English-language publications, his name appears as Sano Gaku; however, he prefers the alternate reading, Sano Manabu. (Letter from Manabu Sano, Dec. 30, 1949). His name sometimes is confused by Japanese authors with that of Fumio Sano, a less important figure in the early Communist movement.

the police version of the story runs—would indulge in too much sake and in the loud singing of revolutionary songs, thus attracting the attention of the authorities, could hardly have been anticipated.* Subsequent police search of his home uncovered the fateful documents and touched off a chain reaction which threatened the very existence of the Party.[8]

On June 5, 1923, Tokyo police arrested over a hundred individuals for radical activities. Few, if any, of the details were made public by the authorities; and in the absence of a satisfactory official explanation, Tokyo newspapers seized upon the story that the Thought Police† had stumbled upon a plot to assassinate every member of the Cabinet and to set up a Communist government in Japan.[9] The majority of suspects were released immediately for lack of evidence. Those who were held, however, constituted a large segment of the young Communist cadre. About the only members to elude the police were Manabu Sano, Kondo, and four accomplices who already had embarked upon a well-timed trip to Russia.

Investigation of the alleged Communists arrested in June was still under way on September 1 when the great Tokyo earthquake shook the Kanto area, causing extensive damage and confusion. Amid the smoke, fire, and fear several thousand Koreans and hundreds of Chinese suffered at the hands of angry mobs, incensed by wild rumors that these foreigners were looting the homeland. The police found this an excellent excuse to round up scores of "undesirable elements," especially socialists, anarchists, Communists, and radical labor leaders. Ten union organizers were summarily shot, and the anarchist, Osugi, was strangled in his cell by a captain of the military police. Violence reached its peak in December with an attempt on the life of Prince Regent Hirohito. The Prince was on his way to a morning session of the Diet when a Japanese youth opened fire with a cane-gun. Although the future Emperor escaped unharmed, his assailant was less fortunate. An angry crowd mauled the would-be assassin before police could rescue him. He was branded a Communist, tried, and eventually hanged.‡ This abortive attack upon the Imperial family did not improve the Communist Party's dwindling reputation.

By this time a Party convention might well have been held at Ichigaya prison in Tokyo where—with the exception of Arahata and the Sano

---

*Sano himself takes exception to this version of the incident. See Jokichi Kazama, *Mosko to tsunagaru Nippon kyosanto no rekishi* (A History of the Moscow-linked Japanese Communist Party). Tokyo, 1951, I, p. 112.

†Although the literal translation of the Japanese term *Tokubetsu Koto Keisatsu* is Special Higher Police, the more widely known and descriptive designation "Thought Police" has been employed throughout this study.

‡Some of the details of this incident must remain obscure, as the writers' letter of Jan. 14, 1950 to the Japanese Emperor, requesting further information on the matter, went unanswered.

group, still in Russia—most of the important Communists had taken up forced residence. What was left could scarcely be called a Party.

Arahata was busy in Moscow, inspecting model factories, attending official Soviet functions,* and conferring with the Comintern policy makers, Zinoviev, Radek, and Bukharin, when news of the virtual annihilation of the Japanese Communist Party reached him. Upon Comintern recommendation, in the winter of 1923, he departed for Vladivostok. Sano and Kondo by then had reached the safety of that Russian port. They stayed only a short time in the Soviet Far East, however, before being ordered to Moscow as Japanese delegates to the Comintern and Profintern,† respectively. When the Russian relief ship "Lenin" sailed from Vladivostok with medical supplies and food for the victims of the Tokyo earthquake, it carried also a Japanese Communist and a small cargo of mimeographed reading matter prepared by Arahata. The cargo did not reach Japan, however, as the vessel was refused permission to enter Japanese waters.

Arahata's return home was speeded by rumors that the remnant of the Party in Japan was disintegrating. The situation he found there was worse than anticipated. Not only had the June arrests crippled the Party physically, but they had shaken the confidence of its members in the organization's future. A faction, centering around Yamakawa and Sakai—by now out of prison and advocating temporary disbandment of the Party—found increasing support among the disheartened revolutionists. Arahata, in opposing this trend, stood virtually alone. In the spring of 1924, Yamakawa left the Party never to return; his followers succeeded in pushing through the dissolution of the organization, causing its premature death less than two years after its inception.

This action met with the violent disapproval of the Comintern. On June 12, 1924—five days before the Fifth Congress of the Comintern opened at the Grand Theater in Moscow—a special committee was formed to deal with the "emergency" in Japan. Throughout the sessions of the Congress, Comintern leaders, including Katayama, refused to acknowledge any change in the progress of the revolutionary movement in Japan. In fact, Katayama's speech (July 1, 1924) at St. Andrews Hall within the Kremlin, strongly implied a continuing, active Party: "The Communist Party of Japan," he said, "is growing steadily in influence and has established ties with the Korean and Chinese movements."[10] By the end of the year the Comintern, conceding the seriousness of the situation, had demanded in no uncertain terms the immediate revival of its Japanese

---

* Arahata took part in the May Day celebrations of 1923 and addressed (in English) the Twelfth Convention of the Communist Party of Russia. Arahata, *Kyosanto wo meguru hitobito*, p. 33.

†The Russian designation of the Red Trade Union International.

branch. In January 1925, Sano, Tokuda, Arahata, and several other Japanese Communists gathered in Shanghai to confer with Comintern and Profintern specialists.* Soviet dissatisfaction, by this time, had become outspoken. The official history of the Japanese Communist Party records the text of the Comintern's criticism: "The nonexistence in Japan today of any organization to unite all Communists represents a grave danger to the revolutionary movement in that country. Our Japanese comrades . . . have fallen prey to opportunism."[11]

The Shanghai Thesis, which emerged from a week of day-and-night sessions, called for immediate revival of the Party organization, a stronger emphasis upon the role of the worker within the Party hierarchy, and establishment of a propaganda organ for the working masses. The Thesis was adopted unanimously—partly owing to the revolutionary atmosphere in Shanghai† and partly as a result of Comintern insistence.

The delegates returned to Japan, where they were to find implementation of the Comintern recommendations unexpectedly difficult. Enactment of the Peace Preservation Law in April 1925 furnished the government with an effective weapon to combat "the spread and infusion of dangerous thoughts." This drastic measure, imposing a maximum penalty of ten years in prison, banned all "organizing of, joining, or inducing others to join any society which aims at altering the national constitution or repudiating the system of private property."‡ The Law was applied for the first time on the campus of Kyoto Imperial University and simultaneously at other schools in western Japan. University social science study clubs had been organized into the nation-wide Social Science Student Federation, a fulcrum of Marxism. When it was discovered (December 1, 1925) that the Kyoto chapter was engaged actively in a drive against military training, the Thought Police raided dormitories on the campus at dawn and seized printed material, notes, and a number of students.[12] Thirty-seven of them were indicted for "dangerous thoughts."§

In the face of such severe anti-Communist activity, the Party organizers proceeded cautiously. A "Communist Group" was set up in August

*Present at this conference were Voitinsky, Chief of the Far Eastern Bureau of the Comintern, and Heller, Chief of the Profintern's Far Eastern Section. (Letter from Kanson Arahata, Feb. 10, 1950.)

†During 1925 the Russian adviser, Borodin, was at the zenith of his influence over the Chinese Nationalist Government.

‡*The Japan Yearbook.* Tokyo, 1927, pp. 264-265. A similar law was introduced in 1922 but failed to pass. To curb radicalism, which rose with the dust of the Great Earthquake, the government promulgated on September 7, 1923 the Peace Preservation Ordinance. The Peace Preservation Law was submitted to Parliament in February 1925, was passed by the Lower House on March 7 and by the House of Peers on March 19, and became law on April 22, 1925.

§*Asahi Shimbun,* May 31, 1927. Two of these students were to play an important part in the Japanese Communist movement in the early thirties: Eitaro Noro and Yoshimichi Iwata.

1925 to lay plans for the formation of a more substantial organization. At a secret gathering held at Manabu Sano's Tokyo home, members of the Group discussed ways and means of meeting so as to attract as little attention as possible.* The core of this Group comprised Arahata, Tokuda, Sano, and a radical labor leader, Masanosuke Watanabe, who, from this point on, was to play a prominent, if short-lived, role in the Party.

Watanabe was born in September 1899 in a small village not far from Tokyo. As in the case of many of his fellow students, financial considerations did not allow him to continue beyond grammar school. To help his family, Watanabe left the farm and went to work in Tokyo; but a growing, active interest in Marxism resulted in his dismissal from one factory after another. One of the most promising among the young labor leaders, Watanabe became a founder of Tokyo's Nankan Trade Union, representing the extreme left wing of the labor movement. From this position it was a short step into the Communist Party.

The Japanese authorities chose to equate the labor movement, the Communist Party, and Soviet Russia. By 1925, in the case of one major Japanese labor organization, such a point of view was not entirely without justification. On May 24, 1925, the Japan Labor Union Council (*Nippon Rodo Kumiai Hyogikai*) was established by leftist elements formerly associated with the General Federation of Labor when an attempt on the part of Communist union leaders, under Watanabe and Nabeyama, to regain their once-dominant position within the Federation failed and the left wing was expelled en masse. The Japan Labor Union Council, affiliated with the Communist-sponsored Pan Pacific Trade Union Secretariat,[13] was controlled by Communists. Its program spoke of "capitalist exploitation" and of the "total emancipation of the working classes."[14] The emergence of a radical labor group of more than ten thousand members was looked upon by the authorities with apprehension. A strike at a large musical-instrument factory at Hamamatsu (near Nagoya)—organized by the Labor Union Council shortly after its formation and lasting more than three months—served to intensify the government's concern.

To what extent the Japanese government had come to fear Communist influence on the labor movement is strikingly illustrated by circumstances surrounding a visit to Tokyo, in the fall of 1925, by four Russian trade-unionists who had been invited by the Japan Labor Union Council.†

*Two government agencies were responsible at this time for "supervision" of the "social movement": a special section of the *Kempeitai* (Military Police) and the *Tokubetsu Kotoka* (Special Higher Police). The latter maintained resident agents in the major cities of Japan. Blacklists of subversive elements were kept. Individuals considered particularly dangerous (such as Yamakawa and Arahata) were placed under twenty-four-hour surveillance.

†A treaty had been signed between Japan and Russia on January 20, 1925, restoring relations between the two powers.

An elaborate reception planned by the Japanese laborites was thwarted by five hundred police and Thought Police agents who were on hand to welcome the Russian guests when they stepped from the train at the Tokyo station. As an added precaution, all active Marxists in the metropolitan area were arrested and detained until the Russians prematurely departed a few days later.[15]

In December of the same year, members of the Communist Group held a secret "expansion meeting" at the Tokyo home of Sanzo Nozaka,* a lecturer and researcher, and one of the most active members of the organization. On this occasion the first tangible result of the Shanghai Conference—a Comintern-financed propaganda sheet, the *Proletarian Newspaper (Musansha Shimbun)*—was laid before the Group. An initial issue of thirty thousand copies of the newspaper had appeared only a few weeks earlier. Its editorial policy, calling for a single proletarian party (led by the Communists), was to result in the confiscation by the police of two of the five issues which were printed during the first three months.[16] Immediately after the "expansion meeting," Tokuda, by this time Chairman of the Group, left again for a short trip to Russia.

In spite of the government's concern with Communist activities at home and abroad, Tokuda and numerous other Communist agents apparently were able to travel freely between the islands and Soviet Russia. By piecing together bits of information from Japanese government reports, Japanese Communist accounts, Chinese and Russian documents, and a few other sources, it has been possible to reconstruct the route to Moscow as well as the details of the trip.

During this early period police operations were neither efficient nor well integrated; as Sano chose to phrase it: "Up to 1928, the police were rather loose."[17] Comintern standard procedure obviated the need for special training in "communications" and made the journey almost routine. At Tokyo the Party member was furnished with funds, credentials typed in English on white silk, and an alter ego complete with "cover name," calling cards, and a fictitious personal history. The traveler then was ready to embark for Shanghai, a trip for which, at that time, a passport was not required. The new arrival put up at a Chinese inn and soon made contact, through a Chinese comrade, with a Soviet representative in Shanghai's International Settlement. After checking credentials, this Comintern representative notified the Soviet authorities at the scheduled transit points and attended to the paper work necessary for entry into Russia. Then, under cover of darkness, the Japanese Communist was helped aboard a Russian freighter by a Chinese agent. At Vladivostok,

---

*Known also by the names Tetsu Nozaka, Sanji Nozaka, Susumu Okano, Lin Che, and Tetsu Hayashi; today perhaps the outstanding personality in the Communist Party of Japan.

which, with Shanghai, had served from the outset as Far Eastern Comintern headquarters, he was met by a Russian or a Japanese liaison man and directed to the International Seamen's Club. From Vladivostok, the Trans-Siberian Railway carried him directly into Moscow.

In order to reduce the possibility of detection, an alternate itinerary sometimes was chosen for the return trip. This route involved the crossing of the Russian-Manchurian border and subsequent entry into Korea. Border crossings were effected at night and on foot, with the help of a local Communist guide provided by the GPU (Soviet secret police). Once in Japanese-controlled Korea, the Communist lost himself in the stream of travelers returning to Japan proper. Contact with the Party was renewed through the good offices of the *Proletarian Newspaper,* while a seemingly innocuous advertisement in the internationally subscribed Tokyo *Asahi* informed the Moscow comrades of his safe arrival.

Over this route since 1924 young Japanese Marxists had been dispatched at regular intervals for training in Russia. By far the most important institution devoted to the education of Japanese and other foreign revolutionists was the Communist University for the Toilers of the East, known also as Stalin University. This school, organized into two divisions, one for Russian citizens and the other for non-Russians, had an enrollment of from fifteen hundred to two thousand students (among them five hundred women), representing more than sixty nationalities. The number of Japanese trainees varied between ten and twenty-five.[18] Indoctrination covering a period of two to three years, depending upon the aptitude of the trainee, included courses in Russian language, history of the world labor movement, interpretation of basic Marxist writings, and history of the Communist Party of Russia, as well as military and certain other technical training.[19]

While the future Japanese Party cadre thus was being trained in Moscow, the few Communists still at large in Japan made final preparations for the Party's resurrection.

On the evening of December 3, 1926, two men got off a train at Itaya station and made their way up the steep mountain road to the Munekawa Lodge at Goshiki, a well-known but secluded spa in northern Japan. There they made arrangements for a company party. The next morning the "President of the Tokyo Storage Battery Company" and fourteen "employees" arrived just in time for breakfast. The group gathered behind closed sliding doors to listen to some well-chosen words from the chairman. That evening there was sake and song, and party members retired in high spirits. On the morning of December 5, the proprietor of the Munekawa Lodge hardly knew what to think when the members left a large tip but, without exception, refused the customary—and incriminating—monogrammed towel as a keepsake. This "company party" at Goshiki Hot Springs was the Third Convention (Congress) of the Com-

munist Party of Japan.* A skeleton organization and a program emerged
from the short session.

This program, the first official platform of the Communist Party of
Japan, contained thirteen planks:

Abolition of the Emperor system;

Dissolution of the Diet;

Universal suffrage;

Freedom of speech, the press, assembly, and association;

Abolition of all antilabor and antifarm legislation;

Eight-hour working day;

Unemployment insurance to be borne solely by the capitalists (i.e.,
employers);

Confiscation, without compensation, of land belonging to large land-
holders, religious institutions, and the Emperor;

Steeply progressive income taxes;

Defense of Soviet Russia;

Nonintervention in the Chinese Revolution;

Fight against the danger of war;

Complete independence for the [Japanese] colonies.[20]

Although the Comintern appeared pleased with the results of the
Goshiki Convention, as evidenced from a congratulatory message conveyed to the revitalized Party,[21] there was, in fact, considerable concern
with Kazuo Fukumoto's influence on Party strategy.

Fukumoto, a young professor, well versed in the writings of Marx and
Lenin, clearly had been the spirit behind the Party's resurrection. An unknown figure in the social movement of Japan until his return, in the
early twenties, from an extended trip through Europe and America, by
1925 Fukumoto had established himself as one of the leading Japanese
authorities in the field of Marxist doctrine. Japan's young intellectuals
admired him for his brilliant mind and profound knowledge of economic
theory. Some saw in him a second Lenin. When the Party's recognized
leaders temporarily disappeared into prison, Fukumoto's views came to
guide the radical intellectuals who formed the core of the re-created
Party.

A comparative study of capitalism in Europe and Asia led Fukumoto
to the conclusion that Japanese capitalistic society already had entered
the advanced stage which characterized the "declining and distintegrating
capitalistic societies of the West," a thesis which contradicted the Comintern interpretation of the stage of development in Japan. Fukumoto's
emphasis on the study of Marxian theory and his contention that a thorough understanding of Marxian writings should be considered a *sine qua
non* for Party membership threatened to turn the Japanese Communist

*The convention took place in the absence of several of the leaders of the Communist
movement. Arahata, Tokuda, Nozaka, and others were then serving a prison term.

Party into an organization of completely indoctrinated, professional revolutionists, thereby isolating it from the masses.

When Arahata, Tokuda and the rest of the experienced Communist leaders were released from prison a few weeks after the Third Party Convention (Congress), "Fukumotoism" became a major issue. Arahata, advocate of a proletarian mass party, flatly refused to participate in the organization; others fought Fukumoto within the ranks of the Party. The anti-Fukumoto found active support in the Russian Embassy's trade representative, Jacob D. Yanson,* who had been doubling in Tokyo as an undercover agent of the Comintern. His reports to Moscow resulted in the summoning of seven Party leaders to the Russian capital where a special committee to deal with "the Japanese problem" had been set up by the Comintern.

This committee, headed by Bukharin, met with Fukumoto, Tokuda, Watanabe, and other Japanese Communists to help the "Japanese comrades overcome these ideological and political distortions and to lay down a right line of action."[22] Fukumoto was given an opportunity to expound his theory and questioned as to the basis and consequences of his approach. The "second Lenin" recanted; and the Japanese delegates unanimously endorsed a lengthy report on the situation in Japan. This document, which was submitted to the Presidium of the Comintern and approved by that body on July 15, 1927, became known later as the "1927 Thesis" or "Bukharin July Thesis."

After a detailed analysis of political, economic, and social conditions in Japan, the Thesis noted that the development of Japanese capitalism was still following an upward curve and that political power lay with capitalists and landowners. The immediate aim of the Party, the Bukharin Thesis recommended, was to be a bourgeois-democratic revolution designed to eliminate the remnants of feudalism (i.e., the Emperor, landowners, etc.). Once this stage was attained, the successful and rapid completion of a socialist revolution would be assured. The document emphasized the absolute need for uniting not only the proletarians but also the farmers and the small bourgeoisie into a single block. The document rejected two "dangerous deviations": Yamakawaism and Fukumotoism. Yamakawa's policy was criticized for its refusal to appreciate the "evident need for an independent, disciplined Communist Party," whereas Fukumoto's views were attacked for "going too far in the opposite direction, and thus exposing the Party to the danger of isolation from the masses."[23]

The Bukharin Thesis came to the significant conclusion that "objective conditions" for a revolution in Japan were present but that "subjective conditions" were as yet lacking. That is to say: the time was right, but the Communist Party of Japan was not prepared.

*Formerly Foreign Minister of the Chita Goverment (Far Eastern Republic).

CHAPTER IV

Systematic Suppression

ON April 20, 1927, General Baron Giichi Tanaka, leader of the ultra-conservative Seiyukai Party, took office as Premier of Japan. The period of relative freedom which had characterized the early twenties had come to an end. To the new cabinet, the growing strength of the foreign-inspired Marxist movement became a matter of increasing concern; and when, toward the end of 1927, radical activity suddenly grew more intense, the government embarked upon a policy of determined and systematic suppression. A bitter struggle between the established authority and its avowed adversary ensued—a struggle which was to last, with brief spells of apparent calm, for nearly a decade.

In the realm of politics, the battle opened in the early part of 1928 with the Diet elections in which, for the first time, all adult male citizens, regardless of social status or income, were entitled to vote. The political party which was most active—and, in a sense, most successful—did not appear on the ballot. This party, the Communist Party of Japan, had formulated its plans several months in advance of the general elections.

At Nikko, a mountain resort near Tokyo, leading Party members met in December 1927, shortly after the return of the Japanese who had participated in the deliberations of the Comintern Committee on Japan.[1] Strategy was revamped along lines suggested in Moscow.

Up to this time the Party roster never had exceeded a grand total of one hundred revolutionists.[2] The same sectarianism which had resulted in the Party's loss of Yamakawa, Arahata, and other more moderate leaders had made it difficult to enlist the support of the people.* A less doctrinaire approach characterized the new policy: Communist leaders mapped out a plan designed to increase contact with the working masses and to rally the latent revolutionary forces around the new "mass party of the workers."

The revitalized organization was to be built up from basic units, called "Cells." The term itself was not new. "Five-man Cells" had been operated by the Party in the past, but relations between Cell members had been informal and activities had centered about the study of Marxist doctrine.

In the winter of 1927, active Communist Cells began to appear in educational institutions, agricultural communities, factories, and govern-

*Yamakawa's and Arahata's group came to be known as the Labor-Farmer Faction (*Rono-ha*).

27

ment agencies, and even within the armed forces. In line with the Marxian concept of the role of the industrial proletariat as a vanguard of the revolution, a more determined effort was made to increase the number and quality of factory Cells.

The Communist members of the Japan Labor Union Council played a significant part in the formation of these Cells. A union organizer would approach a fellow worker who appeared sympathetic and involve him in a discussion on wages or working conditions. If his reaction were favorable, a supply of reading material was forthcoming. A few weeks of daily contact usually proved sufficient to determine whether an individual should be considered a "Party candidate" (a term used in Communist circles to designate a potential member whose background and "character" had not been fully investigated). Conditions forced the Communists to take special precautions: no candidate was admitted to Party membership until he had been thoroughly tested, thus minimizing the changes of inducting bad security risks.

Two or more members (seldom more than ten), employed in the same organization, constituted a Cell. Here again the Party protected itself against possible police infiltration. Cell members formed an intimate group. Only the Cell captain had knowledge of the personnel or specific location of other Cells. In case of arrest. although a single Cell might disappear, the Party structure remained intact. Implementation of Party orders at the lowest level was not the only function of the Cell; it also served as a training center for young revolutionists, preparing them for political action and leadership among the "masses."

Contact between the Cell and the Central Committee—top level of the Party hierarchy—never direct, was maintained through intermediate echelons, the District and Regional Committees. This system, in addition to its administrative utility, provided added protection for the Central Committee.

A collapsible Party headquarters, nerve center of the organization, generally enabled the Communist cadre to keep secret files out of reach of the authorities, despite frequent police search of "questionable" homes and offices.

The top echelon of the Party hierarchy consisted of an Organizational Bureau (Orgburo), a Political Bureau (Politburo), and a Secretariat. The Organizational Bureau was responsible chiefly for agitation and propaganda. Work among the youth and Japan's disfranchised women, however, was considered important enough to warrant a special section for each in this Bureau. Another section, euphemistically designated as the "International Relations Section," was possibly the most indispensable part of the whole set-up, since through this channel funds and instructions were furnished the Party from abroad.* The Political Bureau was concerned with political affairs, agrarian problems, Party publications, and electioneering. Into this last category the Party poured much of its physical and spiritual resources.

The Universal Manhood Suffrage Act had been passed in the spring of 1925 in an effort to pacify widespread discontent among the working classes, previously excluded from representation in the Imperial Diet because of discriminatory legislation. This electoral reform raised the number of eligible voters from three million to thirteen million, although women still were barred from the polls. The first general elections under the new law, scheduled for February 1928, were viewed by the Communists as an opportunity to acquaint the common man with the Party's plans for Japan.

The illegal Communist Party of Japan now began to utilize for the first time the apparatus of legal political parties, although the "seizure of political power through mass struggle, civil war, and revolution" continued to constitute basic policy.[3] An active Communist minority had been successful in infiltrating one of the several proletarian parties formed by left-wing labor groups, preparatory to the forthcoming elections. This was the Labor-Farmer Party *(Rodo-nominto)*, an organization controlled by Communists and under the leadership of Ikuo Oyama, a Communist sympathizer. By the time the campaign got under way, the Party had succeeded in placing the names of ten of its members on the ballot in the guise of Labor-Farmer Party candidates. These representatives were thoroughly briefed for their new roles. In the Communist Party's own words:

> The candidates were under the absolute discipline of the Central Committee [of the Japanese Communist Party] . . .
> Our comrades were cautioned against the slightest deviation from the Party line in their campaign speeches. They were obliged to include in every speech certain Communist doctrine.[4]

The activities of the proletarian parties culminated in one of the most lively elections in the comparatively brief history of parliamentarianism in Japan. Wherever a Labor-Farmer candidate appeared, Communist Party members went along. Strategically scattered throughout the crowd, they responded to the campaign speeches with shouts of "Down with the

*There were transmitted from Moscow through the Comintern's Far Eastern Bureau in Shanghai. Naimusho (Japanese Home Ministry), *Nippon kyosanto undo gaikyo* (Outline of the Japanese Communist Movement). Marked "Confidential." [1935], p. 1. Manabu Sano, *Kyosanto no seitai* (The Organism of the Communist Party). Tokyo, 1948, p. 173. Sadachika Nabeyama, *Watakushi wa kyosanto wo suteta* (I Discarded the Communist Party). Tokyo, 1949, p. 124. Kyuichi Tokuda, *Waga omoide* (Memoirs). Tokyo, 1948, p. 175.

reactionary Tanaka government!" and "Give us liberty!" Such shouts we frequently the signal for the police to step in, arrest the speaker and h enthusiastic supporters, and disperse the rally.

The authorities found it more difficult to suppress written Cor munist propaganda. Here, the extent of Communist influence often w less obvious, as, for example, in the case of the numerous election poste bearing the slogan, "Toward a government of workers and farmers." Tl line of demarcation between legal and illegal publications thus w extremely fine. Some of the items, of course, were less controversial, ar in a few cases the issue was quite clear. Inflammatory appeal signe "Communist Party of Japan" turned up in the flood of proletarian car paign literature and left no doubt as to their origin or objective.

To supplement the Communist-front publication, *Proletarian New paper,* and the more theoretical *Marxism (Marukusushugi)* under th editorship of Shiga—by this time a Communist—the Party began th secret distribution on February 1, 1928 of an official organ, a mimec graphed newssheet bearing the title *Red Flag (Sekki).*[5]

The Party's efforts were rewarded when, on February 20, 1928, despil police interference and intimidation, half a million votes were cast fc the proletarian parties. Although none of the Communist candidate was elected, the Labor-Farmer Party received 193,027 votes and gained tw seats in the Diet.[6] This substantial showing caused increased fear i government circles that the revolutionary movement might get out c hand. Even though the authorities had been concerned with radica activities in Japan since the recrudescence of Marxism after the Russia Revolution—and particularly since recognition had been extended t Soviet Russia in 1925—the Japanese government up to this time had beei content with the confiscation of propaganda literature and the arres of "subversive" individuals. No systematic effort to stamp out the Com munist Party had been made.

The government now decided that concerted action could be post poned no longer. On March 15, 1928, in the early morning hours, th police began a nation-wide roundup of "dangerous elements." Singlec out for special attention were the headquarters and members of th Labor-Farmer Party, the All Japan Proletarian Youth League, the Japar Labor Union Council, and a number of left-wing publications anc "research centers," including the *Proletarian Newspaper* and a research institute operated by Nozaka.

When the drive had been completed some weeks later, more than fifteen hundred individuals accused of Communist sympathy were in jail. A Japanese Ministry of Justice statement, released shortly after the March arrests, purported to clarify the basis for the government's drastic action:

The Communist Party of Japan, as the Japanese branch of the revolutionary proletarian world party, the Third International, is luring our Empire into the whirlpool of world revolution. It strives to change fundamentally the perfect, unblemished character of our nation and to establish a dictatorship of workers and farmers.

In line with its basic policy, the Party stands with Soviet Russia and advocates complete independence for the colonies.

Looking toward the establishment of a Communist society, Party policy calls for revolution . . .

In this way the doctrine and program of the Communist Party of Japan strike at the very foundation of our nation, constituting a capital crime which under no circumstances can be tolerated.[7]

Despite the growing determination of the authorities and the apparent success of the government's initial measures, the key figures of the Communist Party had escaped arrest—with the exception of Shiga, Nozaka, and Tokuda.*

One of the first to slip through the police network was Manabu Sano, who made his way to Moscow where he reported to the Comintern on the critical situation at home. The dark picture painted by the Japanese leader prompted an immediate decision: in order to strengthen the crippled Party, all available Japanese Communists undergoing training in Russia were to be returned to Japan. These reinforcements arrived by way of Manchuria and Vladivostok and at once made contact with what remained of the organization.†

When the Moscow-trained Japanese reached the islands, the outlook for successful propaganda work was even more discouraging than had been anticipated. The Japanese Home Minister on April 10, 1928 notified the leaders of three organizations that their activities were "harmful to peace and order" and violated the Peace Preservation Law. The Labor-Farmer Party, the Japan Labor Union Council, and the All Japan Proletarian Youth League were dissolved by government order. In this way the backbone of the Communist Party was broken. Membership alone in these organizations now became sufficient reason for prosecution under the provisions of the Peace Preservation Law.

That Party workers were able to reëstablish a nation-wide communication system, within three weeks after the dissolution of these front organizations, is a striking commentary on Communist zeal and revolutionary training.[8] It is all the more surprising in view of the fact that

*Yoshio Shiga, *Nippon kakumei undo-shi no hitobito* (Men Who Made Japan's Revolutionary History). Tokyo, 1948, p. 201. Today these three men are considered the triumvirate of the Japanese Communist Party.

†By the end of 1928 some fifteen such students had returned from Russia to Japan.

the Japan of the late twenties, under its parliamentary varnish, was basically a police state.

The Japanese police official, with his conspicuously displayed sword, seldom considered himself a servant of the people. An effective tool in the hands of the military, he rarely hesitated to assert his authority. His word was law; his actions, however unrestrained, beyond reproach. While operating within the framework of the constitution, the police force too often proved expert at circumventing the existing laws. When "dangerous thoughts" were involved, the freedoms guaranteed by the constitution did not always obtain. The "guilty" remained in police custody for months and sometimes even years before being brought to trial, and in court signed confessions often were produced as evidence by the public prosecutor. Indeed, rare was the case when severe treatment* and "spiritual reëducation" failed to achieve the desired result. From the very beginning the final verdict was seldom in doubt.

The Japanese government felt a definite need for an even more "efficient" police system and for more stringent legislation governing political agitation. On June 29, 1928 an emergency decree signed by the Emperor amended the Peace Preservation Law to include the death penalty. The following month saw the creation of an independent centralized administrative organ for the control of social movements throughout Japan. This agency, the Special Higher Police, operated under the jurisdiction of the Home Ministry's Chief of the Peace Preservation Bureau, an official appointed by the Emperor upon ministerial recommendation. Several thousand resident and itinerant agents, trained in the detection of "dangerous thoughts" and familiar with "un-Japanese" political and social doctrines, were on duty in the various prefectures and metropolitan districts. Working in close collaboration with the local police force, these men specialized in the study of local developments and forwarded regular as well as special reports to the Home Ministry, where a number of high-ranking experts integrated data on "subversive" organizations.

The Peace Preservation Bureau included specialists in anarchist, socialist, and Communist theory and experts on the history and organization of political groups advocating these doctrines. Korean and Formosan nationalist movements too were surveyed and evaluated by qualified

---

*A book of reminiscences entitled *A Woman Communist in Prison*, published in Japan in 1930 and immediately suppressed by the Home Ministry, describes conditions in a Japanese jail and the treatment accorded political prisoners: "They beat us, kicked us, and pulled our hair. They forced wood between our fingers and smashed our hands . . . As to food . . . they brought us rice which appeared to be rotting. The miso-soup and the pickles seemed fit only for pigs . . . They call a jail a pigsty, a befitting name. A pigsty, indeed!" Kikue Hara, *Joshi toin gokuchu-ki* (A Woman Communist in Prison). Tokyo, 1930, p. 27-28.

officials, and certain other specialists devoted their time exclusively to the study of trade-unions or cultural organizations. In case of a strike, the Home Ministry was in a position to send an expert on the particular industry or organizing union to the source of trouble in order to direct, supervise, and guide the resident agent in the field.

Special agents were also assigned to important international centers such as Shanghai, London, and Vladivostok to keep close watch on "subversive" movements or individuals in these areas. Information thus supplied helped a central intelligence agency in Tokyo to establish the international ramifications and connections of groups designated by the government as "potentially dangerous."

The Ministry of Justice, responsible for the prosecution of "subversives," also maintained a certain number of specialists in the offices of the Procurator General. Thoroughly acquainted with all facets of the Marxist movement and with its Japanese proponents, these officials— known as "thought procurators"—ably presented the government's case against those indicted for crimes of thought.

The tightening of security measures which had accompanied the arrests of Communists in March 1928 and the subsequent dissolution of the three major Communist-front organizations had, at least temporarily, eliminated any immediate threat to the maintenance of peace and order. The government, however, was not yet satisfied with the scope of its anti-Communist drive. During the months of April and May all radical student organizations, including the influential New Man's Society at Tokyo Imperial University, were dissolved and a number of professors suspected of leftist leanings forced to resign—among them Dr. Hajime Kawakami, Chairman of Kyoto Imperial University's Economics Department and Japan's leading authority in the field of Marxist theory.[9] A few months later "student supervisors" were added to the staffs of government universities and colleges to prevent the revival of undesirable organizations and to "guide" the students' thinking. The decision of August 1928, at a conference of Special Higher Police (Thought Police) officials, to prohibit all outdoor assemblies and mass demonstrations and to require the filing in advance of programs, proclamations, and resolutions of indoor meetings, completed the series of government measures aimed at airtight control of the Communist movement.[10]

There was, however, one obvious weakness in the government's position: the real source of strength of the revolutionary movement lay beyond the boundaries of the Japanese Empire.

The Communists—among them the union leader Kenzo Yamamoto and the Party organizer Shoichi Ichikawa—who had escaped the March arrests reached the safety of Russian soil and joined Manabu Sano at

Moscow, in time for the opening of the Sixth Congress of the Comintern.[11] The theme of the Congress, stressed by Bukharin and repeated faithfully by delegate after delegate, found expression in Katayama's opening address on July 17, 1928:

> In the name of the Communist Party of Japan, we greet you and tell you that the time has come to prepare ourselves for the fight against world imperialism which threatens our fatherland, the Soviet Union.*

Another Japanese delegate was even more outspoken in his call for action:

> The most important tasks the Communist Party of Japan faces on the international level are to make sure that not a single [Japanese] soldier remains in China; to counter all attempts on the part of the Japanese bourgeoisie to interfere in the affairs of the Soviet Union; and to transform the imperialist war into a civil war against the Japanese bourgeoisie.[12]

The Comintern's fear of Japan had some basis in fact. By the spring of 1928 the Tanaka government had abandoned the conciliatory foreign policy of its predecessor and was preparing for action on the continent. Tanaka's "positive policy" eventuated in the dispatch of Japanese troops into the Tsinan area on the Shantung Peninsula, ostensibly to protect the interest of Japanese nationals held to be in danger as a result of a new Nationalist offensive in the area. Fighting between Japanese and Chinese units broke out in May, and Chiang Kai-shek's troops soon were forced to withdraw. It appeared that the Japanese army had come to China to stay.

Within Japan, opposition to the expansionist policy on the continent became articulate almost immediately. From Nagoya, where the Third Division was being mobilized for transport to China, a new wave of anti-war sentiment swept the nation.[13] Behind this movement stood the Japanese Communist Party, which had regrouped its scattered membership under the command of three labor leaders who had been the driving force in the creation of the now defunct Japan Labor Union Council: Watanabe, Nabeyama, and Shiro Mitamura,[14] a former policeman converted to the Communist cause.

---

*While the Comintern Congress was in session, Sano, Ichikawa, Yamamoto, and Sadaki Takahashi, an advanced student at Moscow, met intermittently, from July 15 to September 1, to formulate new strategy for the Japanese Party. Shakai Shiso Taisaku Chosakai (Research Association for Counter-measures Against Social Ideas), *Nippon kyosanto jiken kyoto hikoku Sano Manabu nado no koso-kohantei ni okeru chinjutsu no gaiyo* (Outline of the Deposition Made by Manabu Sano and Others on the Occasion of the Trial of Communists before a Court of Appeal). Kyoto, 1934, p. 15.

Apparently the Comintern still entertained hope that the Japanese branch might regain its strength, for toward the beginning of September 1928 Watanabe and Nabeyama were summoned to the Far Eastern Bureau in Shanghai.

The Comintern's Far Eastern Bureau was principally responsible for the direction of the Communist Parties of China, Korea, and Japan. In 1928 Yanson, of the Soviet Embassy in Tokyo, headed the organization. Allocation of funds for the support of revolutionary movements throughout the Far East was handled from Shanghai. A steady stream of representatives from the Communist Parties of Asia and America, on their way to and from Moscow or simply in Shanghai to confer with the Comintern staff, passed through its offices. In the fall of 1928, when Watanabe and Nabeyama appeared for consultation with the Chief of the Far Eastern Bureau, Earl Browder of the American Communist Party and Chou En-lai of the Chinese Communist Party were active members of the organization. Ho Chi-minh, head of the Communist Party of French Indo-China, was a frequent visitor.[15]

After a number of conferences, during which Yanson and Chou En-lai acquainted the Japanese Communists with the resolutions of the Sixth Congress and discussed their application to Japan, Nabeyama and Watanabe received funds to carry on their work. Separately, the Japanese left for home despite a warning from Yanson that one of them should remain abroad in accordance with Comintern strategy not to commit all of its forces simultaneously.

Although the police drive against radical elements had netted some two thousand individuals by the fall of 1928, the Home Ministry realized that the potential threat posed by the Communist Party had not been eliminated. It was becoming increasingly apparent that the authorities could not hope to eradicate the Party as long as a single leader was allowed to remain at liberty.

The government scored its first success,* unexpectedly, on the island of Formosa. On October 6, 1928, police agents removed a dry-goods dealer from aboard the "Kohoku Maru," which had entered Keelung harbor en route to Japan. The passenger's travel papers were not in order, and a subsequent search of his baggage disclosed fairly large amounts of American, Chinese, and Japanese currency. While being escorted to the police station for further questioning, he suddenly brandished a revolver in an attempt to escape. In the scuffle the chief of the police detail was fatally wounded, and the assailant broke away. When the police finally closed in, the suspect took his own life. Information in the files of the

---

*It is true that Fukumoto had already been arrested in the early summer of 1928. He was, however, no longer considered a key figure by the police or by the Party itself.

Home Ministry revealed that the "dry-goods dealer" had been none other than Masanosuke Watanabe, the new Secretary General of the Communist Party of Japan.*

Watanabe's death did not have the effect anticipated by the Japanese government. The old cadre—the majority Moscow-trained—had been indispensable to the organization; as individuals, however, they were expendable. Although the administrators of Party policy were certain to be among the members of the Central Committee, even their chairman, the Secretary General of the Party, was by no means all-powerful or irreplaceable.

Ichikawa entered Japan from Russia in November 1928 to fill the position vacated by the late Secretary General. His return coincided with a radical shift in Communist strategy. The *Proletarian Newspaper*, ever faithful to the Party line, in October had supported the "popular demand" for a new Labor-Farmer Party; but an article in the same paper on December 5, 1928 represented an editorial about-face dictated by the recommendations of the Sixth Comintern Congress. The editorial said:

> Lacking a clear understanding of the distinction between a "mobilizing organization" and a political party, we fell into the error of assuming the necessity for a legal political party apart from the Communist Party. We must speedily liquidate this "disbandment view." [16]

The Japanese Communist Party, abandoning all pretense of legality, turned its attention toward the radicalized working masses which, since the dissolution of the Japan Labor Union Council in the spring of 1928, had been without organized leadership. The National Conference of Japanese Trade Unions *(Nippon Rodo Kumiai Zenkoku Kyogikai* or *Zenkyo)* was set up illegally on December 25, 1928, with headquarters in Tokyo under the auspices of the Communist Party of Japan.†

By March 1929 active Party membership equalled that of the previous peak—March 1928—and was still growing. [17] The gain actually was greater than this comparison implies, as police arrests had been continuing.‡ A communication of March 4 from the Chief of the Police

---

*Naimusho (Japanese Home Ministry), *Gokusa bunshi no buki shiyo ni yoru keisatsu-kan shogai-cho* (Data on Police Officials Wounded by Leftist Elements). Mimeographed. [1934], p. 1. According to a notation on this document, Watanabe had committed suicide. The Japanese Communists, however, continue to insist that their leader was murdered.

†The president of the Conference, Tamotsu Ito, was a member of the Communist Party. The real directors of the organization were the veteran Communist labor leaders, Nabeyama and Mitamura, both on the Party's Central Committee.

‡These interim arrests had eliminated among others a certain number of influential members: Ichiro Soma, member of the Russian Communist Party, just back from Moscow; Goichiro Kokuryo, a trusted friend of Nabeyama; Watanabe's wife, Setsu; leaders of the Communist Youth League; and several members of the *Sekki* staff.

Division, addressed to prefectural governors throughout Japan, illustrates the proportions which the movement had assumed. The document told of plans for nation-wide mass demonstrations, "directed by the Communist Party of Japan," and scheduled for March 15. It instructed subordinate echelons to prohibit all assemblies and "where the prevention of demonstrations is feared to be impossible, to take in advance appropriate measures against dangerous individuals."*

Two weeks later the arrest of a Tokyo local organizer turned up an organizational chart which led to the Party's chief organizer, Sueyoshi Maniwa.† A coded Party roster, in Maniwa's possession when he was apprehended toward the end of the month, furnished the police with clues to the whereabouts of Party members still at large.[18]

A second wave of nation-wide searches followed on April 16, 1929, resulting in the arrest of more than one thousand suspects; but Ichikawa, Nabeyama, Mitamura, Sano, and Yamamoto, the real leaders of the Party, were not among them. Time was running out for the remaining handful of hunted leaders. Each new arrest reduced still further the dwindling number of loyal comrades and sympathizers whose homes had served at one time as meeting places and later as hideouts. The Communists were forced to seek sanctuary in hotels and teahouses; but even there safety was only relative, as the police had distributed photographs everywhere. On April 28 the police arrested Ichikawa in a Tokyo home. The following day Mitamura and Nabeyama were picked up at a teahouse in the capital's fashionable entertainment district of Akasaka. Of the leaders, only Yamamoto and Manabu Sano remained at large. With the arrest of Sano in Shanghai on June 16, 1929,‡ the government felt it had completed the smashing of the "inner circle" of Party leaders, as Yamamoto, Japanese representative to the Profintern in Moscow, was known to be seriously ill and considered out of the picture.§

Developments of the following years seem to confirm the govern-

*Naimusho Keihokyoku Hoanka, *Tokko keisatsu reiki-shu*, cited, pp. 105-106. These mass demonstrations were preceded by the distribution of inflammatory handbills and were in protest of the March arrests, Watanabe's "murder," and the assassination at the hands of an ultranationalist, on March 5, 1929, of Diet member Senji Yamamoto, exponent of the extreme left-wing position.

†Maniwa, known in Russia by the names Shirai and Shima, had joined an American Communist group early in 1921. He arrived in Russia in August of the same year, where he served as a Japanese-language instructor. He later was connected with the International Seamen's Club at Vladivostok and returned to Japan in October 1928.

‡Manabu Sano had been serving on the staff of the Far Eastern Bureau since March 14, 1929. He was apprehended by Chinese police at the request of the Japanese authorities. Extradition proceedings were initiated at once and Sano subsequently was returned to Japan to await trial.

§A *New York Times* correspondent reported from Tokyo toward the end of the same year: "The authorities are satisfied that all the leading Communists are under lock and key, although a few 'cells' may still be functioning feebly in various factories.' *New York Times*, Nov. 7, 1929.

ment's assumption that the real strength of the Communist movement in Japan had resided in a small corps of a seasoned revolutionists. The sudden disappearance of the experienced leaders unquestionably dealt a severe blow to the Party. Contact between isolated cells was rendered increasingly difficult and perilous, as a consequence of relentless police pressure. By the summer of 1929 nothing remained of the Party but a small group of desperadoes, advocates of total violence, determined to resist arrest at all cost.

CHAPTER V

Armed Interlude

Th E lull produced by removal of the Party's seasoned leadership was broken in the spring of 1930 by a young and reckless revolutionist whose armed-action squads, for a brief span of time, posed the greatest "threat to peace and order" the authorities had yet encountered.

Seigen Tanaka, a student at Tokyo Imperial University, had entered the Japanese Communist Party in the fall of 1927. Tanaka recalls:

> At the time, I felt absolutely no dissatisfaction with the existing social order. I was only searching painfully for truth and for something which I might wholeheartedly accept as my way of life—a common phenomenon among young people. It was just after entering preparatory school that I first experienced this longing. From the spring of that year I shut myself up in the library . . . searching in vain, until the day when I came upon Dr. Hajime Kawakami's book, *The Story of the Poor*. I was touched by its unselfish love and moved by its humanism. Later I read *Studies in Social Problems*, and finally I undertook the study of materialism and capitalism. Intellectually, during my first years in preparatory school, I, who had started from humanism, had reached only the stage of social democracy.
>
> What especially attracted me to Communism (Bolshevism) were [the stories of] the activities of the self-sacrificing Russian Bolsheviks. I was deeply moved by the biographies of the heroes of the Russian Revolution . . . and by the old Russian revolutionists . . . who selflessly worked for their people and their country. These were the motives behind my advance toward Communism.[1]

Tanaka was an organizer in charge of one of the Tokyo districts when the April 1929 arrests deprived the Party of its veteran leaders and of the bulk of its memerbship. Shortly thereafter, Tanaka, then twenty-three years old, appointed himself head of the Japanese Communist Party and began to gather together the few remaining Communists in the Tokyo-Yokohama area. In this way the Tokyo District Provisional Committee was formed and the foundation laid for an underground organization which, Tanaka apparently believed, would eventually reach sufficient strength to overthrow the established government by violence.*

A few weeks later, the young leader transformed the Provisional

---

*Documents of the period confirm this interpretation, although Tanaka, writing in the postwar period and now strongly anti-Communist, denies such ambitions.

Committee into a Central Group with branches in Tokyo, Yokohama, and Osaka;[2] new members were inducted through the efforts of Hiroshi Sano, Moscow-trained leader of the Communist Youth League *(Kyosan Seinen Domei)*, and through contacts within several labor organizations. Membership dues from this small group proved insufficient to create a genuine Party and, because of the unpredictable situation in Japan, allocation of funds from abroad had been temporarily suspended. The Central Group, therefore, appealed to the many sympathetic intellectuals who were ready to give financial support to any organization which opposed government interference with academic freedom.* These contributions permitted a boost in circulation of the Communist-influenced *Second Proletarian Newspaper (Dai-ni Musansha Shimbun)*† and stimulated the revival of *Red Flag,*‡ which was surreptitiously printed and distributed by Youth League members, principally students of Tokyo Imperial University.

A Party purge in the fall of 1929 eliminated those members who, in the light of developments of the preceding year, were convinced that aggressive tactics were doomed to failure. This group of "moderates" advocated a complete break with the Comintern and was willing to sacrifice the Party's perennial, if at times muted, demand for abolition of the Japanese monarchy in the hope of obtaining legal status for the organization. Strengthened by the expulsion of the deviationist faction, a militant group of at least two hundred members emerged toward the end of 1929.§

During the early part of the following year, in a secluded section of Wakayama Prefecture, south of Osaka, Tanaka assembled ten of his trusted followers. This group, which met for a week in January, selected a six-member Central Committee, headed by Tanaka, and officially constituted itself "The Communist Party of Japan." The Committee resolved to abide by the decisions of the Comintern and formulated strategy aimed at the "speedy development of revolution in Japan."

Armed-action squads sprang up unexpectedly in Tokyo during the election month of February 1930. Units of from three to five young Communists, trained in *karate,* the art of self-defense, and equipped with pistols and knives, emerged throughout the industrial areas of Tokyo and Yokohama to incite the workers against their employers and the government and to pass out handbills attacking, in vitriolic language,

---

*Approximately twenty professors, writers, and artists were arrested in 1930 when it was learned that they had contributed to such a fund.

†An illegal publication (circulation about ten thousand), successor to the *Proletarian Newspaper,* which by court order (summer 1929) had been forced to suspend operation.

‡Publication of *Red Flag* was resumed in July 1929.

§The breakdown of the known membership at the time was as follows: Tokyo, 100; Yokohama district, 20; Osaka-Kobe area, 50; Kyushu, 10; and others, 15.

the existing order in Japan. In the past, radical propagandists always had scattered as soon as a policeman appeared on the scene, but Tanaka's gangs were instructed to fight back. This militant strategy produced clashes in which a number of police officers were wounded.*

By the end of February most of the ringleaders had been apprehended, and the armed-action squads had disappeared—or so it seemed. Only Tanaka remained at large.

The Tokyo municipal streetcar strike of April 1930 was the occasion for further disturbances. This time, Tanaka mobilized radical elements of the National Conference of Japanese Trade Unions and instructed his followers: "Strikes are in progress throughout the country . . . We must take the next step toward our objective by transforming these into armed revolt."[3] When moderate elements among the workers pressed for an amicable settlement of the strike, Tanaka is reported to have attempted to assassinate them after ordering his squads to set fire to the Aoyama streetcar barns.

Tanaka launched his most ambitious scheme on May 1, 1930. As a throng of orderly workers marched through Tokyo in their traditional May Day parade, members of the armed-action squads suddenly broke ranks with shouts of "To the Diet! To the Diet!" Their unexpected action provoked clashes with the police but little else, for the workers were not willing to follow. The police had no difficulty in quelling the disorder.[4]

Discouraged by these failures, Tanaka now accepted the advice offered by his chief assistants, Bunkichi Imamoto and Iesada Iwao, who had been sent back from Russia during the spring under Moscow's reorganization program. The youthful leader apparently had realized that armed action on a small scale could only injure the Party's reputation and supply the government with additional grounds for repressive measures. Toward the middle of May Tanaka abandoned his hopes for an immediate revolution.

On July 14, 1930, more than forty armed police officers, specially trained for the mission and led by a former wrestler (protected by a bulletproof vest), converged upon the Tanaka headquarters. When the

*The Japanese government maintained extremely detailed files on such occurrences. One document from the files of the Home Ministry lists incidents involving police officers wounded by leftists (October 1928–January 1934). Information is arranged by date, place, weapon, name of police officer, and name of assailant. In one case the weapon is indicated as "a piece of glass," while the notation under the heading of assailant reads: "unknown—not yet arrested!" *Kyokusa bunshi no buki shiyo ni yoru keisatsukan shogai-cho* (Data on Police Officers Wounded by Extreme Leftist Elements). Mimeographed. [1934].

Another document cites 160 cases involving alleged Communists having pistols in their possession when arrested. Information is equally detailed. *Kenju hakken-cho (kyosanshugi kankei)* (Data on the Discovery of Pistols—Related to Communist Activities). From Japanese government files. Marked "Secret." 1934.

action was over, Tanaka's chief lieutenant had been arrested. The leader himself was apprehended later in the day near Tokyo, thus bringing to a close the brief era of armed action.*

*Naimusho (Japanese Home Ministry), *Kyosanshugi undo gaikan* (An Outline of the Communist Movement). [1934]. Tanaka announced his defection from the Japanese Communist Party in the summer of 1933 but was not released from prison until 1942. During the war he entered the construction business and is now president of the Sanko Construction Company. Tanaka's current political activity is limited to the occasional contribution of an anti-Communist article to the Japanese press.

CHAPTER VI

Reorganization from Moscow

I<small>T</small> is doubtful whether the Communist Party of Japan could have survived the series of mass arrests in the late nineteen twenties without a base of operations beyond reach of the Japanese authorities. Since its formation, the Japanese Communist Party had operated as an obedient subsidiary of the Comintern which, always dominated by high-ranking members of the Russian Communist Party, to an increasing degree had come to function as an agency of the Soviet government. Accordingly, any shift in the policy or personnel of the Soviet one-party government had its inevitable repercussions within the international Communist movement.

In Japan, shifts in the Communist Party line during the early thirties may be traced back directly to the factional struggle for political supremacy in the Soviet Union. As early as 1927 a Japanese delegation, summoned to Moscow to discuss basic policy with the Comintern staff, had been drawn unwillingly into a serious controversy between Stalin and Trotsky. Fukumoto, the leader of the group, had found himself identified with the Trotsky faction and had been branded a left-wing deviationist. The struggle for control of the Russian Party apparatus thus directly affected the destiny of the Japanese Party. On the ideological level, it will be recalled, this was reflected in the 1927 Thesis, drafted under the personal supervision of the Russian, Bukharin, then President of the Comintern. Reëlected in 1928, Bukharin, who had allied himself with Stalin in the fight against Trotsky, seemed powerful and secure. By 1929 he had been ousted from his position of leadership, accused of right-wing tendencies—a victim of Stalin's political machine. Anything associated with Bukharin now became automatically a "mistake."

A one-time worker in Tokyo's automotive industry, Jokichi Kazama, who was being groomed in Moscow for leadership in Japan, answered a call to appear before the Far Eastern staff of the Comintern early in 1930. The matter of revision of the 1927 Thesis figured prominently in the conference, and Kazama was informed that everything "Bukharinistic" should be eliminated from Japanese Communist policy.[1] In the late summer, a special committee on Japan drew up a document to replace the discarded Bukharin Thesis; and toward the end of 1930—after five years in the Soviet Union—Kazama was sent back into Japan with instructions

43

to bring order to the chaotic situation and with full authority to reorganize the Communist movement.*

A few months later, Kazama and a small group of collaborators formed the Central Committee of the Communist Party of Japan, Japanese Branch of the Comintern; and Kazama reproduced from memory the Moscow resolutions in the form of a thirty-page document entitled "The Japanese Communist Party's Political Thesis—A Draft." Presumably a product of the same Marxist premises which had served as a basis for the 1927 Thesis, Kazama's new thesis, however, arrived at different conclusions. The Bukharin commission had defined Japanese capitalism as following a "rising curve," but the new Central Committee, four years later, reached the verdict that capitalism in Japan had leveled off at the final stage of its development—the stage characterized by the domination of monopolistic capital. The new interpretation attached little importance to the role of "feudalistic remnants" within Japan's capitalistic structure and viewed Japanese society as divided into two distinct classes: the proletariat and the bourgeoisie. The Kazama committee thus revised the timetable for establishment of a Communist Japan by deleting the intermediate stage from the revolutionary schedule. The 1931 Thesis advocated an immediate proletarian revolution.

None of the experienced Communist cadre was on the Kazama committee which sought to implement the new policy. All but one were in prison awaiting trial. Sanzo Nozaka had succeeded in freeing himself after two years in custody and, in March 1931, reached the safety of Russian soil.

In Moscow, Nozaka stepped almost immediately into a key position as assistant to the permanent Japanese Comintern delegate, Sen Katayama. The venerable Katayama, in his younger days champion of the Japanese and American socialist movements, was perhaps the best-known and most respected of Asia's Marxists. A member of the Presidium of the Comintern—the highest honor accorded a foreign Communist—the seventy-year-old Katayama officially ranked with Lenin, Trotsky, and Stalin. Delegates from the Eastern countries seldom failed to pay him a visit whenever they were in Moscow. As a part of the Comintern's inner circle, Katayama could have exerted decisive influence on Communist policy in Japan. He seemed content, however, to pass his remaining years reminiscing and giving friendly advice to the younger generation while allowing formulation of Comintern Eastern policy to be guided more and more by Westerners.

---

*Kazama had been preceded by Iesada Iwao (arrested in July 1930 with Seigen Tanaka) and Yojiro Konno (now a member of the Central Committee of the Communist Party of Japan), who had departed for Tokyo immediately after the Profintern Congress held during August and September 1930.

The arrival of Nozaka in the Soviet capital marked the beginning of a new era—an era which was to see more active Japanese participation in the planning of Communist strategy toward Japan and even stricter Comintern control of its Japanese branch.

Nozaka's first assignment in Moscow consisted of rewriting the document which Kazama had reproduced in Tokyo in the belief that it represented Comintern policy. The theory that an immediate proletarian revolution could succeed in Japan already had been discarded by the Comintern. Kazama was behind the times.

The Comintern's new instructions, "providing the Japanese Communist Party with a Marxist-Leninist scientific basis,"[2] reached the Kazama committee over a devious route. Toward the end of June 1932, the former head of the Department of Economics at Kyoto Imperial University, Dr. Hajime Kawakami, whose Marxist studies had led him into the Communist underground, received a lengthy document from Germany. He at once translated it from German into Japanese. Within a few days a copy of his translation was in the hands of the Kazama committee. This was the 1932 Thesis. Another copy was smuggled to the Communists in prison among materials which the defense was allowed to provide for use in the trial then still in progress.

The document originally had been published in the spring of 1932 by the Comintern under the title, "The Situation in Japan and the Tasks of the Japanese Communist Party." When Kawakami's translation appeared as a special issue of *Red Flag* in July of the same year, it was accompanied by a manifesto which pledged "absolute obedience to decisions of the higher echelons" and asserted, "Only the Communists admit before the masses their errors and deficiencies—only the Communists can overcome these by faith and sacrifice."[3]

The Kazama committee's faith was apparent: without explanation the Comintern had shifted its policy and abandoned the 1931 Draft Thesis, but Kazama and his group accepted the criticism and supported now with equal fervor the new 1932 Thesis.

The new Thesis for Japan cannot be fully understood unless it is considered in the light of political and military developments on the Asian continent. In the fall of 1931 Japanese troops had seized the capital of Manchuria; during the succeeding months Japan deployed its forces beyond the main line of the Russian-controlled Chinese Eastern Railway and throughout Manchuria; in February 1932 a Japanese-sponsored Manchukuo proclaimed its independence from China. Japan had embarked upon what appeared to be a well-planned program of military conquest.

"As a result of the recent Sino-Japanese Incident," the 1932 Thesis begins, "an extremely complex international situation has developed.

This imposes serious responsibilities on all branches of the Communist International and especially on the Japanese revolutionary proletariat and its Communist vanguard." These introductory remarks imply what the authors of the Thesis set out to prove: that the "aggressive character" of the Japanese government's domestic policies and its "imperialistic war" on the continent were but different aspects of one and the same thing— "a dictatorship of the exploiting class." The revolutionary struggle at home would have to be augmented by a determined fight against Japanese imperialism designed to "protect the revolutions of Soviet Russia and China." A two-pronged struggle was deemed essential.

Like its predecessors, the new instrument of Communist policy was based on an analysis of social and economic conditions in Japan. This assessment of the relative strength of the elements constituting the "exploiting class" led the architects of the 1932 Thesis to conclusions that differed considerably from those reached the preceding year.

The Communist Party of Japan was severely criticized for lacking "a clear and correct understanding . . . of the character and the tasks of the revolution in Japan," and the Party was advised to "correct its mistaken views." What did the Comintern in 1932 consider "mistaken views"? The new Thesis is specific on this point:

> Japan's Emperor institution is based principally on the land-owners—a parasitic, feudalistic class; it rests also on the bourgeoisie . . . constituting with these two classes a solid and permanent block . . .
>
> The Emperor institution forms the backbone of the present dictatorship of the exploiting class. To destroy this institution must be considered the very first of our revolutionary tasks in Japan. A tendency has prevailed within the ranks of the Japanese Communist Party to underestimate the role of the Emperor institution. Thus some hold the belief that the Diet and a cabinet formed by representatives of political parties should be regarded as organs of a bourgeois state, in distinct contrast to the Emperor institution. Such views are erroneous . . .[4]

Whereas the Draft Thesis of 1931 had placed Japan on a par with the industrialized nations of Western Europe where capitalist development was considered to have reached its final stage, the new document stressed the importance of "feudalistic remnants" within the social structure of Japan. Revamped Comintern strategy now called for a bourgeois-democratic revolution as a first stage on the road toward a Communist Japan. The plan for an immediate proletarian revolution, conceived in 1931, had, by 1932, become a "Trotskyist scheme." The 1932 Thesis emphasized and reëmphasized the new "immediate task" of the Japanese worker: "All signs of dissatisfaction, protest, and struggle," it concluded, "must be channeled into the political fight against the war and the Emperor institution!"[5]

Meanwhile in Tokyo the trial of Communists arrested in 1928 and 1929 finally opened in 1931 after months of investigations and preliminary hearings. At the initial session, on June 25, more than two hundred alleged Communists stood before the Tokyo District Court, accused of participation in an illegal organization which sought to destroy private enterprise and to alter the existing form of government.

In an unprecedented concession on the part of the prosecution, the imprisoned Communist leaders had been permitted to confer with each other. They agreed upon an integrated defense and set up a "Prison Central Committee," including Manabu Sano, Ichikawa, Nabeyama, Mitamura, Tokuda, and Shiga.[6] The Committee formulated three demands which it served upon the Court and which the Court accepted:

(1) The trial must be open to the public. The defendants will assume responsibility for order within the courtroom.

(2) The defendants desire to be tried as a group. Designated representatives will present the Party's case in terms of program, policy, organization, and activities, thus precluding the necessity for independent questioning [of each of the two hundred defendants].

(3) . . . The Prison Central Committee must be recognized by the Bench [as representing all of the accused].[7]

The writings of both Communists and former Communists make it clear that the Party looked upon the trial as an opportunity to advance its aims one step further—even at the cost of losing its case. Nabeyama recalls:

Our depositions were not intended for the Court. They were directed toward the outside through the medium of the courtroom audience. We took full advantage of the fact that this was a public trial and that our statements were carried in the [non-Communist] press.[8]

The Prison Central Committee, consisting of ten members, attended all sessions of the trial. Though other defendants sometimes were called to the courtroom for consultation, the burden of defense rested upon the Committee's principal spokesmen who presented the Party's case: Sano defended the Communist Party's program; Nabeyama answered questions on organization; and Ichikawa integrated and presented the requested data on Party history.* Clearly the Party—not the individual member—was on trial.

*Ichikawa's "Party History" was secretly published by the Propaganda and Agitation Section of the Kazama Organization in 1932. A revised edition, entitled *A Short History of the Struggle of the Communist Party*, with a preface by Secretary General Tokuda, was published in 1946.

The courtroom, always filled to capacity, was frequently the scene of sharp exchanges of words between the defendants and the public prosecutor, Sano, Nabeyama, and Ichikawa regularly refusing to answer certain questions.

Excerpts from Ichikawa's testimony before the Court, on July 23, 1931, reflect the tenor of the sessions:

> ICHIKAWA: The threat of war is daily becoming more serious . . . As soon as hostilities open, the proletariat must overthrow the bourgeois government and transform the imperialist war into revolution. My words must be communicated to the workers and farmers of the world!
>
> THE JUDGE *(pounding on his desk):* If the defendant continues to engage in such propaganda, I shall be forced to bar the public from the trial.
>
> ICHIKAWA: I am not indulging in propaganda. I am only relating. . .
>
> .   .   .   .
>
> ICHIKAWA: Then I will touch upon the Rice Riots.
>
> THE JUDGE: If you touch upon the Rice Riots, I shall see myself obliged to indict you.
>
> ICHIKAWA *(laughing):* Well then I suppose that means another trial. *(Without paying any attention to the Judge's words, he continues to talk about the Rice Riots).*[9]

The Manchurian Incident of September 18, 1931 added weight to Ichikawa's words and provided the defendants with additional ammunition. In his memoirs Nabeyama re-creates the atmosphere: "Amid interruptions, objections and oppression, we shouted our opposition to the dispatch of [Japanese] troops abroad. We began to utilize the courtroom for an antiwar fight."[10] Party members both inside and outside the courthouse participated in the antiwar campaign. At the entrance to the courtroom all spectators were searched. Even so, handbills, concealed within a Communist's kimono, sometimes slipped by the guards. A newly established Trial Section of the Kazama committee—official headquarters of the Communist Party at large—prepared and circulated secretly mimeographed copies of the Court proceedings.

For more than twelve months the trial raged on. By the end of the second summer, public sentiment was running high. On the eve of the final verdict, students from ultranationalistic organizations blocked the entrance to the courthouse to prevent friends of the Party from securing passes to the closing session. They succeeded in cornering virtually all of the tickets that had been allotted to the general public. Three hundred police agents stood along the route from Ichigaya prison to the center of Tokyo as the defendants made their final trip to the courtroom on the morning of October 29, 1932. An additional two hundred guards were stationed within and around the courthouse to maintain order during the sentencing. In the early afternoon—at the end of one hundred eighteen sessions and sixty thousand pages of stenographic notes—the trial came to an end. The defendants, without exception, were found guilty. Central Committee members were given stiff prison sentences ranging from ten years to life: Manabu Sano, Shoichi Ichikawa, Sadachika Nabeyama, and Shiro Mitamura—life; Goichiro Kokuryo and Sadaki Takahashi—fifteen years; Kyuichi Tokuda, Yoshio Shiga, and Kazuo Fukumoto—ten years.

Certain non-Communist groups were dissatisfied with the outcome of the trial. In an open letter to the presiding judge, a representative of the Society for the Defense of Greater Japan voiced the sentiments of many nationalistic groups. He wrote:

> Your Honor: During the more than a year that you have been in contact with members of this pernicious movement, have you yourself not been contaminated by its microbes? . . . More dangerous than ten thousand Communists is a judge who sympathizes with red ideas.[11]

He concluded by offering a definitive solution to the problem: "Kill these microbes! Kill the Communists!"[12]

The upsurge of ultranationalism in Japan, as an immediate consequence of the victory of Japanese arms and diplomacy on the continent, produced in Moscow a new feeling of insecurity. "In defense of the Soviet Union," the Comintern intensified antiwar propaganda and called upon its Japanese expert, Nozaka, to address the Executive Committee in September 1932. He reported:

> The war of Japanese imperialism in Manchuria marks the beginning of a new series of imperialist wars directed primarily against the Chinese Revolution and the USSR. . .
>
> The United States opposes the seizure of Manchuria by Japan, simply because it would like to subject all China to the American dollar. At the same time the dollar diplomats make every effort to embroil Japan in a war with the USSR.[13]

Nozaka ended on a note of militant confidence:

> Should the imperialists of the whole world hurl their challenge at our fatherland, the USSR, we will show them that the world proletariat will arise in arms against them. We will show them that nothing awaits them but the grave.
>
> Down with Japanese imperialism!
>
> Down with the international counterrevolutionary conspirators!

Long live the Red Army of the Soviet Union and the Red Army
of Soviet China!

Strengthen the revolutionary struggle of the world proletariat
against war and war machinations!

Long live the Comintern![14]

The Japanese people, in the throes of an economic crisis, had readily
embraced the idea of military expansion, as their government's attempt
to mitigate the effects of the 1929 world-wide depression by a policy of
economic retrenchment had failed to produce anything but a serious
deflation, widespread unemployment, and dissatisfaction. More nearly
ideal conditions for the propagation of extremist ideas could scarcely be
imagined.

The 1932 Comintern strategy, aimed at creating a Communist mass
party, substantially increased the number of potential Party members.
The shift from a demand for an immediate revolution to the more cautious
approach characterized as an "intermediate stage, the bourgeois-
democratic revolution," allowed the Party to draw new strength from a
vast, untapped reservoir of sympathizers and potential sympathizers.

Kazama, taking his instructions from Nozaka in Moscow, by the end
of the trial in the fall of 1932 had rebuilt a vigorous Party which implemented the new Comintern orders directly by an intricate Party apparatus
and indirectly through a host of front organizations.

The Anti-imperialist League, a "nonpartisan" antiwar organization
with definite Marxist overtones, was affiliated with its international namesake after 1922. By the fall of 1931, the League had gathered twelve
hundred active members in its fight against war on the continent.[15] The
organization was listed by the Japanese government as "Communist-
dominated" and "subversive," and its members were treated accordingly.
A judge of the Tokyo District Court, for example, stated in sentencing
a League member:

> The defendant is fully cognizant of the fact that the League sup-
> ports the Communist Party of Japan and aims principally at spread-
> ing among the Japanese people the seditious slogans, "Down with
> Imperialist War!" "Down with Intervention in China!" and "Protect
> the Soviet Union!"—slogans which also are being advocated by the
> said Party."[16]

The League carried on its antiwar work through the medium of an
illegal propaganda organ, the *Anti-imperialist Newspaper*, by means of
antiwar pamphlets, and by use of antiimperialist squads. On Army Day,
1932, a pamphlet bearing the intentionally misleading title "Army Day

and the Resolute Spirit of Our Imperial Nation" was circulated by League members operating within schools and factories.[17]

The same type of work within the armed forces was handled directly by the Military Affairs Section of the Communist Party. The Japanese government reported, for example, activities of members of this Section in various Tokyo army barracks and military hospitals as well as at the important naval bases of Yokosuka and Kure.[18] The police further reported the seizure from time to time of copies of *Red Flag* and other Communist antiwar publications at arsenals and in munition factories.[19] On September 19, 1932, the Military Affairs Section began publication of a monthly propaganda sheet, *The Soldier's Friend.* Another paper, *The Lofty Mast,* made its appearance about the same time.[20] Both attacked Japanese imperialism and urged the soldiers to "revolt against their commander . . . and . . . transform their units into a Red Army which will turn its weapons against the Mikado."[21]

Military Affairs was but one section of the elaborate Party structure. The chart in Fig. 1 depicts the organization of the Communist Party of Japan as it was in 1932, under the leadership of Kazama.

The Party, a relatively small organization in itself, reached all strata of the population and projected its activities and propaganda into even the more remote regions of Japan through the medium of specialized agencies called Sections. Three Sections—Mass Organizations, Agrarian, and Assistance—will serve to illustrate.

The Mass Organizations Section was charged with the development of "cultural front organizations." Ever since the Russian Revolution many of Japan's outstanding writers, educators and artists had been friendly disposed toward Marxism and the various political groups and associations which fostered its development. By establishing "fractions" within left-wing groups dedicated to intellectual activities, the Communists could mobilize for their purposes a large segment of the nation's intelligentsia. As Communist activity gradually increased in Japan, a number of cultural organizations were drawn into the orbit of the movement. The influence they exerted upon public opinion was out of all proportion to the numerical strength of the Party.

Cultural organizations of distinct Marxist orientation had appeared in Japan in the early twenties. Victims of internal dissension like the rest of the proletarian organizations and persecuted by the government for their "subversive" leanings, these organizations were forced to regroup from time to time, shedding in the process some of their less radical members and gathering more militant elements en route. What had started out as cultural groupings of artists, writers, and scientists developed into a semipolitical association with a pronounced interest in social problems. This process of crystallization was brought to a logical conclusion in

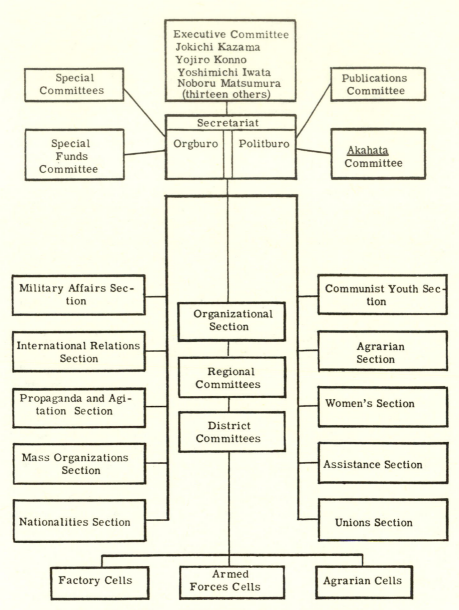

Fig. 1. Organization of the Communist Party of Japan (1932).

1931 when Koreto Kurahara,* an active Communist and well-known writer, returned from the Profintern Congress in Moscow and succeeded in establishing an over-all organization, the Proletarian Cultural Federation.[22] At the time of its establishment, the Federation had a dozen affiliates. A list of these twelve groups will convey an idea of the wide scope of the Federation: Japanese Proletarian Authors' League, Japanese Proletarian Theatrical Guild, Japanese Proletarian Fine Arts Guild, Japanese Proletarian Motion Picture Guild, Japanese Proletarian Musicians' League, Japanese Proletarian Photographers' Association, Japanese Proletarian Esperanto Association, Japanese Proletarian Science League, Proletarian Library, Institute for New Education, Japanese League for Militant Atheists, and Proletarian Birth Control League.

The Proletarian Authors' League exerted the greatest influence of any of the groups within the Proletarian Cultural Federation. An outstanding representative of the many proletarian writers who refused to heed the government's warnings, continued to write as they saw fit, and as a result not infrequently landed in jail,† was Takiji Kobayashi. Kobayashi, an ardent Marxist, expressed his political views through the medium of fiction. His novels, *The March 1928 Arrests, Absentee Landlord,* and *The Factory Cell,* written in a realistic style and depicting a facet of life previously neglected by Japanese writers, were an immediate success. He soon began to take part in Communist activities, for which he subsequently was arrested. In 1933, while still under investigation for "subversive activities," Kobayashi died, probably at the hands of the police.

An Agrarian Section had been part of the Communist organization from the beginning, but the Party had made little headway in its attempt to entice farmers into the movement up to 1930. The Japanese tenant farmer, rooted in the Imperial soil and generally willing to accept his miserable lot—unless driven to direct action by a series of crop failures and starvation—did not readily accept the seditious slogans voiced by Communist organizers. The Japanese government's policy of economic retrenchment and Moscow's new mass party concept afforded the Communist Party its first real opportunity to enlist the support of farmers and fishermen, who together comprised more than half of Japan's population. A sharp decline in the price of agricultural and marine products and a

*Kurahara is a member of the postwar Central Committee and Chief of its Cultural Branch.

†Yuriko Chujo, another member of the Proletarian Authors' League, wrote a number of books on life in Russia after several years there. In 1931 she founded the Society of Friends of the Soviet Union and soon thereafter was arrested and imprisoned for her activities and writings. After her release she married another proletarian writer, who was still serving a prison term for "radical activities." Her husband, Kenji Miyamoto, is a member of the postwar Central Committee of the Communist Party of Japan and former Chief of its Control Commission.

general deterioration of economic conditions about this time produced sporadic riots in farm and fishing villages throughout Japan.

The Communist Party made its first concerted attempt to utilize this situation in the summer of 1931. The All Japan Peasants' Union (formed in 1928 by a merger of moderate and left-wing farmers' associations) was then sharply divided in a struggle between right- and left-wing factions. The right wing, favoring legal procedure, emerged victorious; and the opposition withdrew to form, in January 1932, the All Japan Peasants' Conference, a secret organization under the direct control of the Agrarian Section of the Communist Party. The Conference called for ultimate State ownership of all land and advocated the use of illegal methods (such as riots and refusal to pay taxes) in order to accelerate the process of revolution. According to Japanese government figures, the organization numbered more than twenty-five thousand members in 1932. Its strength began to decline the following year as the result of the apprehension of its leaders, all of whom were members of the Communist Party. The number of arrests and convictions of Conference members, which totaled 137 for the year of 1933, dropped to 28 for the following year;[23] and the government, satisfied that the "level of political consciousness" of the remaining members had sufficiently subsided, reëvaluated the All Japan Peasants' Conference as "of little danger."[24]

The Assistance Section of the Japanese Communist Party was established under Kazama's reorganization program to answer a definite need. Victims of the arrests and their families had been provided assistance in the past by a joint committee of liberals, socialists, and Communists. By 1928, the year of the first Communist mass arrests, only Communists and Communist sympathizers remained within the organization; and the group faced the tremendous task of bringing aid to more than three thousand political prisoners—not all of them Party members—who had been arrested under the Peace Preservation Law. The number of imprisoned Communists and Communist sympathizers further increased during the following year. In 1930 alone more than six thousand individuals suspected of Communist sympathies were apprehended. The growth of the revolutionary movement and the intensification of the government's drive to eradicate the last vestige of "dangerous thoughts" are reflected in the official statistics on the number of persons taken into custody during the ensuing two years for violation of the Peace Preservation Law: 10,422 in 1931 and 13,938 in 1932.* The problem of giving financial and moral support to this ever-growing body of imprisoned Party workers, sym-

*Statistics cited are those which appear in Shihosho Keijikyoku (Criminal Affairs Division, Japanese Ministry of Justice), *Sayoku zenrekisha no tenko mondai ni tsuite* (On the Conversion of Individuals with Leftist Records). Marked "Secret." 1943, p. 3. These figures are identical with those quoted in a number of other Japanese government publications.

pathizers, and their families proved beyond the scope of any privately sponsored organization. Consequently, the Red Aid Association—a legal organization which in 1930 had become an affiliate of its international (Communist) namesake—was placed underground in 1931 as an appendage of the Communist Party's Assistance Section.

Indications of the steady growth of the movement since Kazama took over the reins of the Party, and especially since the arrival of the 1932 Thesis, had caused concern in the Home Ministry that "dangerous thoughts" were becoming more profound and widespread. During the summer and early fall of 1932, law-enforcement agencies had confiscated a large number of issues of *Red Flag* (printed in movable type and boasting a circulation of several thousand),* of the *Party Builder (Tokensetsusha)*—a new organ devoted to the discussion of theory—and of the Communist trade-union paper, *Under the Banner of the Zenkyo Unions.* The discovery of a fully equipped Party printing shop, ready to begin operation, in the suburbs of Yokohama and the detection of plans to effect the release of the imprisoned Communist leaders by force were certain signs that the Party again had taken the offensive. Early in August the Japanese press reported that robbers, captured after having removed thirty thousand yen in broad daylight from a Tokyo bank, were Communist Party members determined to replenish the empty Party treasury.

Only a few months later, the Japanese Communists were compelled to call for replacements from Moscow as Kazama and his staff succumbed to the authorities.

Through an agent planted within the Party's Executive Committee, the Thought Police had learned of a meeting of Communist leaders, scheduled for October 30, 1932 at the resort town of Atami, not far from Tokyo. On that day special agents raided the hotel where delegates were staying and arrested a number of them. These arrests initiated a series of police raids in every major center of Communist activity in Japan. Kazama, Yojiro Konno, Yoshimichi Iwata—key figures in the Party— were arrested in the Tokyo region on the same day the Atami raid had taken place. By December 1 the remainder of the Kazama committee and more than a thousand suspects had been rounded up. The only committee member who managed to escape was Noboru Matsumura, whose Party affiliation dated back to the days of Tanaka and his armed-action squads. All indications point to the fact that Matsumura had been in touch with the police. After these raids, which had eliminated the majority of the Party's members and all of its leaders, the police began to round up the intellectuals who had contributed directly or indirectly to

*During the first three months of 1932, circulation of *Red Flag* was reported to have increased from 800 to 7000. Naimusho Keihokyoku, *Shakai undo no jokyo*, 1932, pp. 30-32.

the rise of Marxism in Japan. A large number of professors, writers, and artists were taken into custody, among them Dr. Kawakami, translator of the 1932 Thesis.

Barely two months after Kazama's arrest, Nozaka sent into Japan another Moscow-trained organizer, Masami Yamamoto, a graduate of the Moscow Communist University and one of the framers of the 1932 Thesis. By January 1933, Yamamoto had reassembled the few remaining Party members. Hampered by the opposition of those who proposed the establishment of a new Party—to be made up of workers, not intellectuals—he consumed three months in mapping out plans for reorganization; but his efforts were in vain for, like his predecessors, Yamamoto was trapped by the Thought Police.*

The shock experienced in Moscow upon receipt of a report that Yamamoto too had been arrested was probably mild compared to the effect which must have been produced by the news that two of the Japanese Party's most experienced and able leaders had announced from prison a complete defection from Communism and bitterly denounced the Comintern.

Manabu Sano and Sadachika Nabeyama submitted a written "apology" to the authorities in the summer of 1933. This document was given the greatest possible publicity by the government and was widely discussed in the press. Sano and Nabeyama had come to the conclusion that the Japanese Communist Party was nothing more than a "society of friends of the Soviet Union" and its effectiveness like the "distant barking of a skinny dog." The disappointed leaders related how they had organized a party for the working classes, but that it had now become a "playground for petty bourgeois pacifists," while its incapable leaders hardly dared express an opinion without first consulting *Pravda* or *The Communist International*.[25] Their former comrades labeled them "ugly traitors" who had "put some socialist syrup on Japan's imperialistic program of conquest,"[26] but Sano's own explanation of the break with the Party runs as follows:

> In June 1933 I issued a statement and left the Communist Party. Many of my comrades agreed with me and joined me. This event marks the important line of demarcation between those who believe that Japanese socialism must develop along national lines and those who hold to internationalism with major emphasis on the class [struggle].†

*Yamamoto was arrested in May 1933. Naimusho (Japanese Home Ministry), *Saikin ni okeru kyosanshugi undo no gaikyo* (Recent Developments in the Communist Movement.) Typewritten. [1934].

†Manabu Sano, *Shinzenbi*, June 1946. In rapid succession Shiro Mitamura, Sadaki Takahashi, Seigen Tanaka, and Jokichi Kazama also announced their defection from the Japanese Communist Party.

The government, which had countered successfully every attempt from abroad to reorganize the Japanese Communists and seemed to be making progress even on the ideological level, now launched a direct attack against the Party's peripheral organizations.

On the day of Yamamoto's arrest—May 3, 1933—the Chief of the Police Division issued instructions to all security agencies to pick up members of the National Conference of Japanese Trade Unions. "This Conference," the official cautioned, "proposes a change in Japan's national structure. It recently revealed its true colors by adding to its program the demand for abolition of our monarchy."[27] In rapid succession the organizations which had constituted a reservoir of Communist sympathy were neutralized by the apprehension of their leaders and scores of members. Nearly fifteen thousand such individuals were taken into custody during 1933.[28] Few of the associations, unions, and federations which under Kazama had linked the Party to the people remained by the end of the year. The Party itself, after the arrest of Yamamoto, was back to the position it had occupied during the early twenties: a scattered group of professional revolutionists, pursued by the police and torn by internal dissension.

All attempts at reorganization from Moscow ended in failure as, one after another, the Russian-trained replacements were apprehended by the Japanese authorities almost as fast as Nozaka could send them into the country. The series of successful government raids—beginning with the arrest of Kazama and netting Yamamoto and his successor, Eitaro Noro,* as well as several subsequent Moscow returnees—had convinced the remaining cadre in Japan that police spies were at work. Fear and distrust among members of the Party reached its climax in the so-called "lynching incident," involving Kenji Miyamoto, Satomi Hakamada (a graduate of the Moscow Communist University), and several other Central Committee members.† The arrest of Noro, a few months after he had taken over direction of the Party, had aroused suspicion among Party leaders. Miyamoto, Noro's successor, summoned a "board of inquiry" to grill the suspect Central Committee members. After several days of questioning, one of the spy-suspects "fainted and did not regain consciousness."[29] This was the first in a series of similar "lynchings."

---

*Chairman of the Central Committee from May to November 1933, he belonged to the "intellectuals" within the Party. A former student of Nozaka's at Keio University, Noro was the author of the well-known *History of the Development of Japanese Capitalism* and one of Japan's outstanding writers on economic theory. The Party's "worker faction" attempted to wrest the leadership from Noro and his group. When Noro was arrested unexpectedly on November 28, 1933, responsibility was laid quite logically at the door of the "workers." In this connection, it is interesting to note that the ratio of workers indicted for membership in the Party had dropped from a high of 45.5 percent in 1927 to 17.4 percent in 1933.

†Hakamada is a member of the postwar Central Committee.

Symptomatic of the atmosphere of dissension was the appearance of the Majority Faction, in the spring of 1934, shortly after the Thought Police had captured every member of Miyamoto's Central Committee except Hakamada. This faction, composed of members from the Party's lower echelons, accused Hakamada of being a police agent and questioned his right to head the Party. News of the split and of the chaotic conditions within the Party soon reached Moscow. Nozaka, by this time officially in charge of the Comintern's Japanese branch as a result of Katayama's death in November 1933,* attempted in vain to save the Party. From the Soviet capital, he wrote: "The Party organization must as a rule quietly remove from Party activity Party workers who are suspected of being provocateurs."[30]

It is uncertain whether Nozaka's message reached Hakamada, whom the Comintern continued to support. A courier dispatched from Moscow was apprehended aboard a ship in Nagasaki harbor before he could set foot on Japan. On March 3, 1935, Hakamada, the last important leader entrusted by Nozaka with reorganization of the Party, was apprehended, and an official of the Japanese Home Ministry tersely stated:

> The Communist movement is now in a state of complete decay. This is the perfect moment for its eradication. We must pursue the retreating enemy more relentlessly than ever; but at the same time, let us intensify our efforts to reform those in prison and to guide and protect the converts. In one hand the sword; in the other, the Koran![31]

*Sen Katayama was given a state funeral. The impressive ceremony took place in front of Lenin's tomb, Stalin, Molotov, and Comintern dignitaries serving as pallbearers. A twenty-gun salute was fired to honor Soviet Russia's most famous Japanese. He was buried within the walls of the Kremlin.

CHAPTER VII

Ties with America

Foreign support for the Japanese Communist Party had always come directly from Soviet Russia and revolutionary China. Without this backing the organization could hardly have survived as long as it did. Yet suddenly, in 1935, Comintern directives and funds began to arrive in Japan from across the Pacific. Sanzo Nozaka's "Letter to the Japanese Communists," conceived in compliance with the resolutions of the Seventh Comintern Congress which called for a popular front of all antifascist forces on a national and international scale, did not travel from Moscow to Japan over the customary route.* Instead, it was printed in the United States and forwarded to Japan in a special issue of *International Correspondence (Kokusai Tsushin),* organ of the Japanese Section of the American Communist Party. At about the same time a Comintern agent, dispatched to Japan by Nozaka, was instructed to use instead of facilities in Shanghai a new contact point in Brooklyn, U. S. A.[1] What was behind this shift of advanced liaison bases from China to the United States?

In 1935 the Soviet Union felt threatened by the rise of fascist movements abroad. Areas, such as Germany or Japan, once considered ripe for a Communist revolution, had come under aggressive anti-Soviet governments. Hitler had begun to rebuild a powerful Reich. Steadily the Japanese were inching forward into regions which, though formerly in the Russian orbit, were now viewed by the Kremlin as springboards for aggression against the Soviet Union. European fascism and Japanese militarism appeared on the offensive everywhere.

Ever since the Siberian expedition of the Japanese armed forces, Russia had realized the importance of mobilizing antimilitarist elements in Japan to hamper and, if possible, to contain Japanese expansion on the continent. This had been attempted for a time by utilizing Soviet Russian agencies, as well as Comintern personnel. The practice, however, was

*The Seventh Comintern Congress, last congress of this organization before its official dissolution in 1943, convened in Moscow in July and August 1935. On the opening day, Nozaka was elected to the Presidium, filling the vacancy which Katayama's death had left. Nozaka was then still a comparative unknown among Moscow Communists. The stenographic record of the Congress makes this point quite clear. According to this document, applause accompanying the election of delegates to the Presidium, ranged from "applause" for the minor figures of the Communist heirarchy to "stormy prolonged applause, ovations, shouts of 'hurrah'" for Stalin at the top. Nozaka rated only "loud applause." The "Letter" was signed also by the Japanese representative to the Profintern, Kenzo Yamamoto, who subsequently disappeared. His fate remains a mystery.

abandoned subsequently for good reason. The disadvantage of assigning Soviet officials abroad to act in a dual capacity as representatives of their government and as secret Comintern operatives had been amply demonstrated by the disastrous set-back in China in 1927, where the defeat of the Comintern-backed Communist forces was followed by a rupture of diplomatic relations with the Soviet Union, by the ouster of the Soviet advisers, and by a general weakening of Soviet influence. At about the same time a similar development appeared imminent in Japan: the Japanese government confronted the Russian Embassy with evidence that Japanese Communists had received support and instructions from official Soviet agencies. The Tokyo authorities threatened to take appropriate action.[2] The Soviet government apparently decided to change its approach rather than risk a major diplomatic clash with Japan, and after 1928 the Comintern was assigned sole responsibility for liaison with the Japanese Communist Party. Communications were now handled through Comintern centers in Shanghai and Vladivostok. By 1935 the route through China, Manchuria, and Korea had become both impractical and dangerous. The Japanese Foreign Office as well as the Ministry of Justice and the Home Ministry maintained counterespionage agents at Asiatic danger spots, such as Vladivostok, Harbin, and Shanghai.[3] This interlocking network of Japanese observation posts on the continent proved increasingly effective after 1933, as evidenced by the number of Communist liaison agents arrested the moment they landed in Japan. A gradually stiffening Japanese attitude over the matter of Comintern-Soviet collaboration (the Soviet government contended that there was none) made it necessary finally to devise a plan which would allow continued operations in Japan but which, at the same time, would minimize or entirely eliminate the risk of Soviet diplomatic or military involvement.

It is hardly surprising then that some time in 1935 the Comintern opened a new route to Japan. In March of that year the Chief of the Criminal Affairs Division, Ministry of Justice, stated in cautious terms that there were "indications that Russia was withdrawing its support somewhat from the Japanese Communist movement."[4] About a year later the Chief of the Japanese Home Ministry's Police Division, in a confidential communication to prefectural governors, revealed that the Communist movement in Japan, which had shown signs of decline, was regaining its strength "owing to an influx of propaganda literature from the Communist Party of America."[5] In the interval between the two statements, the switch from the Asian to the American route apparently had been carried out.

It would be a mistake, however, to assume that the United States' importance for the prewar Communist movement in Japan dates from 1935. Ties have existed between Japanese and American Communists since 1919, when Katayama, the "father of Asian Communism," founded a Japanese Communist group in New York. He participated simultaneously in the establishment of an organization which subsequently grew into the Communist Party of America. Almost ten years later, Katayama—by then a member of the Presidium of the Comintern and its chief adviser on things Japanese—proudly declared in Moscow that his past intimate association with the American labor movement had earned him the right to be considered a member of the American Communist Party.[6] Several of the Japanese delegates to the Far Eastern People's Congress (1922) which laid the foundation for the Japanese Communist Party were drawn from Katayama's American Communist group, while the first left-wing organization in Japan to designate itself "Communist" (the Dawn People's Communist Party) was established by Katayama's friend, Eizo Kondo, a long-time resident of the United States and well-known figure in a number of American radical organizations. In the late twenties, when reëstablishment of diplomatic relations between Russia and Japan facilitated direct communication between Moscow and Tokyo, the ties with America tended to be less conspicuous. For a while they appear to have been limited to occasional financial assistance afforded the Japanese Party by the American Communists and by sympathetic Japanese residents in the United States.* Even so, there are indications that the close coöperation which had existed between the two Communist movements did not cease during this period. In Moscow, Katayama spoke for the Japanese as well as for the American Communist Party when, in 1928, he presented a joint manifesto to the Sixth Congress of the Comintern.[7] In Shanghai the (Communist) Pan Pacific Trade Union Secretariat, headed for a time by Earl Browder,[8] served as a convenient meeting-place for representatives from the United States and Japan.

Communist propaganda in the United States and Canada found considerable response among the Japanese minority on the Pacific Coast, where racial prejudice was reënforced by discriminatory laws. The Los Angeles, San Francisco, Seattle, and Vancouver areas with their sizeable Japanese populations early developed into centers of Communist activity. In the late twenties Japanese residents in the section of Los Angeles known locally as "Little Tokyo" formed numerous Marxist study societies. At least one of these was affiliated, after 1927, with the California branch of the American Communist Party. In 1929, a Japanese Section of the American Communist Party was formed in San Francisco. This group published several newssheets and periodicals, the two most significant

---

*Yoshio Shiga recalls, for example, in his memoirs, that a contribution from the United States made possible in the twenties the expansion of the "legal mouthpiece" of the Party, the *Proletarian Newspaper*. Yoshio Shiga, *Nihon kakumei undo-shi no hitobito* (Men Who Made Japan's Revolutionary History). Tokyo, 1948, p. 168.

being *Class War (Kaikyu-sen)* and *Labor News (Rodo Shimbun)*.[9] Similar activity was recorded in and around Seattle and in New York.

Anarchists and Communists were considered of sufficient import in Southern California to warrant a special "Red Squad" within the Los Angeles Police Department. During the thirties, arrests of Japanese residents for Communist agitation increased, and a number of noncitizens were deported. The files of the Los Angeles Police Department reveal, for example, that several Japanese, identified as militant Communist Party members, "accepted voluntary departure at their own expense on August 8, 1932 from San Pedro, California on the German motorship Portland—Destination: Russia."[10]

Liaison with Japan thus was facilitated by an extensive Communist network of Japanese residents which reached up the West Coast as far north as Vancouver and which was tied directly into American Communist Party headquarters in New York.* While precise data on these Communist organizations and their membership are difficult to establish, the carefully compiled statistics of the Japanese Overseas Police give a fairly accurate picture of the situation. This agency's report for 1935, for instance, placed the total of Japanese Communists in the Los Angeles area alone at close to two hundred individuals.[11]

Japanese sailors and Japanese ships formed the principal link between these organizations and the homeland. After 1935 this highly mobile means of communication assumed an increasing importance. Much of the traffic apparently went undetected until after the Sino-Japanese Incident (1937) when large-scale warfare in China and American hostility toward Japan resulted in considerably tightened security. Even today, when Japan's defeat has opened the archives of the Japanese government agencies once responsible for investigating and checking all subversive activities directly or indirectly affecting Japan, it is still difficult to evaluate the intensity and scope of Communist American-Japanese relations. From the data now available, it appears that the peak in coöperation between the two Communist movements was reached in the period from 1935 to 1937. A few examples will illustrate the character of liaison work during these years.

Early in 1937 at Yokohama the Japanese authorities arrested a sailor by the name of Hoyu Okamoto. Search produced a number of Communist

---

*One Japanese document notes that orders to the Japanese Communist Party were dispatched through what is referred to as the "Comintern's liaison office at 39 E. 12th Street, New York City." The same document asserts that during the period from January to April 1935 on at least two occasions the Japanese Communist Party received orders from the Comintern through the American Communist Party. Testimony of a number of Japanese Communists apprehended during this period appears to confirm these assertions. Shakai Shiso Taisaku Chosakai (Research Association for Countermeasures Against Social Ideas), *Saikin ni okeru waga kuni kyosanshugi undo no gaiyo* (An Outline of the Communist Movement in Japan during Recent Years). Kyoto, 1935, p. 3.

pamphlets and proof that Okamoto had belonged to the Maritime Communist Group, an organization of Japanese sailors, mostly former members of the outlawed revolutionary National Conference of Japanese Trade Unions. Representatives of this illegal Group, with headquarters at Kobe, had been in close touch with the Japanese Section of the American Communist Party which had supplied them with literature and funds. Further investigation of Okamoto established the fact that he had served as a liaison agent traveling regularly between Japan and the United States. In this capacity he had left Kobe on October 9, 1935 on the "Belfast Maru" sailing for the United States; he had returned to Japan on December 7, leaving from Kobe again on the same ship toward the end of the month; back in Yokohama in May 1936, he had sailed again from Kobe on the "Florida Maru" in September, bound once more for the United States. The Japanese authorities finally arrested him in Yokohama in January 1937.[12] Okamoto's subsequent testimony confirmed the suspicion that he had been engaged in gathering information on the political and economic situation in Japan as well as material concerning the Japanese revolutionary movement. Before returning to Japan, Okamoto had been supplied in the United States with propaganda literature and specific instructions.

To judge from the material seized over a number of years, more than a hundred different kinds of Communist periodicals, newssheets, or pamphlets (including the organ of a Chinese Communist group in New York) were smuggled into Japan from the United States.[13] Three of these Japanese-language publications apparently constituted the principal vehicles for Communist propaganda, serving concurrently as a means of conveying instructions and important news from the outside world to Japan. With the gradual tightening of censorship over news of foreign origin, such material assumed an increasingly important role in stimulating the popular-front movement in that country. These publications— *International Correspondence (Kokusai Tsushin)*, organ of the Japanese Section of the American Communist Party; *Pacific Worker (Taiheiyo Rodosha)*, published in New York and Chicago; and *Maritime Correspondence (Kaijo Tsushin)*, a monthly put out in Seattle—carried a varied assortment of reading material. This generally fell into one of three categories: Instructions, Information, and Propaganda.

Instructions were often disguised as "letters to the comrades at home." For example, the October 15, 1936 issue of *International Correspondence* contained a letter printed on the occasion of the reappearance in Japan of the illegal Communist organ *Red Flag*. The "editors" advised:

> While we shall extend you from abroad all possible assistance, we sincerely hope that you will make every effort to establish intimate and organic relations between the [Japanese Communist Party Re-

construction] Central Committee and us . . . Only through such liaison will it be possible to internationalize the Japanese movement, now on the verge of isolation. . .

The contents of *Red Flag* follow, in principle, the instructions of the Comintern . . . The publication of *Red Flag* must not constitute, however, a reason for neglecting legal publications . . . A Communist who is incapable of carrying on legal activities must (with a few special exceptions) be considered a bad Communist . . . A delicate division between legal and illegal writing must be worked out.[14]

The same issue carried an appeal to Communists in the United States to raise three thousand yen (about one thousand dollars) in order to assist the Party Reconstruction Committee in Japan in revitalizing the organization. A subsequent issue of January 20, 1937 contained a brief statement from Los Angeles to the effect that some progress meanwhile had been made toward assembling the badly needed funds. Part of the money apparently came from American sympathizers.

Conversely, Communist pamphlets printed in the United States appealed to the Japanese worker to support and collaborate with striking American seamen. For instance, one item read:

Japanese sailors, dock workers, and other workers! Lend a hand to the American maritime strike! The Japanese workers, intimately linked to the American worker by the Pacific Ocean, must not remain distinterested![15]

Communist publications smuggled into Japan also contained much information then unavailable there. Carried "for reference," this material consisted of editorials from the *Daily Worker,* Soviet articles on German-Japanese relations, and statements by prominent Japanese opposed to the policies of their government. Such literature continued to turn up in Yokohama, Tokyo, Osaka, Kobe, Nagasaki, and elsewhere, despite the fact that to distribute it in Japan meant to risk long imprisonment or worse.

Most of the items that reached Japan from the United States were disguised by covers which bore such titles as "Suggestions for the Improvement of Japanese Wearing Apparel," "A Painless Cure," or "Honeymoon Apartment."[16] Identical with Communist literature of the period in other countries in their emphasis on the necessity for the creation of a popular front, they were skillfully tailored to the Japanese scene. That they found considerable response is evident from the numerous enthusiastic letters which the three major American-Japanese Communist publications carried in each issue.

How such "letters to the editor" could be sent from Japan without involving the writers with the police may be deduced from a brief notice in the September 1, 1936 issue of the *Pacific Worker:*

> We welcome questions from the readers in our question and answer column. We also welcome criticism and suggestions in the form of short articles. *You need not give* your real name or address. Any address will do. If you number among your friends reliable sailors, you may also use the convenient method of having them mail your letter from a foreign port.[17]

It was probably also through such "reliable sailors" that Stalin's writings reached Japan.

If the frequency with which the Japanese authorities devoted confidential memoranda to the matter of confiscation of foreign popular-front literature is any indication, a considerable quantity of Communist literature must have found its way from the United States to Japan even during the late thirties. Sanzo Nozaka, in discussing his famous "Letter to the Japanese Communists," revealed that a "substantial number" were carried into Japan.[18] This is indirectly confirmed by the Japanese authorities, who recorded in a confidential report that between January 1935 and December 1936 1256 items of Communist literature of American origin had been picked up in Japan. "A considerable amount of the same type of material," the report concludes, "must be assumed to have gone undetected."[19]

The extent to which the Japanese government was concerned over these ties with America may be judged from two documents which turned up in the mass of classified material seized by the Allied authorities after Japan's surrender. The first consists of a list of Japanese Communists in the Los Angeles area, arranged by name, membership number, and Party assignment. Copies of the document, compiled by Japanese Foreign Office agents in the United States and dated August 31, 1938, were supplied to all prefectural governors with a covering letter requesting an immediate report should any of the suspects appear in their respective areas of jurisdiction.[20] The names of some four hundred suspect Japanese and of a few "dangerous" Chinese and Koreans residing within the United States are listed in a second Japanese government document which clearly represents only a portion of the original. The roster, though not complete in every case, generally contains information on the individual's address, occupation, and Party status or left-wing political affiliation.[21]

The tightening of security measures which accompanied Japan's advance into North China and her subsequent involvement with the United States inevitably reduced the amount of liaison between the Japanese and American Communist Parties. The above may not be the whole story. Part of it was destroyed along with Japanese government records during the war, while some of it must remain, for obvious reasons, within the files of the Federal Bureau of Investigation. Many of the events and most of the details may still be known only to the participants. It is precisely this latter possibility which suggests the real significance of the issue; for, although Communist liaison between Japan and the United States apparently was checked and the Party organization virtually destroyed during the wartime period, it is not unlikely that, with the re-creation of a strong Communist Party in postwar Japan, these ties with America—as is true of contact with the Soviet Union, China, and Korea—may have been reëstablished or even strengthened.

CHAPTER VIII

Communism in Wartime Japan

THE Japanese Communist movement reached its lowest ebb during the Second World War. In Eastern Asia the war began in 1937—fully two years before the outbreak of hostilities in Europe. The China Incident, as the Japanese government preferred to call the full-scale operation on the Asiatic continent, marked the climax of a long power struggle in Japan between militant nationalists and their heterogeneous opponents.

For a time after World War I it appeared that the dominent current of Japanese political thought might be moving closer to the Western concept of party government. In 1918 the Emperor appointed as premier the leader of a political party, a civilian and commoner, who formed Japan's first party cabinet. Civilian influence on the formulation of foreign and domestic policy gradually increased during the twenties, strengthened by enactment of a universal-suffrage law which brought Japan as close as it was to come to representative government. The Japanese people enjoyed new freedom of action and thought; and, stimulated by Western ideas, many began to dissect and scrutinize traditional values. It was in this atmosphere of intense intellectual curiosity that the Marxist movement in Japan left the realm of theory for the field of action. The closing years of the decade, however, produced a resurgence of militant nationalism. In 1930 Japan was poised between parliamentarianism and military rule. The issue was decided by the Manchurian Incident of 1931 when the Japanese army, on its own initiative, launched a war of conquest, and the government, if reluctantly, endorsed the venture. By 1937, after six years of assassination, intimidation, and coercion, an authoritarian regime which acknowledged few of the freedoms guaranteed by the constitution was firmly entrenched in Japan.

The Communist underground which, since 1928, had functioned under increasingly difficult circumstances found operations in wartime almost impossible. Nevertheless, Nozaka, writing from Moscow in 1938, stated: "In the factories, in the villages, in the schools, in the barracks and at the front, everywhere the Communists are trying to win the people for the demand that the war must be ended immediately and unconditionally."[1] Actually, by this time, the Communist Party of Japan as such had long since ceased to exist. Short-lived, isolated groups of former Party members, whose effectiveness—either individually or collectively—was practically nil, constituted the entire wartime movement. In 1932, when Communist strength in Japan was at its peak, the Japanese authorities had arrested fourteen thousand individuals for Communist sympathies, but

even the vastly more elaborate wartime police system was unable to un-
cover in any single year more than a few hundred offenders among the
six thousand "Communist suspects" kept under varying degrees of surveillance.[2]

A number of factors account for the decline in Communist activity
during the war years. The defection of the early leaders of the Japanese
Communist movement, who had renounced the Party because of its
"abject submission to the Soviet Union," had the effect of demoralizing
the rank and file of members and had started a process of disintegration.
Outbreak of the war in China hastened this development. After Japan's
initial gains on the continent, a wave of nationalism swept the islands,
carrying along even the left-wing worker who, more concerned with his
own livelihood than with the defense of Soviet Russia, saw in victory the
promise of prosperity. At about the same time the use of "antifascist
popular-front language" was added by order of the Chief of the Peace
Preservation Bureau to the long list of actions considered "harmful to
national solidarity and deplorable from the point of view of public
order."[3] Since Dimitrov's speech before the Seventh Congress of the
Comintern in 1935, the "popular front" slogan had guided Communist
policy throughout the world. Nozaka's appeal to the Japanese Communists
to "enter liberal groups . . . and to work from within"[4] had little effect in
Japan, where the government countered the popular-front strategy by
dissolving the Proletarian (left-wing socialist) Party for its outspoken
opposition to the war. The sole remaining political organization of
workers, the Social Mass Party, escaped the same fate only by swinging to
the support of the militarists.

The government applied a similar technique to labor. Left-wing trade
unions were dissolved and their leaders imprisoned. Enactment in the
spring of 1939 of the National Mobilization Law, aimed at "control of
the allocation of manpower," practically eliminated strikes. By 1940 all
but the government-sponsored trade-unions had disappeared.* Without
these organizations, the few Communist Party members who had succeeded in regrouping after release from prison were forced to operate
entirely on their own. Assistance from abroad, which reached Japan for a
time by way of America, had dwindled to a mere trickle as strict control
of international communications was rendered more effective by an exchange of intelligence information with Germany and Italy under the
terms of the Anti-Comintern Pact, concluded in November 1937. Consequently, Communism in wartime Japan—denied a solid basis for development, short on veteran leadership, and weakened by the detention or

---

*Statistics of the period (1937-1940) showing the number of participants per year
in strikes, sabotage, or lockouts reflect this trend: 1937, 123,720; 1938, 18,341; 1939, 50,162;
1940, none. *The Japan Yearbook.* Tokyo, 1943-44, p. 628.

conversion of its proponents—lost most of the ground it had gained during the prewar years.

A survey of organized Communist activity in Japan during the first phase of the wartime period may be reduced to an account of four abortive attempts to revive the defunct Party.

By far the best-organized Communist group created during the war was led by Shojiro Kasuga, a graduate of the Moscow Communist University.* Kasuga, who had been chief organizer in the Osaka area before his arrest in March 1928, was released after nine years in prison and at once went underground.[5] Toward the end of 1937 Kasuga assembled a handful of former Party members who were eager to rebuild the Communist organization. This was only a few months after the outbreak of war in China, and the Communist Group, as Kasuga called his preparatory committee, agreed to concentrate on the "antiwar struggle." The China Incident was considered by the Communists a prelude to Japanese action against Soviet Russia, a view seemingly confirmed by the conclusion of the Anti-Comintern Pact; and the program worked out at Osaka in the winter of 1937 listed "determined opposition to aggression in China and an active fight against the military dictatorship in Japan" as the prime objectives of political action. Thousands of antiwar handbills distributed by the Group among ammunition-industry workers were the first tangible evidence of Kasuga's determination to carry out his program. Attesting to the unexpected revival of Communist activity were three new publications, which the Kasuga Group secretly printed in Osaka and circulated among workers and students in western Japan—*Party Builder, Braving the Storm,* and *Voice of the People.*[6] Copies of these publications even appeared in the United States and in the Soviet Union, where they produced undue optimism among sympathizers regarding the scope and potential of Communism in wartime Japan.

Kasuga's long-range plan called for the formation of a limited preparatory committee which would establish contact abroad. When a sufficient number of "reliable" Communists had been assembled, the Group would then obtain Comintern recognition and, under the designation of "Central Committee," proceed with the systematic reorganization of the Party. But Kasuga's Communist Group, still in the "preparatory committee stage," was uncovered by the Thought Police in the fall of 1938. Kasuga and 157 of his followers were arrested.[7] The smashing of this Communist Group ended organized wartime activity in western Japan.†

*One of the postwar leaders of the Japanese Communist movement, a member of the Central Committee.

†At the same time a group of Communist workers from factories in the Tokyo-Yokohama area, headed by a member of the Japanese National Planning Board, was discovered by the Thought Police. Among literature confiscated at the time of arrest were copies of Kasuga's *Party Builder.*

To guard against the reappearance of organized "threats to peace and order," at about this time the Home Ministry amended its regulations relative to "individuals requiring surveillance." All persons judged potentially dangerous to the "national structure" were placed under observation and assigned to one of six categories in order of importance: Communists, Socialists, Anarchists, Other Extremists, Koreans, and Formosans. Each category in turn was subdivided into "A" (poor security risk, requiring constant surveillance) and "B" (minor security risk).[8] The Japanese government maintained detailed files on all suspects residing in Japan and abroad;* and since Communists and former Communists suspected of "feigned conversion" were placed in category I, group A, it is hardly surprising that all subsequent attempts by former Party members to reëstablish a Communist Party in Japan ended in failure.†

In the spring of 1940 three Communist groups were operating independently in the Tokyo-Yokohama area. Each group was led by a former Party member who had spent years in prison, and each was working for the same cause—the reëstablishment of the Japanese Communist Party— but apparently none was aware of the others' existence.

The first of these groups was headed by Shoichi Kasuga,‡ an electrical worker, and Teikichi Sakai, a graduate of the Moscow Communist University, who secretly had conferred with three other Communists in March 1940. Barely sixty days later the leaders were arrested together with more than forty new members whom they had by this time recruited.

The second group, despite years of cautious preparation, had not reached even the stage of organized political action when its ringleaders, Yasoji Kazahaya, Hiroshi Hasegawa, and Ritsu Ito,§ were arrested in the summer of 1940.‖

A third group began limited operations in the Tokyo-Yokohama area under the leadership of a Communist, Shigeo Kamiyama,** whom the Japanese authorities characterized as "an outstanding example of feigned

*The United States was not the only country in which the Japanese agents kept watch on Communist suspects of Japanese extraction. A document seized after World War II, bearing the notations "Secret" and "Copy to His Excellency Prime Minister Koiso" lists "leftist converts" residing in Central China, their places of employment, age, background, etc. Naimusho (Japanese Home Ministry), *Zaika-chu sayoku tenkosha ryakumeibo* (A Short List of Left-wing Converts in Central China). [1943].

†During 1938 even members of such groups as the Society for the Study of Materialism, composed of scholars and writers—among them Kiyoshi Miki, Nyozekan Hasegawa, and Goro Hani—were arrested for having contributed to the Communist cause by furthering the study of Marxism.

‡Shoichi Kasuga is a member of the postwar Central Committee.

§All three became ranking members of the postwar Party, Ito and Hasegawa serving on the Central Committee.

‖Thirty students of Tokyo Imperial University were arrested at the same time for their connection with the group.

**Kamiyama also played an important role in the postwar Communist movement.

conversion."[9] Released from prison in 1937, after pledging to abandon all interest in Communism, Kamiyama had begun immediately to work for the recreation of a Communist Party. So strict were wartime police control and surveillance that it took the veteran labor leader and organizer more than two years to locate his former associates and to establish a functional organization. "Step by step," Kamiyama instructed his followers, "we must work our way into legal organizations."[10] But agents of the Thought Police, who had been keeping close watch upon movements of the "former Communist," apprehended most of the members of his group, about seventy in all, in February 1941, and the leader himself in May of the same year. Kamiyama was returned to prison, where he remained until the end of the Pacific War.

The only major Communist incident in wartime Japan involved a group of individuals who had no direct connection with Japanese Communists. An extensive Soviet espionage organization which had supplied high-level military and political intelligence to the Russian government for a number of years was discovered by the Japanese authorities in the fall of 1941. This spy ring, directed by a German correspondent and ex officio member of the German Embassy in Tokyo, had agents in a number of Japanese government departments and good contacts in most of the foreign embassies, but was careful to avoid association with the Japanese Communist movement. The leader of the group, Dr. Richard Sorge, was arrested a few weeks before the beginning of the Pacific War but only after he had forewarned Moscow of the planned German attack and of Japan's intention to move south rather than against the Soviet Union.[11]

The Japanese attack on Pearl Harbor ushered in the second phase of the war in Asia and a dark age for Communism in Japan. In the name of national unity, the slightest opposition to the militarists' plans was labeled "un-Japanese" and ruthlessly suppressed. Liberalism and Communism were lumped together and dealt with as a single evil. A Japanese government spokesman, appearing before a Diet committee in 1943, asserted: "Communist thought and liberal thought have a common origin. They do not differ."[12] As the war progressed, the last traces of organized Communism in Japan disappeared under mounting wartime restrictions.

It is difficult to evaluate the amount of sabotage in wartime Japan which should be attributed to the Communists. Clearly there was no systematic destruction of equipment or military supplies. Sabotage of machinery and other vital equipment was reported, but neither the scope nor the circumstances surrounding the incidents suggest any over-all, effective Communist plan to wreck the Japanese war machine.

Reports of strikes throughout Japan on the eve of the Pacific War seem to have been grossly exaggerated by members of the pro-Communist

(Japanese) Antiwar League in China, anxious to paint Japan as on the verge of revolution. Nozaka's picture of Japanese Communists engaged in "antiwar work" within Japan is misleading. In North China, he stated: "During the Pacific War our revolutionary workers have been able to carry on the struggle . . . On the second day following the opening of the Pacific War, the Tojo government arrested three thousand antiwar elements, but the Communists did not cease their activities for even a single day . . . The strike at the Kawasaki Military Arsenal in 1941 was organized by Communists."[13] Such speeches and writings convey an erroneous impression of the strength and character of the Communist movement in wartime Japan. True, work stoppages and strikes did occur from time to time, but the Communists could not justifiably claim responsibility for either the widespread unrest or for specific labor incidents.

During the closing months of the war, Communist activity in Japan was restricted to the occasional appearance of an untimely pamphlet. There were also incidents involving individuals labeled "red" by the police, but in most of these cases "sympathizer" or even "liberal" would have been a more accurate description. After more than fifteen years of prying and scraping, the Thought Police had reached the bottom of the barrel. Communism in Japan had been effectively, if temporarily, checked.

CHAPTER IX

Preparations at Yenan

IT is usual to date the resurgence of the Japanese Communist Party from the Allied Occupational Directive of October 4, 1945, which gave new freedom to Japan's political prisoners. Actually, by that time the spark of the postwar Party already was glowing brightly on the continent. It had been kindled in the spring of 1940 with the unexpected arrival in Yenan of Sanzo Nozaka.[1]

Nozaka's decision to leave Russia for Yenan, the Chinese Communist capital, was reached only after years of fruitless efforts and frustration. By 1940 ruthless police action and the upsurge of nationalism which followed the outbreak of war in China had rendered ineffective the scattered remnants of the revolutionary movement in Japan. Repeated attempts to establish liaison with the Japanese comrades had resulted in failure. Nozaka had received only a modicum of tangible support from the Russian leaders, who were then, despite the Russo-German Non-aggression Pact, perhaps more concerned with the growing power of Nazi Germany and the outcome of the Soviet venture in Finland.

In the early part of 1940 the Japanese leader decided to leave the Russian capital. Nozaka describes the period immediately preceding his departure for China:

Two years had passed since the outbreak of the China Incident and I had come to the conclusion that I must find a way to reënter Japan. The Moscow comrades supported this idea . . .

During nine years in the Soviet Union, I had spent relatively little time in Moscow. I operated in a number of areas closer to Japan, engaging in various activities directed against that country . . .

Liaison with Japan was becoming increasingly difficult. The crews which had been engaged in liaison work were frequently transferred to other positions or arrested by the Japanese authorities. Moreover, as the war progressed, fewer ships arrived and departed. We attempted to use foreign crews, but even this type of liaison was ferreted out by the police. We also sent quite a number of comrades back into Japan; contact with them proved difficult. In fact, most of them were arrested. Therefore it was up to me to enter the country. But from where? And how? These were the questions which puzzled me. Japanese security measures had been tightened. In my case standard procedure would not be adequate. The only way open seemed to be through a Chinese port. But my Chinese comrades had been away from their country for many months—and in some cases, for years. Consequently, they were out of touch with the situation there. I even asked Li Li-san,* but found him of little help.

Then, unexpectedly, I learned that a certain Chinese Communist leader was to visit Moscow for a short time. I was as happy as a lark. I met him and his group and inquired about the situation. Of course, they could not guarantee anything, but they felt that once I had reached Yenan, something could be worked out. Even if I should be unable to reach Japan, at least I might fight militarism on the battlefields of China and give revolutionary training to Japanese prisoners of war—a significant and challenging prospect!

I submitted this plan to Comrade Dimitrov, then Secretary General of the Comintern. He fully approved and was most helpful in the implementation of my plan.[2]

By March 1940 all preparations for the trip into China had been completed. The details of the long and dangerous journey were first made known by Nozaka in the summer of 1949. Up to that time it had been widely reported and generally assumed that the Japanese Communist leader had arrived in Yenan in 1943.[†] Nozaka's own account indicates otherwise:

It was in the early part of 1940. Moscow was still blanketed by heavy snow. I spent the days preparing for the journey. A famous Indonesian Communist was slated to make the trip with me. Without a word to anyone we left Moscow. I told my wife only that we were going to China and that we would probably not meet again until the war was over. . .

How to conduct two foreigners secretly through the Chinese Nationalist and Japanese lines to Yenan[‡] was a serious problem for our Chinese comrades. Neither I nor my Indonesian friend knew a single word of Chinese. We were really perplexed . . . Finally we decided that I should be an Overseas Chinese who had lived in the

*One of the early leaders of the Chinese Communist Party; he resided in Moscow from 1931 until his return to North China in 1946. With the establishment of the Chinese People's Republic, he became one of the most powerful figures in Mao Tse-tung's regime.

†In a conversation with U. S. intelligence agents in Yenan in September 1944 Nozaka stated: "I came to Yenan in the spring of 1943 as a member of the Central Committee of the Japanese Communist Party." U. S. Government, Office of War Information, China Division, Yenan Report No. 8, Sept. 25, 1944.

‡In 1937 an agreement between the Nationalist government and the Chinese Communists had been reached for a common front against Japan. By 1940 relations between the two parties again had deteriorated to the extent that a Nationalist blockade of Yenan virtually isolated the area from the rest of China.

Philippines and Japan and that my Indonesian comrade would be a Chinese from the South Seas. En route, this "Japanese-looking Chinese" and this "Chinese from the South Seas" were watched with suspicion by the innkeepers and authorities alike. We found ourselves in more than one tight spot. But our Chinese comrades always managed to save the day. Had we been caught, it would have meant the end . . .

We finally arrived in Yenan . . . It was the beginning of April, and the snow had begun to melt.[3]

Yenan was unique among the cities of China. Most of its forty thousand inhabitants made their homes in caves cut into the brown loess cliff sides flanking a narrow valley. Here the Communist armies had ended their Long March and established a new capital in 1936. Three years later a series of heavy Japanese air raids had reduced the city to a heap of rubble. By force of circumstances, the capital was transformed into a cave city.

When he arrived in Yenan, Nozaka was received by Mao Tse-tung, leader of the Chinese Communists, at the latter's cave residence. Only a few members of the Yenan hierarchy were on hand, as Mao had deemed it advisable not to make the Japanese Communist leader's presence known for the time being. Present was a Chinese whom Nozaka had known in Moscow, who embraced him and—in Nozaka's own words—"shed tears of joy."[4]

To protect himself from Japanese agents, known to be operating in the area, Nozaka found it necessary to add another cover name to an already lengthy list of pseudonyms. He identified himself as "Lin Che," a simple Chinese name, which might be assumed to be a Japanese name, in which case the written characters are read as "Hayashi Tetsu." For a short while "Tetsu Hayashi" confined his activities to the study of the Chinese language. During this period in his isolated cave home, a Chinese bulletin, distributed in the evening, was his only source of news from the outside world.

Whether Nozaka seriously considered continuing his trip beyond China and into Japan is questionable. In any case, barely a month after his arrival in Yenan, he readily accepted Chou En-lai's* proposal to join the staff of the political section of the Chinese Communist armies. In this capacity he was to take over the direction of psychological warfare against the Japanese forces in North China, especially the indoctrination of Japanese prisoners. The political education of Japanese prisoners in China was first inaugurated in 1938. Toward the end of that year ten Japanese prisoners of war were organized into a psychological-warfare

*After 1949 Prime Minister and Foreign Minister of the Chinese People's Republic.

unit, under the auspices of the Eighth Route Army.* This was the first Japanese antiwar organization in North China. Soon, similar groups made their appearance throughout Communist-held territory.

In assuming this new role with the Chinese Communist armies, Nozaka had by no means abandoned his original plans for Japan. Up to this time a research group had been maintained in Yenan to advise Mao Tse-tung's staff on matters related to Japan. Nozaka agreed to take over the direction of this work. "The Chinese Communist Party and the Eighth Route Army are pursuing the same objectives," Nozaka said; "with common aims, we must fight together in unity."[5] Wang Hsueh-wen, head of the Eighth Route Army's Psychological Warfare Section, soon assigned him a specific task: the preparation of analytical studies of the military, political, and economic situation in Japan.

About the same time Nozaka's first policy statement since leaving Moscow was distributed anonymously among Japanese soldiers and residents in North China. This pamphlet, entitled "The Present Duties of the Revolutionary Proletariat in Japan," emphasized three points: the development of a proletarian mass movement in Japan favored by the foreign and domestic situation; the necessity for friendly ties with the Soviet Union; and the importance of carrying on the fight under a number of specific political slogans. These three points were developed in detail. In Nozaka's opinion, the position of Japanese imperialism had been weakened substantially by the outbreak of war in Europe and the resulting neutralization of the Anti-Comintern Pact. A series of military defeats on the continent—at Nomonhan by the Soviet Union and at Changsha by the Chinese—had seriously shaken the nation's confidence in its leaders. Wang Ching-wei's puppet government in Nanking, sponsored by the Japanese imperialists, had not brought about the anticipated end of hostilities in China. Japan's blitzkrieg had become a protracted war.

Nozaka knew that this drawn-out war had given rise to a serious economic crisis in Japan. As a result, enthusiasm for the war on the continent was cooling off, and dissatisfaction was becoming evident throughout the homeland. The "National Spiritual Mobilization" of the Japanese nation had failed, Nozaka concluded.

Nozaka explained that the Japanese ruling classes were trying to form an anti-Soviet alliance which was bound to be dangerous and detrimental to the interests of the Japanese people. He emphasized the importance of friendly, neighborly ties with the Soviet Union. Nine slogans were provided with the recommendation that these be used to arouse the masses:

*In the spring of 1937, as part of the united-front agreement, Communist forces in North China were nominally incorporated into the Nationalist armies under the designation "Eighth Route Army."

Immediate termination of hostilities!

Immediate withdrawal of Japanese armed forces from China!

Down with the General Mobilization Law!

Reallocation of military funds! Toward the stabilization of the daily life of the people!

Freedom of speech, press, assembly and association!

Down with the militarists and their government!

Establishment of a democratic people's government!

Establishment of a peaceful and free Japan!

Sino-Japanese unity!

Nozaka's conclusion:

> The Bolsheviks, while fighting valiantly against extreme reaction, waged an all-out war against defeatism, party dissolution factions, and social-democratic trends. They put all their efforts into preparation for the 1917 Revolution. And under their glorious leaders, Lenin and Stalin, they won a brilliant victory and established the first Socialist State in history, covering a sixth of the surface of the globe.
>
> Comrades! Japan's "1917" is rapidly drawing near! Indeed, will we not by our efforts hasten that day![6]

At no time were Nozaka's efforts confined to purely military matters, nor did he ever lose sight of his final objective, "the establishment of a free and democratic Japan." Thus, his proposal in the spring of the year to establish a school "for the democratic education of Japanese prisoners of war,"[7] was dictated not alone by the demands of the situation in North China. Nozaka is explicit on this point: "The establishment of the school was not only for the immediate task of propaganda activities, but looked toward the establishment of a democratic Japan in the postwar period."[8] The Chinese Communists gave Nozaka a free hand to go ahead with his plans. Mao Tse-tung personally endorsed the project.

The establishment of a new school in wartime Yenan presented less of a problem than might have been expected. Nozaka's "Japanese Peasants and Workers' School" was allotted a large whitewashed cave right in the center of the capital. The school opened in October 1940 with a student body of ten Japanese prisoners of war who had volunteered for this unusual assignment.

Instruction was designed with a single purpose in view: the conversion of militarists into "revolutionary fighters for peace and democracy." Indoctrination was handled rather cautiously, a characteristic of Nozaka's approach. At first, the students were not directly confronted with Communist dogma. Rather, the Marxist interpretation was placed on such subjects as "What causes war?" or "The future of the worker in Japan." Gradually, as the pupil came to doubt the validity of many of the concepts which up to that time he had accepted without question, the dosage of pure Communist doctrine was increased. This was a slow process, and occasionally a student who seemed to be "advancing satisfactorily" reverted to his past beliefs. Nozaka relates the story of several students who secretly climbed the hill above the school to celebrate the Emperor's birthday by shouting the traditional *Tenno Heika Banzai.**

In spite of such relapses, the atmosphere among the students slowly "improved," and within a year a number of graduates were ready to put their knowledge to use in propaganda work with the Antiwar League *(Hansen Domei)*. The League had been created in 1939 by combining a number of smaller antiwar groups.† From the very beginning, this organization was more than its name implies. It aimed at the destruction of the Japanese fighting spirit as a prelude to the "establishment of a democratic Japan."

Methods of making contact with the enemy were diversified: a nostalgic song with special lyrics played over a loud-speaker; a mysterious telephone call from one of the League members; or a mimeographed leaflet, carried back into the Japanese lines—all were calculated to produce a receptive frame of mind within the enemy camp. The material was subtle and effective, another example of the Nozaka "go-slow" approach.

What these little songs may have lacked in musical quality, they more than made up for in homely appeal. Consider the following:

> My cherished home
> I had to leave behind
> And now—
> Beneath those crumbling eaves
> In utter loneliness
> A wife and child await
> That spring which never comes.[9]

Such songs conditioned the soldier psychologically for antiwar propaganda of the more conventional type:

> This constant talk of dying for the Emperor or the homeland—
> what nonsense! War brings only suffering to the Japanese people.
> The rich coin money, while you die a needless death in this robber
> war.[10]

*Long live the Emperor!
†The first branch was established at Kweilin on December 25, 1939 by Wataru Kaji, a left-wing refugee in Nationalist China.

By 1943 Nozaka-trained propagandists were operating with Chinese Communist units throughout North China. The Peasants and Workers' School was growing. The number of students had increased to about a hundred, and the original Chinese staff had been completely replaced by Yenan-trained Japanese.

The Japanese Communist leader "Tetsu Hayashi," primarily responsible for the political training of Japanese prisoners, appeared now for the first time in Yenan under his Moscow name, Susumu Okano. At a meeting of the Chinese Communist Politburo, which had been called to discuss the dissolution of the Comintern,* Mao Tse-tung proposed that Nozaka lend his prestige to the antiwar drive by making his presence in Yenan officially known. His existence in the Chinese Communist capital was no longer a secret, in the strict sense of the word.†

"An Appeal to the Japanese People," on July 7, 1943, the sixth anniversary of the Sino-Japanese Incident, marked the beginning of a new phase of preparations at Yenan. In fiery language Nozaka predicted the inevitable defeat of Japan, a defeat which he saw as a blessing in disguise —a rare opportunity for the "progressive forces" in Japan, led, of course, by the Communist Party. He called on the laboring people and especially on members of the proletarian parties, the trade-unions, and farm associations to rally under the banner of the Communist Party and to establish a "people's government":

> My fellow countrymen! My fellow soldiers! The bugle for the advance has sounded. March! Raise the glorious banner of the people. Under this flag we shall fight and, if need be die![11]

The blueprint for the organization which was to implement the establishment of a people's government after the imminent defeat of Japan emerged toward the end of 1943. In January 1944, Nozaka set up a preparatory committee composed of leaders of the Antiwar League to make plans for a Japanese Emancipation League. The League was to work for the political and economic emancipation of the Japanese working classes to be carried out with the help of the Allied military forces. Nozaka visualized a world-wide organization capable of uniting the more than five hundred thousand Overseas Japanese and ready to lend support to "democratic elements" within Japan. The new plan went beyond anything envisaged by the Antiwar League.

Although the platform of the Emancipation League embodied the antimilitarist slogans of its predecessor, beginnings of a political and

---

*The Comintern was dissolved on May 22, 1943.

†Japanese Intelligence on several occasions had sent spies into Yenan to attempt to assassinate Nozaka.

economic program for postwar Japan were clearly visible. This program was in the nature of a statement of principles. Controversial issues were either excluded—as in the case of the Emperor question—or dealt with in a cursory manner. In the latter category, the agrarian problem, for example, is dismissed with a single recommendation for the establishment of "a land system which will guarantee the effective use of land and permit introduction of mechanized farm equipment in order that our nation may attain prosperity."[12] No mention of either socialism or the Communist Party is found in the League's program.

The factors which determined the make-up of the Emancipation League's platform were clarified by Ken Mori, Nozaka's chief assistant, in the following terms:

> Our program aims to appeal not only to Japanese in Free China, but also to soldiers in the Japanese armed forces (and other Japanese residents) in China, and to the masses of people in Japan. We can even say that it is the latter group we emphasize. Therefore, it is their present morale, ideas, demands, struggles, etc. that we should consider in determining the basis of the program. Thus, those demands which are very far from their present degree of understanding, though correct in principle, are put in reserve and not included in this program. Our program, then, is a minimum one. When great changes occur in the political situation and in the conditions of the masses in the future, this program needs to be complemented and revised.[13]

The pattern of this anticipated revision had been forming in Nozaka's mind during years of "antiwar work" in North China. His conviction that success in transforming Japanese society could be achieved only through a cautious, slow approach had been reaffirmed by experience with Japanese prisoners where the desired result came only at the end of a patient and painstaking process of reëducation. This concept, as applied to Japan, took the form of a three-stage program leading from the destruction of the feudal-militaristic order through a bourgeois-democratic revolution to the final establishment of the socialist state. Nozaka did not hesitate to assert that active coöperation with the capitalist nations would be necessary in the first stage and desirable in the second. During the second stage, completion of the bourgeois-democratic revolution, Nozaka proposed to liquidate all traces of feudalism and to set up a "complete democracy" on a capitalistic basis. He reserved the destruction of capitalism and the establishment of a socialist order for the third and final stage.

In a conversation with a United States government observer in Yenan in the fall of 1944, the Japanese Communist leader implied that his preference for a gradual and peaceful development was subject to change. Nozaka was quoted as having said:

> The aim of this (third) stage will be to carry the development through to full socialism. This will mean the liquidation of capitalism. *But this should be a progressive and gradual development ...* If, however, capitalism is allowed to become so strong and monopolistic that it controls our democracy, then there will be a greater chance of violent revolution.[14]

United States government observers had arrived in Yenan in the summer of 1944, and confidential reports began to flow through Chungking to Washington. To Nozaka, the presence of these Americans offered the first real opportunity to establish direct official contact with the United States forces and to impress Washington with the potential usefulness of his Emancipation League as a vehicle for the democratization of Japan.

The fall of Saipan on July 9 of the same year and subsequent large-scale air raids on the Japanese homeland marked the beginning of the final stage of the war in the Pacific. The tempo of work in North China was stepped up, looking toward the day when the Emancipation League would plant its flag in the soil of Japan. By the spring of the following year (1945) some twenty branches of the Emancipation League had been established throughout North and Central China; concrete plans had been laid to extend activities into South China and even into Mongolia, Manchuria, and Korea.

The Seventh Congress of the Communist Party of China, which was held in Yenan shortly after the surrender of Germany, provided an excellent opportunity for Nozaka to air his views on the future of Japan. His address, as official representative of the Communist Party of Japan, followed a political report by Chairman Mao Tse-tung and a military report by Chu Teh, Commander-in-Chief of Chinese Communist forces. Nozaka, essentially, attempted to correct what he termed "mistaken views" held by the Allies—especially by Americans. He took exception to the tendency on the part of "certain Allies" to deny the existence of democratic forces within Japan, to show indifference to them, or to ignore them altogether. In raising the issue of the political future of Japan, Nozaka pointed to his country's "long history of liberalism" and to the presence of "progressive forces," led by the Communist Party. These, he stated, had continued to fight in the face of severe repression throughout the war and were ready now to shoulder the burden of democratization. It is this group, Nozaka emphasized, rather than the "moderates" or the "pro-Anglo-American faction" * which constitutes the most reliable basis for democracy in Japan.

Even sooner than expected, the war was over; and Nozaka began immediate preparations for his return to Tokyo. One of the last evenings there he spent with Mao Tse-tung in an exchange of ideas on the future of Japan. Nozaka recalls: "When I said good-bye to him, Mao firmly clutched my hand and encouraged me to do my best toward building a new Japan. Promising to meet again when this task had been completed, we said farewell."[15]

A curious climax to these years of preparations at Yenan came shortly after the surrender of Japan when Nozaka boarded an American plane for the first leg of the journey home. He reports:

> I heard that an American plane was scheduled to leave Yenan at the beginning of September with the mission of transporting some American soldiers to Lin Ch'u, a village one hundred miles south of Kalgan. There was no telling when I might get to Japan should I allow this opportunity to slip by. Therefore, I asked United States Army authorities to permit me to board the plane. At the same time I ordered members of the Japanese Emancipation League in North and Central China to move into Japan. The American plane left Yenan around noon, the 10th of September. I, three members of my Emancipation League, and fifteen members of the Eighth Route Army cadre had received permission to board the plane. We reached Lin Chu the afternoon of the same day. From there we finally managed to reach Kalgan by a combination of walking, horseback travel, oxcart transportation, and the train. The trip consumed about seven days.
>
> I had been working for about a week among the Japanese residents in Kalgan when, unexpectedly, a Soviet plane made its appearance at Kalgan airfield. This plane had been on a mission to Peking in search of another Soviet craft which had disappeared in the area. The search apparently had been of no avail, and the plane was scheduled to return from Kalgan to Changchun. The Eighth Route Army cadre members had been negotiating with the pilot for a trip to Manchuria, and we had hoped to go along. At the beginning there seemed to be some difficulty, but eventually the pilot consented. We and the Eighth Route Army cadre thus made the trip into Manchuria.

*These groups, according to Nozaka, were made up of financial magnates, members of the Imperial Household, bureaucrats, old generals, and leaders of the Seiyukai and Minseito parties.

While still in Manchuria, I learned from the radio and telegraph that the Japanese Communist Party had been given legal status and that Tokuda, Shiga, Kasuga, Hakamada, Miyamoto, and other leaders had been released from prison. When I heard this, I was elated. These leaders and I were bound together by the ties of time-tested comradeship. Their health must have suffered greatly during these more than ten years in jail, and I was greatly surprised when they began their work on the very day of their release . . . That such heroes should have come from the ranks of the Japanese workers made me very proud. I was eager to return to Japan as soon as possible in order to lighten their burden.

But my trip was beset with numerous obstacles. Even so, every day I drew a bit nearer to Japan, reaching Mukden, Heijo (Pyongyang), and Seoul; and on the 10th of January, at long last, I set foot on my native land—that land which I had never for a moment forgotten—that land which I had not seen for sixteen years.[16]

Part II

COMMUNISM IN POSTWAR JAPAN

CHAPTER X

Resurgence

O N September 2, 1945 representatives of the Japanese Emperor formally acknowledged their country's defeat. General Douglas MacArthur, as Supreme Commander for the Allied Powers, established headquarters in Tokyo and almost immediately launched a program of sweeping political, economic, and social reform. In line with the provisions of the Potsdam Declaration calling for the removal of "all obstacles to the revival and strengthening of democratic tendencies among the Japanese people," SCAP, during the early weeks of the occupation, concerned itself primarily with the problems of disarmament and demilitarization. The Japanese government, through which Allied objectives were to be realized, came to feel only gradually the full impact of defeat. For a time the Home Ministry continued, as in the past, to enforce "security measures" in an attempt to check the rising tide of "un-Japanese" ideas.

Confidential documents from the files of the Home Ministry reveal that on the eve of the surrender the Japanese government feared a resurgence of Communism in postwar Japan. The Soviet Union's belated entry into the war, only one week before Japan's capitulation, coincided with the first reports of renewed Communist activity throughout the nation. Acceptance of the Allied terms of surrender on August 14 did not alter the Japanese government's stand on the Communist issue. On August 16, a "former Communist" was arrested in central Japan for boasting, "Our time has at last arrived." The following day, Communist suspects were apprehended in northeastern Japan for celebrating their nation's defeat. The same week, police agents reported apprehensively the revival of the pro-Communist Esperanto movement.[1] Alarmed, the Thought Police began an extensive survey of political trends in Japan. A cross section of significant opinion thus obtained was filed by that agency for reference: "In the future, Japan will be a crucible of class struggle between the pro-American bourgeoisie and the pro-Soviet proletariat," one informant volunteered. Another stated: "Before the outbreak of war between the United States and Russia, the Soviet Union will direct a violent anti-American campaign through the Japanese Communists and strive to set up a red government in Japan."[2]

For fully a month after the unconditional surrender, the Japanese government did not relax its wartime censorship nor did the Japanese authorities, acting on their own initiative, hesitate to arrest individuals suspected of Communist sympathies. In one such instance, the Home Ministry was notified by the Governor of Kanagawa Prefecture of the arrest of three journalists for having written "objectionable" articles on the future of Communism in Japan.[3]

During this early transitional period, the Japanese government hesitated to admit the existence of political prisoners. On September 30, an American and two French journalists visited Fuchu Prison near Tokyo and demanded to see the imprisoned Communists. After some prodding, the guards, who at first had pleaded total ignorance of the matter, led the newsmen to the solitary-confinement block where the Communist leaders Kyuichi Tokuda and Yoshio Shiga were being held incommunicado.

Four days later, a SCAP directive, sometimes referred to as the Japanese "bill of rights," ordered the Japanese authorities to release all political prisoners. It further directed the government to "abrogate and immediately suspend the operation of all provisions of all laws, decrees, orders, ordinances, and regulations which establish or maintain restrictions on freedom of thought, of religion, of assembly, and of speech, including the unrestricted discussion of the Emperor, the Imperial Institution, and the Imperial Japanese Government." This directive, by granting unprecedented freedom of thought and political action, removed serious obstacles to the development of democracy in Japan; at the same time, it permitted the revival of latent revolutionary forces and, for the first time in Japan's history, granted the Communist Party legal status.

Reluctantly, the Japanese government released the political prisoners. Tokuda and Shiga were among the handful of Communists freed on October 10. Still clad in a light-green prison uniform, Tokuda delivered a ten-minute address in front of the prison to several hundred sympathizers who had gathered in the rain to greet the veteran leader.

Defeated Japan offered ideal conditions for the revival of a strong Communist movement. Her major cities, with the exception of historic Kyoto, lay in ruin. What remained of the nation's industry was disintegrating rapidly. Despair, hunger, and confusion inevitably followed total defeat. The Communists, who had consistently fought Japanese militarism and the ruling oligarchy, after the surrender constituted virtually the only political group which could convincingly disclaim any responsibility for the war and its consequences. They now appeared as the self-appointed champions of democracy.

Democracy came to Japan suddenly and by decree. The document, "United States Post-Surrender Policy," which formed the basis for the conduct of the occupation, stipulated: "The Japanese people shall be encouraged to develop a desire for individual liberties and respect for fundamental human rights, particularly the freedoms of religion, assembly, speech, and the press. They shall also be encouraged to form democratic and representative organizations."

The Communists were quick to take advantage of the situation.

Within ten days after the Allies had freed political prisoners, the first postwar issue of the Communist newspaper *Red Flag (Akahata)** came off the press. Communists distributed ten thousand copies of this twenty-page pamphlet carrying an "Appeal to the People," which had been conceived by Tokuda in his prison cell.

Before other political parties could effect the necessary transition to democracy, Communist leaders were touring the country to enlist support for the establishment of a "democratic people's government." On October 21 a "Relief Society for Martyrs of the Liberation Movement" held a rally in Osaka to welcome the "freed liberals." Tokuda appeared as principal speaker and outlined a program for "the development of democracy in Japan." He pleaded for the immediate overthrow of the existing order and for the creation of a people's government which he proclaimed "the only road to happiness."[5] The wide publicity given such rallies by the Japanese press tended to create generally the impression that the Communists constituted the mainstay of democracy in Japan.

In Tokyo the small organization which the liberated Communists had formed hailed the American occupation forces as liberators, identified itself publicly with the objectives of the occupation, and made plans to expand in order to "assist" in the establishment of a democratic Japan.

Three hundred Communists convened in Tokyo on the morning of November 8 to attend a special meeting. "May I address a few words of welcome to you at this—the National Consultative Conference," Tokuda greeted the first legal gathering in the history of the Japanese Communist movement. "Since we are Communists," he continued, without dwelling on his eighteen years in prison, "my greetings will be more in the nature of a report." He then appealed to the assembled Party members to step up Cell activity in factories, on farms, in fishing villages, and in schools throughout Japan. At the same time he cautioned against any relaxation of Party discipline and security: "Party democracy—that is, the democratization of Party activities—does not imply that we must publicly discuss Party affairs . . . Stalin has repeatedly said that the aim of Party democracy is the achievement of strict enforcement of Party regulations and the forceful application of Party policy."[6] Under Tokuda's chairmanship, the Conference then proceeded to a discussion of Party regulations and a consideration of a program, which was subsequently endorsed for presentation to the Party Congress scheduled for December.

Less than two months after a "bill of rights" had brought unprecedented freedom to the Japanese nation, the Communist Party of Japan, with a registered membership of more than one thousand, held its Fourth National Congress—the first in nineteen years.

*The Japanese characters for this title were generally pronounced *Sekki* during the prewar period.

CHAPTER XI

Party Organization and Administration

THE Japanese Communist Party is not a political party in the Western sense of the term; attainment of its stated objective, "the establishment of the ultimate form of democracy, a socialist state, culminating in the creation of a Communist society,"[1] would alter not only the existing form of government in Japan but the very structure of Japanese society itself. To accomplish such a goal, a political organization patterned after the Republican Party in the United States or the British Labor Party would be inadequate. The Japanese Communist organization accordingly bears little resemblance, either structurally or functionally, to any of the conventional Western political parties.

In organization, nomenclature, and administration, the Communist Party of Japan—as is to be expected—closely resembles the Communist Party of the Soviet Union and, like its Russian prototype, embraces every aspect of the political, economic, and social life of the nation through an interlocking network of Communist Cells guided and controlled by a hierarchical arrangement of Party agencies (see Fig. 2).

THE PARTY STRUCTURE

CENTRAL AGENCIES

The core of the Japanese Communist Party is formed of four central agencies which represent the highest echelon of the rigid chain of command. These are the Party Congress, the National Consultative Conference, the Central Committee, and the Control Commission.

The Party Congress

The Party Congress officially constitutes the supreme authority within the Communist Party of Japan. Delegates to its conventions are elected by Party members through local organizations. These delegates formulate the Party's platform, discuss its governing regulations and lay down the principles of political action. The Congress elects the Party's Executive Board: the Central Committee members and their alternates and members of the highest investigative and judicial body, the Control Commission. On paper the prerogatives of the Party Congress exceed even those of a legislative assembly in a Western democracy.

The Party Congress, in theory all-powerful, is an example of "Party democracy." All members of the Executive Board are ex officio delegates

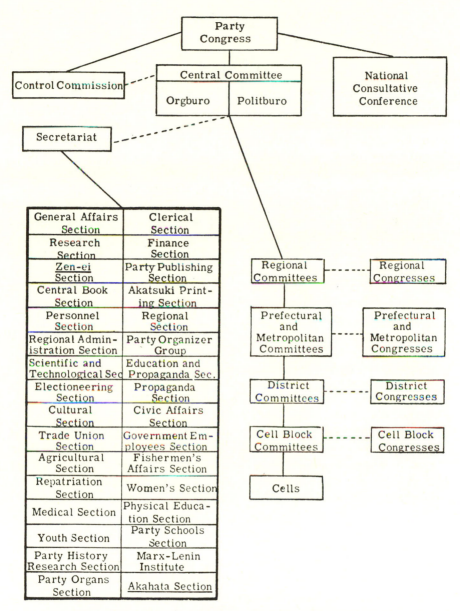

Fig. 2. Organization of the Communist Party of Japan (1950).

to the Congress. They also determine the procedure for electing other delegates; and, since the Central Committee must certify all organizations electing delegates, members of the Executive Board thus control, to a large extent, the actual makeup of the Congress which, in turn, "elects" the Executive Board. The effectiveness of the Party Congress as an "independent forum" has been reduced further by the Secretary General's policy of excluding the public from most sessions to permit "full and open discussion."[2] Accordingly, opposition is given little opportunity to become vociferous, and resolutions prepared in advance by the Party's leadership always have met with the approval of the delegates.

With increasing stress on "concentration" within the Party's concept of "democratic concentration" (democratic centralism), the Party Congress has functioned less and less as the supreme policy-making agency. This trend is reflected in the decreasing frequency of its "annual" conventions: a Party Congress was convened in December 1945, in February 1946 and again in December 1947; but no Congress convened during 1948 or 1949 nor did a Congress, repeatedly scheduled for the fall of 1950 or 1951, materialize.

The National Consultative Conference*

The National Consultative Conference, a small-scale working model of the Party Congress, may be called together at the request of the Central Committee whenever urgent questions of basic policy or serious differences of opinion within the Central Committee make such a meeting advisable. The Conference has the authority to remove a member of the Central Committee for "inefficiency" and to replace him by an alternate. Up to one-fifth of the Committee members may be dismissed in this manner. The Conference cannot, however, convene of its own accord, so this prerogative is of a highly hypothetical nature.

The Central Committee

The Central Committee is the most authoritative agency of the Japanese Communist Party. In theory, its twenty-five members and their nine alternates are elected by the Party Congress to represent the Party and to carry out the program agreed upon by the majority of the Party membership. In practice, the Central Committee has become a self-perpetuating body of veteran leaders whose authority is limited only by extra-Party pressure. Members of the Committee may be purged only by the Party Congress—where they are the predominating influence —or by a two-thirds vote of their fellow members. Thus, they are virtually invulnerable.

*The Fourth National Consultative Conference convened secretly in Japan in February 1951.

The Central Committee, headed by the Secretary General, meets at least once every two months. Plenary sessions (at which the alternates and, at times, members of the Control Commission are also present) are called at least every four months, but only Central Committee members vote at such meetings. A plenary session represents the greatest concentration of power within the Communist Party. All important decisions on strategy and general policy are made by this group, which meets in closed session. A brief of the proceedings of the Nineteenth Plenary Session of the Central Committee which convened in Tokyo on April 29, 1950 will serve to illustrate the nature of such a meeting:

(1) Discussion of the Secretary General's draft of a 1950 Thesis. [This fifty-two page document, "Tasks of the Japanese Communist Party," was to be made public eventually.]

(2) Report by the Secretary General on an urgent matter: the rise within the Party of a "petty-bourgeois sect," supported by the actions of a certain Central Committee member [only in part for publication].

(3) Clarification of the above-mentioned issue by the Chief of the Control Commission followed by concrete recommendations for disciplinary action [secret].

(4) Discussion of the above matter and an "explanation" by the members concerned [secret].

(5) Approval of a brief unanimous statement on Party policy for release to the press.

Although the Central Committee retains the final authority in regard to formulation and implementation of Party policy, it has delegated the daily execution of these tasks to three separate agencies which are staffed by Central Committee members.

THE POLITBURO

The Central Committee's Politburo constitutes the Communist Party's permanent planning board for revolutionary action. Major decisions relative to Communist strategy and tactics are made within this small group which comprises the key figures of the Japanese Communist Party. According to the governing regulations of the Party, "The Politburo has been established within the Central Committee in order to determine the over-all policy of the Party as well as the course of political action."[3]

The Politburo meets whenever the situation requires and continues its deliberations until agreement has been reached on an issue. Its recommendations then are transmitted to the Central Committee, which makes the final decision. The Politburo's approval, however, is tantamount to adoption of a measure since members of the Politburo are concurrently members of the Central Committee and have a decisive influence on the Committee's action. Only in the rare cases when no agreement can be reached within the Politburo does the Central Committee reassume the authority delegated to its branch.

Communist strategy and political action are thus effectively formulated and directed by the eight Party members who make up the Politburo of the Central Committee of the Communist Party of Japan.*

ORGBURO

The Central Committee's Orgburo is headed by the Secretary General of the Communist Party, who is assisted in his duties by another member of the Central Committee. This section directs the organizational phase of Party operations; thus, the training and allocation of Party organizers fall within the jurisdiction of the Orgburo. The section head regularly calls meetings to evaluate past achievements and to instruct the Party workers in methods of propaganda and organization. Such gatherings are further used to focus the attention of the organizer on hitherto neglected segments of the population and to effect an exchange of experience on a national basis.

The fact that a special agency within the Central Committee has been charged with the execution of such specific duties illustrates the importance which the Party attaches to all questions of organization.

THE SECRETARIAT

The Central Committee's executive arm, the Party Secretariat, is responsible for the implementation of Politburo decisions. Its activities are supervised by the Secretary General of the Party and a limited number of experienced Central Committee members. Since the Secretariat must attend to a variety of Party affairs, ranging from the running of nursery schools to the administration of the Marx-Lenin Institute and from the sponsorship of "democratic chamber-music societies" to the propagation of the Word among fishermen, the Central Committee has created a steadily growing number of Special Sections.

The Control Commission

The Control Commission of the Communist Party, appointed by the Party Congress, is an independent central agency. "Its chief tasks," the

*An order from SCAP to the Japanese government on June 6, 1950 resulted in the "removal from public life" of the twenty-four members of the Central Committee. (One had been purged the previous year.) Neither this nor subsequent purge orders, however, appear to have brought about any basic structural changes, although these measures compelled Party leaders to streamline the organization and to place more of the apparatus underground. See Chapter XVIII.

official Party newspaper relates, "are education [of Party members] and the fight against destructive elements."[4] These are, in fact, but two aspects of a single mission: the enforcement of absolute discipline within the Party. The Control Commission is composed of Party members who are selected for superior Party records and outstanding devotion to duty. It enlists the support of central and local agencies in its efforts to maintain a high level of security. The Commission is responsible for the prevention and detection of infiltration from the outside and of information leaks from within as well as for the correction or elimination of opponents of the Party line. (These last-named persons are variously designated as "deviationists," "sectarians," "Trotskyites," or "petty bourgeois.") A continuous check on the operations of local agencies likewise falls within the domain of the Commission.

Disciplinary measures vary according to the nature of an offense. Any one of five corrective actions may be taken: admonition, warning, suspension, imposition of restrictions (as in the case of Central Committee member Shigeo Kamiyama who, in 1948, was asked to refrain from writing on certain subjects), and expulsion (as in the case of the Communist Diet member, Ko Nakanishi, who was expelled from the Party in the spring of 1950 for his outspoken opposition to the Central Committee's line). In principle, each of the Party's units may purge itself of "undesirable elements"; the final decision, however, lies with the Control Commission. Punitive measures taken for infractions of regulations and "conduct harmful to Party interest" are not limited to Party members or individuals. The Control Commission may dissolve Party units and call for a re-registration of members or prohibit executive agencies from handling certain printed matter, as in the case of the magazine *Truth (Shinso)* which, in May 1950, was banned from circulation among Party members when the Control Commission detected in the columns of the hitherto pro-Communist publication examples of "demagogic distortion." In a high-level involvement, the Control Commission acts only in coöperation with the Politburo or the Central Committee.

An important aspect of the Commission's activities consists in measures taken to protect the Party against all outsiders. Throughout Japan the Commission maintains counterintelligence agents who investigate and evaluate the activities, strength, and background of anti-Communist elements, groups, and organizations. Within these categories fall certain Japanese government departments and agencies of foreign powers.

REGIONAL, PREFECTURAL, AND DISTRICT UNITS

Regional, prefectural, and district agencies of the Japanese Communist Party are central agencies in miniature: the Regional Party Congress corresponds to the national Party Congress and the Regional Committee to the Central Committee. Regional agencies form the echelon directly below the central agencies in the Communist Party's chain of command. Personnel of the lower echelon must be certified by the Central Committee in order to guarantee uniform execution of Party instructions and absolute obedience.

Japan is divided into nine regions, following the traditional geographical breakdown: Hokkaido, Northeastern Honshu, Northwestern Honshu, Tokyo, Southeastern Honshu, Osaka-Kyoto, Southwestern Honshu, Kyushu, Shikoku. These nine regions, in turn, are subdivided into prefectural (and metropolitan) areas, each with its own Congress and Committee. These areas are further broken down into districts, with District Congresses and District Committees, similar in structure to the corresponding units of the higher echelons. The size and number of districts vary in accordance with the number of Party members affected, the strategic importance of the area, and the distances involved.* To facilitate work among the farming population, a District Committee may be called a "branch" or "association," although for inner Party communications the official term is used.

The District Committee is only one step removed from the basic unit of the Communist Party structure—the Cell. The main duty of the Communist District Committee consists in groundwork among the "masses" for the expansion of existing organizations and the creation of new Cells.

THE CELL

The word "cell" is a relatively new addition to the Western political vocabulary. Correctly understood in its social and political connotation, the term represents an exclusively Marxist concept, familiar perhaps only in the most general way to the average Western student of political science. To the Marxist, it is the very essence of political organization. Knowledge of the term as used by Marxists, therefore, is essential to an understanding of Communist Party organization. An official handbook of the Communist Party of Japan, entitled "Cell Activities Made Easy," provides an excellent description:

> When a number of individuals function as a group, they unite in some definite form. This is what is meant by organization. Members of labor unions, social groups, and cultural circles are organized appropriately. Similarly, members of a political party, whether they number several thousands or several million, must be organized. The bourgeois political parties and the Socialist Party . . . place

*In July 1950 there were 317 District Committees throughout Japan.

greatest emphasis upon the vote at election time. In focusing their attention upon the election, these parties organize according to their member's place of residence, rather than according to his place of work. Our Communist Party is different. The Communist Party is not interested primarily in obtaining votes. To our Party, the working masses are more important . . .

The Communist Party must fight bravely for the needs of the working masses and, through this fight, develop within the masses a class consciousness. The Communist Party must be organized in a manner appropriate for such revolutionary activity . . .

The basic unit of the Party is called a Cell. Cells are created in shops, agrarian communities, schools, and residential areas. These Cells, each of which has a definite, independent character, serve as the nuclei of Party activity. The situation is exactly the same as in the case of the human body, where each cell functions as an independent organism, contributing at the same time to the function of the body as a whole.

These Cells are combined to form District Committees, Regional Committees, and a Central Committee. Through the Cell, the higher echelons activate the masses. Union of the Party and the masses is effected through the Cell . . .

The Cell is the stronghold of the revolutionary movement.[5]

A Cell is thus the smallest tactical unit of the complex Party organization and, as such, corresponds to the squad in the infantry company. The parallel becomes increasingly apparent as one studies the structure of a Cell and its relation to other agencies.

Four major types of Cells are operated by the Japanese Communist Party: the Agrarian Cell, the School Cell, the Residential Cell, and the Shop Cell. Structurally, they are the same. Ranging in size from three to

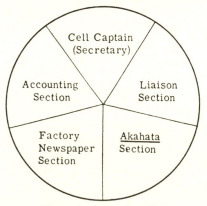

Fig. 3. A young shop Cell.

one hundred members, they may be divided, in terms of development, into three categories: the young Cell, the mature Cell, and the giant Cell.

The young Cell* (Fig. 3), which may consist of as few as three individuals or as many as fourteen, is formed from Party members in the same shop. To become active, the Cell must be recognized by the District Committee. Once out of the "preparatory stage" (fewer than three members), the group begins independent operation, meeting at least once a week under the leadership of a Secretary, or Cell Captain. Cell members are obliged to abide by resolutions adopted at the weekly meetings. The scope of activities of the young Cell is determined by its size; for example, a Cell having only three members might consist of the Cell Captain (also liaison representative with higher echelons), a representative for the Party newspaper, *Red Flag,* who is also responsible for publication of a factory newspaper, and a secretary-treasurer (in charge of collection of Party dues, Cell accounting, and the like). As the Cell expands, new sections are created and operations are stepped up.

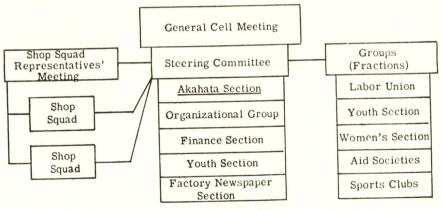

Fig. 4. A mature Cell.

The mature Cell, composed of from fifteen to seventy members (Fig. 4), has been the basis of Communist operations in Japan. A steering committee of not more than five members is elected at the Cell meeting and placed under the direct leadership of the Cell Captain. A number of squads and special sections are maintained to handle the various aspects of the Cell's activities.

The giant Cell (Fig. 5), with more than seventy members (meeting once a month), consists of a steering committee (which meets daily), special sections, shop squads, and Party-member groups (fractions). It represents the ultimate stage of development of the Communist Cell in Japan. In practice, however, even a giant Cell maintains only those sections deemed

*The shop Cell has been used here for purposes of illustration.

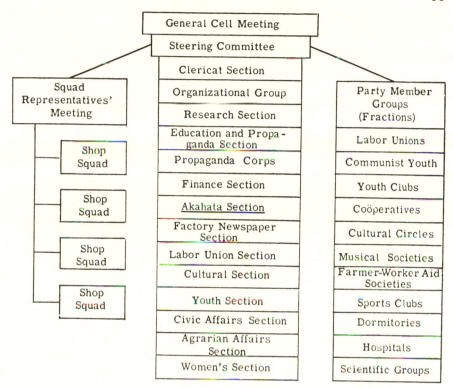

Fig. 5. A giant Cell.

essential to its immediate operations and, therefore, may not always include all of the sections shown in Fig. 5.

In short, as an official handbook of the Japanese Communist Party defines it: "The Cell is the 'home' of the Communist Party."[6]

PARTY FUNDS

Figures released by the Japanese National Election Supervision Committee concerning Party funds for the 1949-1950 fiscal year show that the Communist Party registered 122,876,000 yen as against 42,897,000 yen reported by the Liberals; 11,254,000 yen for the Socialists; and 4,966,000 yen for the Democrats. This striking contrast served to stimulate widespread speculation regarding the source of Japanese Communist Party funds, which generally are assumed to be even more substantial than the Party is prepared to admit.

According to the Party Rules and Regulations, funds are derived from three sources: membership dues, consisting of 1 percent of the member's salary or wages; revenue from Party enterprises; and contributions. It has been suggested repeatedly that such sources as enumerated above produce no more than a fraction of the Party's total actual revenue. Before exploring this question, it may not be out of place to consider how the Japanese Communists spend these funds.

Funds generally are allocated to the various agencies in the following proportions: 10 percent to the Central Committee, 10 percent to the Regional Committees, 30 percent to the Prefectural Committees, 40 percent to District Committees, and the remaining 10 percent to the Cell Committees. Precise data on the use to which the money is put on the various levels of the hierarchy cannot readily be obtained, although the available fragments of the picture reveal a significant pattern.

Normal operational overhead comprises a large portion of the budget, since the nature of the Party organizational structure necessitates the maintenance of more offices and branches throughout Japan than is the case for the conventional political parties.* To these expenditures must be added the salaries of members who devote full time to service with the Party. During 1946, the uniform monthly salary for such individuals was two hundred fifty yen(then about seventeen dollars at the official rate of exchange). In addition, the full-time Party worker received monthly fifty yen for travel, thirty yen for miscellaneous expenses and fifty yen for each dependent—the total not to exceed five hundred yen. The Party's contention that the Party Secretary General receives the same compensation as other salaried members has been viewed with some skepticism even within Japanese Communist circles.

Campaign expenses require another large cash outlay. Since the Communist electioneering pattern has approximated that of other political parties in Japan and, for that matter, has not differed materially from the accepted techniques in the United States, it may suffice to say that, during the several weeks prior to a national or local election, travel expenses, the cost of campaign literature, and related items eat heavily into the Party funds. In the elections of January 1949 the Communist Party put about fifteen hundred candidates in the field. As Japanese experts estimate the minimum cost of the campaign for the House of Representatives at a quarter of a million yen for each candidate (approximately seven hundred dollars at the official rate), it is evident that electioneering constitutes an expensive operation.

The third item on the debit side of the ledger is what the Party terms "aid to democratic organizations" and "support of worthy projects." This category includes the "front organizations," some of which apparently receive intermittent subsidies from the Party—although, in theory,

*Comparative figures on organizations registered with the Japanese Attorney General's Office in 1949 were as follows: the Liberal Party, 728; the Democrats, 293; the Socialist Party, 1336; the Communist Party, 5625.

they are expected to contribute to the Party. Publicity drives to win new members for such organizations as the "Japanese-Soviet Friendship Association" find their place here, as does the sponsorship of cultural circles and the like.

Finally, mention should be made of funds earmarked for espionage, sabotage, and related intelligence work, although these together perhaps constitute only a relatively small percentage of the total cost of running the Party.

It is impossible to calculate Party spending on a precise basis; yet the over-all impression gained from an examination of the available information on Party expenditures is one suggesting resources other than those admitted by the Party.

An investigation into the origin and size of Party funds proceeds logically from a brief analysis of the three sources cited in the Party Rules and Regulations. What is the monthly revenue actually received by the Party from source number one: membership dues? It is clear that the Party has not been able to enforce the rule of 1 percent of the member's fixed income. In July 1948 the Otaru District Committee in Hokkaido reported that from its twenty Cells it had been able to collect only 81.6 percent of the total assessed membership dues, for an average of twenty yen per member.[7] The Tachikawa Cell Group in the Tokyo area gave the following figures on dues collected for May, June, and July of the same year: 81 percent, 77 percent, and 45 percent, respectively.[8] Though Party Committees and Cells at times have claimed 100-percent results, such instances appear to have been the exception rather than the rule, for the Party reported in the spring of 1948 that more than three million yen in membership dues and subscription fees for Communist publications had not been remitted to the Party Finance Section.[9] The organization's income from membership dues in the peak year of 1949 is believed to have been about two million yen monthly.

By "Party enterprises," the Rules and Regulations allude to sale of official and unofficial publications, to cultural festivals, and to numerous small-scale operations such as wastepaper drives and the taking in of washing and selling of soap and towels by women Communists to raise funds for the Party. Proceeds obtained in this manner must remain highly speculative. Certainly the largest item in this category has been returns from publications, reliably reported at fifty thousand yen monthly as early as 1946. The Finance Committee told the Sixth Congress in December 1947 that two Party members who had toured Ishikawa Prefecture selling Communist publications had sold one hundred thousand yen worth of literature in one month.[10]

The same Committee spoke of three hundred yen profit per day in the city of Kobe from the sale of Communist comic books. By 1949, however, owing to the deflationary trend which had set in, revenue from this source dropped off sharply, forcing the Party to depend more and more upon contributions and to launch a major fund-raising campaign. After noting this trend, *Red Flag*, on July 14, 1949, recorded:

> Members of one of our Cells, participating in our nation-wide fifty million yen fund-raising campaign, visited every single home in their area. They explained in passionate words the significance of this campaign and achieved splendid results. For example, the head of a fire brigade—which had been designated by the government as a model brigade—an adherent of the Shintoist sect, *Tenrikyo,* not only responded to our appeal for funds but even joined the Party. It is said that the *Tenrikyo* believer applied for membership because he had been moved by the enthusiastic attitude of our Party members, in which he saw "a vision of God."

Though it is unlikely that the Party achieved its goal of fifty million yen, certainly contributions have constituted a major source of funds, perhaps as high as two hundred thousand yen monthly. They have come from a variety of sources. At the time of the general election of 1947 each member was requested to donate four hundred yen for the Party's election-campaign fund. Party sympathizers have also contributed financial aid. Donations are even reported to have been made by certain capitalists in the hope that they might avoid labor trouble by remaining on good terms with the Communist Party. One of the most enterprising contributors has been the non-Communist Japanese exporter. The Party's contact with such trade representatives, particularly in the Osaka-Kobe area, is a matter of record. A matter of record also is the desire of these businessmen to share in any future trade with Communist China. Since the Japanese Communist Party had been the most articulate champion of trade with the continent, persistent rumors during 1946 and 1947 of substantial Party contributions from "business interests" in Osaka and Kobe are not surprising.

To what extent these legal fund-raising endeavors have been augmented by illegal activities cannot readily be ascertained. Speculation runs high. The Party repeatedly has attempted to refute all such allegations. In his general report to the Fourth Party Congress in December 1945, Secretary General Tokuda denied rumors that the Party had received upwards of twenty million yen from the Soviet Union, stating that, under then existing conditions governing foreign exchange, the transfer of such a sum obviously would be impossible.[11] Alluding to reports of certain secret sources of Party revenue, *Red Flag*, April 22, 1948, carried the following item: "Our funds do not come from some obscure source. They are nothing but the accumulation of many pennies produced by the toil of the working people."

Though no specific information has come to light to substantiate the recurrent rumor that funds have been supplied secretly to the Japanese Communists by the Soviet Mission in Japan, knowledge of other aspects of the Party's operations suggests that some financial aid may have been afforded from that source. There is, further, considerable evidence of other illicit transactions.

The charge that the Party derives some of its revenue from smuggling and from the illegal handling of drugs has been raised from time to time. Here, rumor finds some support in fact. Early in 1949 documents came to light which, if authentic, link the Japanese Communist Party to an extensive and profitable smuggling operation involving the illegal importation from Russia and sale in Japan of the drug Santonin.[12] In July the story received partial confirmation with the announcement that the National Rural Police had made raids upon eleven District Committee headquarters of the Communist Party and had arrested six Communists on suspicion of violating the medical law by the sale of five hundred bottles of medicine tablets for five hundred thousand yen. The bottles were labeled "Made in England."

For many months prior to this time it had been an open secret in Japan that both Allied intelligence and the Japanese government were concerned with the extent of smuggling known to be going on between Japan and the continent. The *New York Times* reported in January 1949 that the Japanese government had plans under way to augment the number of coastal patrol vessels on duty by fifteen modern ships modeled after United States revenue cutters. Other reports involving individual Communist Party members tend to confirm the Party's participation in such illicit traffic. For example, in October 1950 the Chief of the Fukuoka Communist District Committee was arrested by the police on charges of having violated the antinarcotics law by attempting to sell 450 grams of heroin, valued at more than one hundred million yen (which he had received from a Korean).[13] An additional bit of evidence attesting to the Party's clandestine fund-raising campaign was picked up in November 1950 when the nephew of Communist leader Tokuda, after being indicted by the local procurator's office on embezzlement charges, admitted having given two hundred thousand yen of the money in question to a representative of the Communist Party.[14]

The conclusion seems warranted that the terms "Party enterprises" and "contributions," listed by the Party as sources of its funds, can be interpreted only in their broadest sense and that any "financial report" made public by the Party must be viewed with the greatest skepticism.

THE COMMUNIST PRESS

The Japanese Communist press represents an important element of the Party structure. It is organized along the same lines as the Party itself with each echelon publishing and distributing its own propaganda paper. Three Special Sections of the Central Committee's Secretariat have been responsible for the editorial policy and publication of the principal newspapers and periodicals which the Communists have circulated in Japan during the postwar period. These Sections are *Red Flag* Section, *Vanguard* Section, and the Party Organs Section.

Red Flag, the Party daily and official mouthpiece of the Central Committee, was published regularly in Tokyo and distributed on a nationwide scale until its suppression by the Japanese government during the summer of 1950. Its circulation at the beginning of 1950 was approximately three hundred thousand. The paper carried all significant Party reports and resolutions, statements and articles by the recognized Party leaders, and the Moscow interpretation of foreign and domestic news. In addition, the Party published for a time a weekly magazine, the *Red Flag Weekly,* which represented the Communist version of the *New York Time's* "News of the Week in Review."

Vanguard, the Party's monthly periodical, which continued to be published during 1951, has been read by a more limited number of Party members, as its appeal was intellectual with emphasis on theory.* The table of contents of the May 1950 issue will serve to illustrate the nature of the subject matter treated:

> The Significance of the Editorial [on Japan] in the "Organ of the Information Bureau of the Communist and Workers' Parties."
> Fundamental Lessons from the Exposure and Destruction of the Kostov Faction. Deficiencies in Party Operations and Our Tasks.
> Seeing Through the New Budget: Military Colonization.
> Ideology as a Weapon of the Ruling Authority and Our Philosophical Front.
> Research Material from the Second Comintern Congress.
> The New Stage in the Agrarian Movement and Important Factors in Its Development.
> A Realistic Criticism of Ko Nakanishi.
> The Victory of the United Front.
> A New Stage in the [Japanese government's] Traitorous Fiscal Policy.
> The Struggle for Removal of the Deficit in Chinese Economy.

*With Issue No. 59, June 1951, *Vanguard* editorial policy was changed to make it, as the editor stated, "less specialized and more readable."

Postwar Struggle for the People's Liberation in Colonial Areas and Semicolonial Countries.

Comrade Malenkov's Speech on the Occasion of the Elections to the Supreme Soviet of the Soviet Union.

Five other Communist publications were officially designated by the Party as central organs: *A New World (Atarashii Sekai), Intelligence Digest (Chosa Jiho), Science and Technology (Kagaku to Gijutsu), The Friendly Gazette (Nakayoshi Shimbun)* and *A Club for the Masses (Taishu Kurabu).*

Every Regional and District Committee is urged by the Central Committee to publish its own newspaper. In practice, only the fully developed areas attempt to edit and print information and propaganda sheets. The five most important regional publications have been *The Tractor (Torakuta)* in Hokkaido, *The Kanto Weekly (Kanto Shuho)* in the Tokyo area, *Dawn (Akatsuki)* in the Osaka-Kyoto area, *Chugoku Front (Chugoku Sensen)* in Southwestern Honshu, and *Construction (Kensetsu)* in Kyushu.

Many Communist Cells also publish newssheets. The postwar Cell newssheet, like its illegal prewar predecessor, is prepared and distributed in mimeographed form to members and sympathizers. In terms of both quantity and quality the factory newspaper is the outstanding example of this type of Party publication. "Red Tractor," "Spark Plug," "Searchlight," and "Line of Battle" are representative factory newssheets intended "to give workers in a particular factory a Communist consciousness."[15] An effective newssheet contains such varied material as a discussion of problems faced by the worker in the particular factory, concise interpretations of events in Japan, political caricatures, poems and essays by workers, and "letters to the editor." The mission of the Cell newssheet is summarized by the Party's specialist in the field, Central Committee members Shojiro Kasuga: "Not only must the factory newssheet foster the worker's dissatisfaction with the capitalists and the government, it must also voice the general discontent . . . and show the working class . . . how to capitalize upon dissension and strife between the classes of society in order to bring about its own liberation."[16]

PERIPHERAL (FRONT) ORGANIZATIONS

The structure and operational procedure of the Communist Party of Japan, as outlined above, constitutes only part of the plan for eventual domination. The Communist movement in Japan, as elsewhere, draws much of its strength from a host of peripheral organizations —often referred to as "front organizations"—over which the Party exercises a varying degree of influence and control.

No segment of the population is considered insignificant; no group is deemed too small; no field of interest is regarded as too remote. The numerous associations and clubs, which fluctuate in and out of the Communist orbit, range from large labor unions to obscure poetry societies; and their combined strengths must be reckoned with in evaluating the Communist movement in Japan.

The existence within Japan of organized sympathizers is not a recent phenomenon. During the thirties many "proletarian" cultural societies, labor unions, and student groups actively supported the Communist cause. The nomenclature has since been revised to replace "proletarian" by "democratic," but the significance of such peripheral organizations remains essentially the same. By drawing upon this nonregistered strength, the Communist Party of Japan commands an effective force for the revolutionary struggle.

CHAPTER XII

The Leaders

THE BIG THREE—VETERANS OF THE TWENTIES

TOKUDA—THE FIERY SECRETARY GENERAL

KYUICHI TOKUDA, the highest-ranking and nominal leader of the Japanese Communists is perhaps the most dangerous of the antidemocratic elements. Twenty-eight years of unswerving devotion to the international Communist cause, almost twenty of which were spent in prison, have earned him this position. Although at times his policies have been criticized by other Party leaders, his position as the ranking Communist in Japan has never been challenged.

Tokuda was born on September 12, 1894 in the village of Nago on the island of Okinawa, at a time when the Ryukyu archipelago was the Japanese Emperor's most distant possession. An unorthodox family background and an unhappy childhood lie behind his interest in social problems and apparently gave him an early start on the road to Communism. Tokuda related in 1946:

> I became a Communist as a result of very special circumstances. In the days of feudal government, my paternal grandfather, a native of Kagoshima, worked his way up from a position as a common sailor to the status of trader. He sailed his ship to the Ryukyu Islands, where he bought merchandise cheaply and resold these goods at the cities of Kagoshima, Moji, and Osaka. Traders such as my grandfather all kept mistresses in the Ryukyus. My father was born from the union of this Kagoshima trader and his Ryukyu mistress. . .
>
> My paternal grandmother came from a very poor family of farmers. The house in which she was born looked like a pig pen, and her family found it necessary to sell her into prostitution. Thus she became my grandfather's mistress and gave birth to my father. My mother was born of a similar union.
>
> Her mother was also born into a poor family of artisans as one of three daughters, two of whom were sold into prostitution . . . The price at that time (1866) was about twenty yen for a fifteen- or sixteen-year-old girl . . . When I was young, the price varied from thirty to fifty yen.
>
> My maternal grandmother was a usurer. She loaned money at a monthly rate of 10 percent . . . As my own family was poor, I had to

do housework at my grandmother's home until I finished high school. I also helped with the accounts and collected monthly payments. At the same time, I was supposed to be going to school, but actually I went only about twenty [sic] days out of every month.

By the time I was . . . twelve, I understood well the methods by which usurers and their like deceive and exploit the farmer and worker and the poor people. My young heart was filled to the brim with sympathy for the worker and the farmer and with hatred for those—including my grandmother—who engage in such sordid transactions. I told our clients that it was no good to borrow money, that they would only be squeezed, and that they should wait until I would earn some money to help them . . . My grandmother detested me. She wouldn't buy me any shoes. For calisthenics I had to borrow old shoes from my uncle. I usually went to school barefoot. . .

Raised in such an atmosphere, my resentment against the oppression and injustice inflicted on the poor was very strong. Deep down in my heart I felt that in such a society one could not live properly and happily. I awoke politically, and a bright light began to shine upon this dark indignation. . .

When I was sixteen, someone lent me a copy of *Essence of Socialism,* written by Kotoku. In bold type, the words, "Marx said," "Engels said," confronted me on almost every page. From Kotoku's writings I learned for the first time about socialism.[1]

Tokuda's experiences and the resentment he felt toward his Japanese teachers—who traditionally looked down upon the natives of Okinawa—produced several minor crises in the boy's life, including a classroom strike in elementary school in protest against a severe principal; another incident occurred in high school when Tokuda was almost expelled because of a derogatory statement he made about an Imperial prince and princess who visited his school.

After graduation from high school, Tokuda spent an additional year studying in Tokyo before entering the college preparatory school at Kagoshima on the southernmost of Japan's four main islands. He stayed with a distant uncle whose wife refused to associate with this "crude native" of Okinawa and made him eat with the hired help and bathe at a public bathhouse. In school he received similar treatment.

At the end of one year of insults and humiliations, Tokuda returned to Okinawa in 1913 more resentful than ever. For the next few years he earned a meager living as a substitute elementary-school teacher and, later, as a secretary in a district administrative office. This type of work did not seem to satisfy the strong-willed youth, whose urge to see and learn more of the world soon became irrepressible. In 1917, at the age of twenty-three, he returned to Tokyo.

Tokuda—The Fiery Secretary General

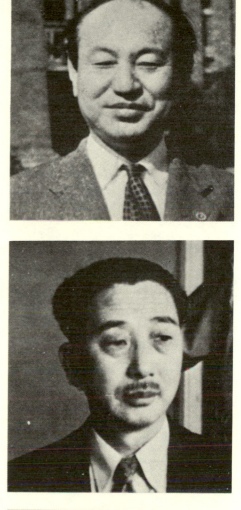

Nozaka—The Astute Strategist

Shiga—The Inflexible Theorist

THE THREE LEADERS OF COMMUNISM IN POSTWAR JAPAN

A year later Tokuda enrolled in the evening classes of the Law School of Nippon University. Like many of his fellow students, he worked during the day, earning a small wage as a clerk in the Communications Ministry. The sudden increase in the price of staple foods toward the end of World War I proved disastrous to many who had been living close to starvation. At the time of the Rice Riots, Tokuda was in the hungry, angry crowd which emerged from the Fukagawa industrial section of Tokyo and advanced on the center of the city, raiding rice storehouses all along the way. Tokuda recalls:

> When we reached Manseibashi, government troops went into action. An officer gave the order to fire, but the soldiers refused to obey. Flanked on both sides by troops and beaten by the police from behind, we were forced to run for our lives. I never will forget how, out of breath, I fled to Hongo and climbed the Tenjin hill. Somehow I managed to escape arrest and to reach my boarding house safely.
>
> These Rice Riots were my first experience in a mass movement . . . I was indignant at the government's terror. This indignation was to remain alive for many, many years.[2]

After three years in Tokyo, Tokuda received his law degree and entered the employ of a Tokyo lawyer with strong socialist sympathies. During this period a continuing active interest in social problems brought him in contact with most of Japan's leading Marxists. Tokuda became a prominent member of a small socialist study group, the Wednesday Society, and was one of the few socialists of the time who made a real attempt to go beyond the study of theory. "I was not particularly apt at writing on Marxist doctrine. . ." he recalls; "I concentrated instead on the preparation of handbills, on factory agitation and propaganda among the workers."[3]

When the Comintern agent Chang T'ai-lei secretly visited Japan in the fall of 1921, Tokuda was among the young Japanese he selected to participate in the Far Eastern People's Congress. Tokuda crossed into Russian territory from Manchuria while fighting between Japanese and Russian Communist troops was still going on in Siberia. He reached Moscow, via Irkutsk, toward the end of the year. The Congress in which he took part, it will be recalled, laid the foundation for the establishment of a Communist Party in Japan. Of his return trip across the Central Asia deserts, Tokuda wrote some twenty-five years later that even these remote areas were not free from exploitation:

> Furs and hides transported by caravan across the Gobi desert are brought together in Kalgan. From here they are shipped into China and to the great cities of the world. The fur coats of gaudy women in New York and London represent the toil of these Mongolian nomads.

Let us not forget that the feelers of imperialism reach even into the daily life of the Mongolian nomad.[4]

The trip to Russia—his first abroad—proved the turning point in Tokuda's life. No longer was there any doubt in his mind as to his own future or the future of Japan. Tokuda took a leading part in the formation of the Communist Party of Japan in the summer of 1922, after his return from Moscow. From this point on Tokuda's life is the story of the Japanese Communist Party's struggle for power.

As one of the leaders of the young Party, Tokuda worked in closest coöperation with Russian and Chinese members of the Comintern staff and made frequent trips outside of Japan. For example, he visited Shanghai in January and in May of 1925 and was in that city again in December on his way to Moscow.

In the first Japanese general elections, held in February 1928, Tokuda ran officially as a candidate for the left-wing Labor-Farmer Party, although he remained a member of the Central Committee of the underground Communist Party. He was already well known to the police, since he had spent short terms in jail, in 1923 and in 1926, for his connection with the subversive movement. Tokuda was one of the first to be apprehended in the mass arrests of March 1928, and while in jail he placed his legal experience at the disposal of the Communist Party for the historic trial of 1931-32. The Central Committee, it will be remembered, was found guilty, and Tokuda, as a member, was sentenced to ten years at hard labor. While Manabu Sano and other prominent Communist leaders renounced the Party or recanted, Tokuda remained loyal to the cause, refusing to bend under police pressure or to subscribe to the new anti-Moscow line of his former comrades.

Tokuda's convictions were put to the ultimate test in the winter of 1934 when he was suddenly transferred to the Abashiri penitentiary on the icy northern shore of Hokkaido facing the Sea of Okhotsk. The climate of that region is perhaps the worst in Japan. Tokuda still speaks of the seven bitter winters in Hokkaido. "It was the kind of cold," he recalls, "which penetrates the very marrow of one's bones. Even now, when I think of those six years in Abashiri, I begin to freeze up again."[5]

During the war years Tokuda was shifted from prison to prison, finally landing in Fuchu penitentiary near Tokyo, where he remained "under preventive custody" until released by order of the occupation authorities on October 10, 1945. He was one of the handful of veteran Communists who survived the treatment aptly described by the motto of the Japanese police: "Don't kill them, but don't keep them alive."

At the Fourth Congress of the Communist Party of Japan, held in December 1945, Tokuda was named Secretary General of the Party. Three times he has been elected to the Japanese Diet on the Communist ticket.

Within the Party, he is a member of the Central Committee and the Politburo and heads the Orgburo; the Repatriation Section is also under his direct supervision. Legally, Tokuda's postwar political career came to a close on June 6, 1950, when—in response to a request from General MacArthur—the Japanese government banned the twenty-four members of the Central Committee from public life. A few days before the outbreak of hostilities in Korea, Tokuda disappeared; and despite intensive search by Allied and Japanese authorities, he remains at this writing unaccounted for.

Kyuichi Tokuda, who directed for nearly five years the varied activities of the legally recognized Party, by background, experience, and character is more fitted for leadership in an underground movement. His nickname *Tokkyu* (meaning "express train"—a play on words), well describes his boundless energy and fiery revolutionary zeal. Tokuda seems to operate at his highest level of efficiency under pressure. These qualities, enhanced by a personal warmth and devotion to his associates, command for him the respect and loyalty of the entire Party. Though other Party leaders may be guided by a process of reasoning, Tokuda tends to act by intuition. His popularity with the rank and file, experience in underground activity, and time-tested devotion to the Soviet Union make it unlikely that the Secretary General will be removed—short of death or imprisonment—from the highest-ranking post in the Party.

Nozaka—The Astute Strategist

Sanzo Nozaka is unquestionably one of the most powerful political figures in Japan. Within the Communist Party, he is outranked only by the Secretary General. His real influence on policy is thought by many, both Communists and non-Communists, to exceed even that of Tokuda. A number of factors have contributed to his preëminent position: long association with the movement; an extended tour of duty on the continent, which brought close personal relations with Russian and Chinese Communist leaders; a sharp mind; and the rare ability to combine theory and practice.

Whenever Nozaka spoke before the Diet, during the four years he served as a member, even the most conservative Japanese politician would listen attentively. The suave and well-groomed former university lecturer appears, least of all, the seasoned revolutionist he is.

Nozaka was born on March 30, 1892, in Hagi, a little town on the shores of the Japan Sea, across the channel from Korea. He was the son of a small businessman who had been driven into bankruptcy, and Nozaka's earliest recollections speak of poverty and unhappiness and of a feeling that the world around him was utterly dark. He was fourteen when both of his parents died. After a short while he went to live with his elder brother, who operated a lumber yard in the city of Kobe. During this period, while attending polytechnic high school, Nozaka began to develop an interest in socialism. The reasons for this interest he explains in his autobiography:

> Even before I graduated from Kobe Polytechnic High School, I was drawn into socialism. There were two reasons: the poverty of my family and the influence of the Kotoku case [involving the anarchist Kotoku, who was sentenced to death for plotting the assassination of the Japanese Emperor]. This historic incident implanted in my mind an interest in socialism and anarchism. I felt that Kotoku was a kind of hero who had fought for socialism. I began to develop an outspoken interest in such ideas when I discovered a chapter on the subject in a book by the old American capitalist Ely.*
>
> For my graduation theme I chose the topic, "Socialism," on which I wrote a short essay. My teacher was furious. He reprimanded me in front of the entire class and stated that I was a disgrace to the school, but I didn't feel that this was true.
>
> At the age of eighteen, I went to Tokyo to enter the Political Economy Department at Keio University. My thoughts were becoming increasingly socialistic. I didn't spend very much time on my lessons, but preferred to devour Japanese and foreign books on socialism which turned up in Tokyo's second-hand bookstores. In 1913, I joined the *Yuaikai* [the forerunner of the General Federation of Labor]. From here on, I participated actively in the social movement.[6]

At Keio University, one of Japan's outstanding private institutions, Nozaka made few friends. He spent most of his time with the workers of Tokyo. That Nozaka's interest in Marxism already was intense may be judged from the fact that, when a friend secured for him an English edition of the *Communist Manifesto,* Nozaka, dictionary in hand, laboriously went over the document word by word.

In 1917, Nozaka graduated from Keio the second in his class, despite his thesis, entitled "Revolutionary Trade Unionism." Almost immediately he was offered a well-paying position with Japan's largest spinning mill, but he refused it for a financially less attractive position as secretary of the *Yuaikai.*

At the end of the First World War Nozaka had an opportunity to visit Europe. He left for England in 1919 to study the labor movement.

*Nozaka refers here to the American economist Richard Theodore Ely, the first head of the Department of Political Economy at John Hopkins University, one of the most influential teachers of economics in the United States in the period before World War I. His students included Woodrow Wilson and Newton D. Baker as well as many of the present-day American economists. Ely is the author of *Socialism and Social Reform,* a book which resulted in his trial in 1894 for teaching socialism in the United States.

His trip was financed by his elder brother, whose lumber business in Kobe had prospered during the war. Nozaka enrolled at the London School of Economics where he did research under the direction of Clement Attlee. Better known in British labor circles than among his professors or fellow students, the young Japanese took an active part in socialist activities and, in 1920, was among the charter members of the British Communist Party. Nozaka attended the First Convention of that organization as a delegate from the London branch. He was a frequent speaker at Communist meetings and one of the Party's most active agitators. As a result of these extracurricular activities, he was summoned to Scotland Yard in 1921, charged with radicalism, and given seventy-two hours to leave the country. Nozaka, forced to continue his research into social problems elsewhere, visited France, Switzerland, Germany, and finally Russia, where he was received by the exiled Japanese Communist leader, Sen Katayama. After a few weeks in the Russian capital, Nozaka returned home via Western Europe and the Suez. Scotland Yard, perhaps fearful that this radical Japanese would engage in "research" in the colonies, apparently had notified British intelligence in the Near and Far East of Nozaka's itinerary. En route home he was refused permission to go ashore at any British port.

Nozaka arrived in Japan in the spring of 1922 and immediately placed his experience at the disposal of his country's growing labor movement. He spent the year editing *Labor,* official publication of the General Federation of Labor, and lecturing at his alma mater, where he offered a course in World Social Problems. He joined the Communist Party of Japan which had been formed in July of that year. In 1923 he was arrested for his participation in that secret society and sentenced to eight months in jail. After his release, Nozaka went back to work for the Party. Through the establishment of the Industrial Labor Research Institute and publication of *Industrial Labor Report* and *International,* he contributed materially to the growth of Marxist influence within the ranks of labor.

When a split occurred within the General Federation of Labor in 1925, Nozaka sided with the left wing. From that time until 1928 Nozaka directed the "legal phase" of the Japanese Communist movement. He was, therefore, among the first to be arrested in the police raids of March 1928, but, unlike Tokuda, he did not remain in prison to face trial and conviction.

The story of Nozaka's disappearance from Japan, for years shrouded in mystery, has come to light only since the end of the war. According to Nozaka, after two years in prison, he was freed temporarily to undergo specialized medical treatment for a serious eye condition. That such an ailment normally was not considered sufficient justification for release suggests a flaw or, at best, an omission in his version of the incident. A secret Japanese government document, intended for the use of authorized agents of the Ministry of Justice, contains a more plausible explanation. In this compilation, entitled "On the Conversion of Individuals with Leftist Records," dated August 1943, Nozaka's case is cited as a significant example of "feigned conversion."[7] The government's notation that Nozaka, a member of the Central Committee of the Communist Party, had satisfied the conditions for release from prison is all the more likely in view of Nozaka's moderate stand on the central issue: abolition of the Japanese monarchy.[8]

In March 1930 Nozaka entered a hospital in the city of Kobe. One ailment after another led him from hospital to hospital for the better part of a year. He was still under a doctor's care when the Party renewed contact with him toward the end of the year. Nozaka disappeared from Kobe in March 1931. His whereabouts remained a mystery until the Buddhist Festival of Souls in the middle of the summer, when the family shrine at his brother's home was opened and yielded a last will and testament which made it clear that Nozaka and his wife had left for Russia.

Nozaka reported for duty at Comintern Headquarters in the spring of 1931. There, under the name of Susumu Okano, he remained for fully nine years as absentee director of the Party in Japan. During this protracted stay in the Soviet Union, Nozaka became a member of the Comintern Presidium and came to know intimately the Russian leaders of the international Communist movement, important Communists from almost every country in the world, and Stalin himself.

In the spring of 1940 Nozaka left Moscow for North China, where he worked for more than five years with the Chinese Communist leader, Mao Tse-tung.*

Nozaka's triumphant return to Tokyo in January 1946 was the occasion of a welcome rally at Communist Headquarters and must be regarded as a milestone in the annals of the Party. The subsequent spectacular resurgence of Japan's Communist Party is due largely to the strategy of this astute leader and his equally experienced wife, Ryo.

Ryo (also known as Tatsuko) is head of the Women's Section of the Party and the only woman member of the Central Committee. Born in Kobe in 1898, the daughter of one of the wealthiest members of the community, her interest in the social movement dates from her acquaintance with Sanzo, whom she knew before he became a Communist. She accompanied her husband on his trip to Europe in 1919. Since that time—with the exception of Sanzo's five years in North China, during which Ryo remained in Moscow—she has been his constant aide and companion.

Nozaka is a member of the Party Central Committte, Politburo, and

*See Chapter IX, "Preparations at Yenan."

Secretariat. He heads four Party Sections: Regional Committee Section, Scientific Section, Party Schools, and Marx-Lenin Research Institute. Up to June 6, 1950, he was leader of the Communist delegation in the Japanese Diet, and, like Tokuda, he disappeared just before the North Korean attack.

Nozaka's tendency toward opportunistic gradualism should not be evaluated superficially as an undesirable quality for revolutionary leadership. His flexibility, sometimes mistaken for weakness, was, in fact, among the Party's greatest assets until the Cominform's criticism of the Japanese Party for "straying from the Marx-Lenin line" forced a change in his approach. The controversial Nozaka seemed singularly well suited to the role he played from January 1946 to January 1950. He perhaps is even better qualified for his present assignment, although his concept of strategy and his approach to underground activity may at times differ from that of the Secretary General.

Shiga—The Inflexible Theorist

The third-ranking member of the Japanese Communist hierarchy, Yoshio Shiga, veteran editor and outstanding theorist, is unexcelled in his field. His is, probably, the best-trained mind in the Party. It is this quality which places him in the same class with Tokuda and Nozaka, both of whom are older and vastly superior in revolutionary experience. Recognition came to Shiga only after years of bitter struggle, imprisonment, and near despair.

Shiga was born on January 1, 1901, in Hagi, the same town where Nozaka was born ten years earlier. His father was one of Japan's first steamship captains. Of his mother, to whom he was very devoted, Shiga says: "She was the kind of person who would not easily show her feelings, even toward her own children." [9]

Shiga was an unusually bright and sensitive boy, deeply moved by the injustices of the society in which he lived. He tells of the indignation which he felt toward his classmates who looked down upon those whose social status was below their own. One of the most memorable events of his youth took place in his high-school classroom, when the teacher told the story of the French Revolution, wrote four numbers on every blackboard in the room, and advised the young students, "Forget your own name before you forget this: Modern history began with the year 1789." [10] In high school Shiga began to read books on the Russian Revolution; but it was not until the Rice Riots of 1918 that he took, as he puts it, his "first step into the social movement." [11]

Shiga entered Japan's best-known college preparatory school, Tokyo's Ichiko, in the fall of 1919. There he began a serious study of Marxist literature, which, by the close of World War I, was flowing freely into

Japan. He soon joined a number of radical societies and clubs, forerunners of the Japanese Communist Party. In his own words: "By 1922 I had definitely accepted the Communist point of view."[12] This was also the year that he entered the Social Science Department of Tokyo Imperial University.

Not yet a member of the Communist organization, Shiga escaped the police roundups of 1923 and thus was free to work on behalf of the Party while most of its leaders were in prison. After graduating with honors from Tokyo Imperial University in March 1925, he joined the staff of Nozaka's Industrial Labor Research Institute and became a contributor to a number of Marxist publications. In January 1927, at the end of a one-year voluntary enlistment in the Army, Shiga resumed his career as a journalist, serving as editor of the magazine *Marxism** until his arrest in March 1928. By his numerous writings he firmly established his reputation as one of the leaders of the Communist movement in Japan.

Shiga's life from this point literally parallels that of Tokuda. Shiga looks back philosophically upon his eighteen years in prison:

> Life in prison is the touchstone of a revolutionist. Whatever oppression a revolutionist may meet, he must never give up. Having overcome one obstacle, man is ready for the next. Even when new and greater difficulties confront him, he will be able to endure them because of his new-found confidence. In the beginning there is only a thin line between success and failure; but, with each successive conquest, man advances. Steel is not perfected without tempering. Man, like steel, hardens only after being tempered many times.[13]

At the end of the war, Shiga, still in prison, was among the few surviving Party members who had remained loyal to the Communist cause. He was, with Tokuda and Nozaka, one of the three veterans of the twenties; and, in addition, he was Tokuda's closest friend. It is not surprising, therefore, that this brilliant theorist and writer who possesses precisely the qualities lacked by the recognized leader, Tokuda, should have been chosen by the Secretary General as his chief lieutenant.

Shiga resumed his journalistic career in 1945 as editor-in-chief of the Party's official organ, *Red Flag*, a position which he held until General MacArthur issued his personal directive of June 6, 1950. Shiga is a member of the Central Committee and of the Politburo and heads two Sections: the Publications and the Party History Research Sections.

Five postwar years of practical experience, including two terms in the Diet (May 1946 to April 1947; February 1949 to June 6, 1950), have added much to Shiga's stature and prestige. Shiga clashed with Tokuda and

---

Marxism was a legally recognized publication, founded in May 1924. It supported the Communist point of view but limited itself to the discussion of Marxist theory.

Nozaka in 1950 over the question of Communist policy in Japan. Temporarily estranged from the two leaders through his advocacy of a more radical approach, Shiga returned to the fold in 1951 to assume—somewhat belatedly—an important role at the side of his elders in the Communist underground.

LEADERS FROM THE THIRTIES

RITSU ITO

Ritsu Ito, although youngest of the leaders, has been the Party's official spokesman during the postwar period. Ito was born in 1913 on a small farm in central Japan. His interest in the "agrarian problem" stems from an uncle who was active as an organizer in the farm villages of Gifu Prefecture. Ito was a bright pupil in high school and a brilliant student at Tokyo's First College Preparatory School, Ichiko, until expelled during his senior year for radicalism. Arrested for the first time in 1933 as a Communist, he remained in prison until the end of 1934 and was released only after swearing to begin a new life apart from Communism. In and out of prison from this date on, Ito was imprisoned in 1940 along with Hiroshi (Ko) Hasegawa* and listed by the Japanese authorities as another case of "feigned conversion." He also is reported to have been unintentionally instrumental in the discovery by the police, in 1941, of the Sorge spy ring. He spent the war years in jail.

Ito—one of Tokuda's staunchest supporters—occupies a number of strategic positions within the Party; he is a member of the Central Committee, the Politburo, and the Secretariat. As head of the Agrarian Section, Ito personally is responsible for the Party's projected program of agrarian reform. The versatile Ito was also assistant editor of *Red Flag* until General MacArthur's directive of June 6, 1950. He dropped from sight soon thereafter. Although Ito's precise role in the Communist underground is difficult to ascertain, there is reason to believe rumors which suggest that Tokuda has delegated to him much of the organizational work.

KENJI MIYAMOTO

Kenji Miyamoto, born in 1908 in Yamaguchi Prefecture, made a name for himself as a literary critic soon after his graduation from the Department of Economics of Tokyo Imperial University. At a time when Marxist literature flourished in Japan, Miyamoto was one of the most prominent members of the "Proletarian School," as was his late wife, Yuriko Chujo.

Yuriko Chujo, almost ten years her husband's senior, had her first novel, *Poor Folks*, published at the age of seventeen. After a year in the

*Also a member of the Central Committee and the Politburo.

United States and three years in the Soviet Union, Yuriko returned to Japan in 1930. The police arrested her in Tokyo for Communist sympathies shortly thereafter. She married Kenji in 1935. Her husband was still in his twenties when he joined the Communist Party. He became head of the Central Committee in 1933 and, it will be recalled, was arrested a few months later in connection with the "Lynch Incidents." From this time until the end of the Second World War he was held in prison.

Kenji Miyamoto, head of the Party Control Commission up to the spring of 1950, must be regarded as one of the most powerful individuals within the Japanese Communist movement, despite a temporary reassignment to a less sensitive position of leadership after supporting Shiga's stand against Tokuda and Nozaka. The exact nature of Miyamoto's tasks in the new Communist underground remains somewhat obscure.

Shigeo Kamiyama

Shigeo Kamiyama ranks as one of Japan's leading Marxist theorists, although the views of the prolific writer and union organizer have often brought him into conflict with the Party's orthodox authorities.

Kamiyama was born in 1905 in the city of Shimonoseki on the southern tip of Honshu, the main island of Japan. At an age when most of the other leaders of the Party were in college, Kamiyama, whose formal education ended with his graduation from high school, was leader of the Kanto Free Trade Unions. In 1928 he joined the Communist Party. A newcomer to the Party ranks, Kamiyama was not imprisoned during the mass arrests of that year. By 1929 he had become one of the directors of the illegal National Conference of Japanese Trade Unions. When his faction failed in an attempt to dominate the Conference, Kamiyama temporarily withdrew from active participation. He emerged in 1934 to form a small Communist Group which he expected would grow into a full-fledged Party, but his arrest in July 1935 forced the temporary abandonment of his plans. Sentenced to two years in jail and released on probation toward the end of 1936, Kamiyama resumed his career immediately. In 1939 once more he attempted to build up a Communist labor organization in the Tokyo-Yokohama area, but his efforts culminated in arrest and imprisonment (May 1941) as did his first attempt. He was released in 1945 after Japan's surrender.

In the postwar period, Kamiyama, although frequently at odds with the Party's recognized leadership, has been a prominent—if controversial—member of the Central Committee. It may be significant that Kamiyama chose to remain above ground at the time when most of the Party leaders went underground.

LESSER LEADERS

No discussion of the Japanese Communist Party's general staff would be complete without an evaluation of a certain group of second-echelon Party officials about whom little is known and who, consequently, are regarded by many as of minor importance in a consideration of the Communist movement in Japan. In a situation where one stroke of the Supreme Commander's pen or a purge decree of the Japanese government suddenly may force the Party leaders to disappear temporarily underground—thus producing the need for a reshuffling of the Party's overt executive staff—a second, a third, and even a fourth layer of potential leaders is indispensable to smooth operations. Accordingly, the minor Party officials of today may well be the Party leaders—or at least the directors of legal and semilegal Party activities—of tomorrow. Who may be considered candidates for such positions?

Contrary to a widely held belief, the Japanese Communist Party does not lack capable and experienced members who, if need be, can take the place of men such as Tokuda, Nozaka, or Shiga. There remain today close to a hundred individuals who have been associated intimately with the direction of Communist activity in Japan for two or even three decades. In the postwar period they have served the Party on the Central Committee, on the Control Commission, as chiefs of regional organizations, as Diet members, or, at times, in less conspicuous functions. Some held in reserve for emergencies never have occupied any Party positions; but as purge after purge removes the top layer of leadership, they gradually are being brought to the fore. Of varied background and different temperament, the Communist second and third echelons have in common experience in underground work and a loyalty toward the Party proved in long years spent in Japanese prisons. The Japanese Communist Party increased its membership about a thousandfold during the first four years after the surrender, yet not a single important position was ever entrusted to a new Party member. Despite the exceedingly high casualty rate among Communist leaders during 1950 and 1951, the Party never chose to assign or was compelled to assign key positions to postwar Party converts. A vast reservoir of Communist veterans is guarantee that unless drastic government measures are effectively applied—and it is not certain that effective measures can be applied at the present stage—leadership of the Japanese Communist Party will remain in the hands of men who have proved themselves in prewar times.

Space limitations preclude a full discussion of all who should be considered candidates for Party leadership. The brief sketches of minor leaders presented here thus are selective rather than exhaustive.*

*Some of the other more important lesser leaders are: Katsuji Banno, Hiroshi (Ko) Hasegawa, Yuichi (Muraichi) Horie, Hiroaki Hosaka, Karoku Hosokawa, Iwao Iwamoto,

SHOJIRO KASUGA

Shojiro Kasuga (not to be confused with Shoichi Kasuga, also a member of the Central Committee) is one of the few Communist leaders whose connections with the Party go back to the revolutionary trade-union movement of the early twenties.

Born in Osaka in 1903, Kasuga, at the age of twenty, formed the Kanto Printers' Union and, as a result, was among the young union leaders selected by Tokuda the following year (1924) for study and training in Russia. He graduated (under the assumed name Kawamura) from the Communist University in Moscow in the fall of 1926 and returned immediately to Japan. Admitted to Party membership in January 1927, he was dispatched immediately to direct Communist activities in the Osaka-Kobe area. Arrested in 1928, tried, and sentenced to eight years at hard labor, Kasuga came out of prison in 1937, at a time when the Communist Party as such no longer existed. He formed a small, well-organized Communist group which was responsible for the little success the movement could claim during 1937 and 1938. Several of his collaborators of the period now occupy important positions within the Party: Tsunesaburo Takenaka is a member of the Central Committee and the Party Secretariat, and head of the Clerical Section, but he is perhaps better known as the author of a Party handbook entitled *Cell Activities Made Easy;* Soichiro Matsumoto, another former member of Kasuga's Osaka group, serves on the Control Commission and heads the Personnel Section. Kasuga's group, as has been related, was smashed by the police in the fall of 1938 and he again was imprisoned.

Only Kasuga's poor health has prevented him from assuming a postwar position commensurate with his background and training for underground activity.

KAZUO FUKUMOTO

Kazuo Fukumoto might have been one of the Big Three today, if it had not been his fate to become unwillingly involved in the Stalin-Trotsky controversy. Removed from a leading position within the Japanese Communist Party at a Comintern conference in 1927, Fukumoto never has quite succeeded in making his comrades forget that he once had been called a "Trotskyite." An intellectual with a firm grasp of economic and political theory—comparable in this respect to Shiga—Fukumoto possesses in addition the qualities required for leadership.

Like most of the important figures in Japan's Communist Party, Fuku-

Eiichi Iwata, Kimio Izu, Susumu Kamimura, Kanichi Kawakami, Kenji Kawata, Yujiro Komatsu, Saneki Matsumoto, Ryuji Nishizawa, Bunkichi Okada, Fumio Sugimoto, Ichiro Sunama, Ichizo Suzuki, Tomeji Tada, Zentaro Taniguchi, Wataru Tsuzura, Takechiyo Uno, Ichizo Wada, and Kentaro Yamabe.

moto has spent many years in prison. His prolonged retirement from the Party ended officially in January 1950 when it was announced that, in August 1949, Fukumoto had been readmitted to membership; and the "former Trotskyite" published a statement in the Party press characteristically entitled "Joyful Return to the Native Home." Actually—and this sheds important light upon the tenuous line which often separates the Party member from the sympathizer—it was revealed by the Communist Party that Fukumoto had "worked in liaison with a section of the Central Party apparatus" for more than a year prior to his readmission into the Party.[14]

Fukumoto's name has been mentioned ever since the first Communist purge of 1950 as a possible successor to Party leader Tokuda. As thoroughly grounded in Marxian theory as Shiga or Nozaka and more versatile than Tokuda (Fukumoto is a prolific writer on many subjects and one of Japan's outstanding authorities on Japanese color prints), Fukumoto would most likely occupy one of the foremost positions within the Party, were it not for his past identification with left-wing radical "Trotskyite deviationism." For the time being at least, Fukumoto may be obliged to serve the Party as an assistant to the Big Three until he has proved himself to be a loyal follower of the Stalinist type of Communism. That he apparently was not allowed to join the other Party leaders, when one after another they were going underground after the outbreak of war in Korea, would seem to confirm this view. Arrested in September 1951 in connection with antioccupation activities, he was released soon after for lack of evidence. His considerable ability still may win for Fukumoto the position denied him by the turn of events in the Soviet Union.

ETSURO SHIINO

Despite the much-advertised "proletarian character" of the Japanese Communist Party, "workers" in the Communist sense of the word are few in number among the Party leaders. Etsuro Shiino is one of them. His name was virtually unknown outside Communist circles until on June 6, 1950 he emerged suddenly to head the Interim Central Directorate which replaced—at least in name—the Central Committee purged in its entirety by order of General MacArthur. There can be little doubt today that Shiino, a staunch supporter of Tokuda, has been hardly more than a figurehead for those who, purged, had been compelled to go underground. A former coal miner and union organizer, Shiino has a long Party record (and consequently also a long prison record). His education was limited to primary school, and he has had little opportunity and inclination to supplement this deficiency by studying Marxian theory. Now, as in prewar times, he is essentially a faithful (and sometimes stubborn) supporter of whatever line his superiors have agreed upon. It is exactly this trait which enhances his usefulness to the Party. Whether a member of the Control Commission, charged with enforcing discipline and eliminating deviationists (as from 1946 to 1950), leader of the legal activities of the Party (as from June 1950 to September 1951 when, purged by the Japanese government, he rejoined Tokuda), or as an underground worker, hunted by the police and constantly in danger of arrest, Shiino can be relied upon to do his duty and more. He is one of the small group of experienced Party organizers who will unflinchingly follow the Party line and enforce it strictly and without hesitation. That there are only a few workers like Shiino in the Japanese Communist Party constitutes perhaps the greatest weakness of the postwar organization.

KIN TEN KAI (KIM CHÔN HAE)

Kim Chôn Hae, a Korean, better known by his Japanese name, Kin Ten Kai, is representative of a type of Communist found frequently in the ranks of the Japanese Communist Party. In prewar times the Japanese Communists had worked in close collaboration with their comrades abroad. Their relation to Korean and Formosan Communists has always been particularly close, and members of either racial group have participated freely in the activities of the Japanese Communist Party. In the postwar period, the presence of a large Korean minority group in Japan and the increasing strategic importance of the Korean Peninsula in the struggle between the Communist and the free worlds have, if anything, only intensified this collaboration and raised it to the level of international significance. While Korean Communists have thus participated in the "struggle" of their comrades in Japan, the Japanese Communist Party directly and indirectly has furthered the cause of the Kim Il Sung regime.

Kin Ten Kai, a veteran Communist, is the unofficial liaison man between the Korean and the Japanese Communist movements. Born in Korea in 1900, he came to Japan as a young man among the thousands of workers imported from Korea to do the work Japanese laborers were unwilling to do. Since 1924 he has been engaged in Communist agitation among Koreans and Japanese, first as head of the Japanese section of the Korean Communist Party, then (after a six-year interval spent in a Japanese jail) as a member of the Japanese Communist Party. He was considered dangerous enough by the Japanese authorities to be put under "preventive custody" (together with Tokuda, Shiga, and other Communist leaders) during Japan's war years and was released only in October 1945 after Japan's defeat. His role in the postwar period has grown in direct proportion to the increased importance of Korea as a bridge from Communist Asia to American-occupied Japan. As a member of the Politburo of the Japanese Communist Party and leader of the Communistorientated Korean Residence League, Kin has fulfilled a twofold mission: responsible for coördinating the Korean movement in Japan with the activities of the Japanese Communist Party, he has simultaneously served as the unofficial ambassador of the North Korean (Communist) regime at Party headquarters in Tokyo. His official career was cut short by a purge order issued in the fall of 1949 from General MacArthur's headquarters, but, undisturbed by these measures, Kin apparently has succeeded in continuing his work for the Communist movements of Korea and Japan.

A few days before the attack of the Communist forces against South Korea, Kin disappeared from Japan. He was reported passing through Wonsan (Korea) on June 21, 1950, his destination unknown. Information from North Korean sources, though necessarily fragmentary, indicates that Kin Ten Kai—now under his original name, Kim Chôn Hae—has assumed important functions at Communist headquarters in North Korea. With the intensification of Japanese Communist underground activity and with the increasing tendency of the Japanese Party leaders to look to the continent for support, Kim's role in the international Communist movement may be expected to assume added importance.*

*Information contained in this chapter has been drawn largely from published biographies and autobiographies of Japanese Communist leaders, Japanese government documents, personal correspondence, and interviews. Some of the more significant published Japanese sources have been listed in the authors' work, *Japanese Communism: An Annotated Bibliography of Works in the Japanese Language* (Los Angeles and New York: University of Southern California and Institute of Pacific Relations, 1952), Sec. II-F, "Biography and Autobiography."

CHAPTER XIII

The Communist Program for Japan, 1946-1950

A DISTINCTION must be made between ultimate and immediate objectives when considering the Communist program for Japan during the four postwar years of "peaceful revolution." The goal of the Communist Party of Japan is identical with that of Communist parties throughout the world.[1] But since—according to the Marxist interpretation—Japanese economy up to 1950 had not yet reached the final stage of capitalist development considered essential to a successful socialist revolution, the Japanese Party saw the necessity for an intermediate state. This intermediate stage, characterized as a "democratic people's republic," was to be reached by the early completion of the "bourgeois-democratic revolution," described as then in progress in Japan.

A Japanese dictionary of Communist terminology defines "bourgeois-democratic revolution" as follows: "In its widest sense identical with 'bourgeois revolution.' Especially, a bourgeois revolution which produces thoroughgoing democratic reforms (republican form of government, establishment of maximum political freedom for the people, agrarian revolution)." A "bourgeois revolution" is defined as "a revolution where the bourgeoisie, which has developed gradually within the framework of the feudal system, considers the feudalistic restrictions an obstacle to the development of production, advocates liberty and equality for the human being, demands democracy, seizes power, realizes parliamentarianism, abolishes the entire feudal system, and opens the way for a free development of capitalism."[2]

The Program of Action of the Communist Party of Japan, geared to the requirements of the "bourgeois-democratic revolution," was aimed at the establishment of a "democratic people's republic."

Since the end of World War II the Communist Party of Japan, like Communist parties elsewhere, has found "democracy" a most useful term. Although contemporary political writing at times may suffer from an overdose of semantics, it seems imperative to examine more closely the Communist concept of the term. The interpretation placed upon the word by the Japanese Communists is evident from a statement made by Sanzo Nozaka in 1946, shortly after his return from China. He explained:

> At present there is much talk within Japan of democracy. It seems to me that a distinction must be made between two kinds of democracy. One is the democracy supported by the government,

the capitalists, and certain political parties. It is the kind of democracy which is dominated by bureaucrats, capitalists, and landowners; in other words, a democracy which operates to the advantage of a small minority: the privileged, exploiting, upper class. This is old-fashioned democracy . . .

We are thinking in terms of a new democracy, under the leadership of all those who comprise the working classes: the worker, the farmer, the productive intellectual, and the small and medium businessman. The people of Japan fervently desire this kind of democracy.*

The Program of Action adopted at the Communist Party's Sixth National Congress in the winter of 1947 enumerates in twenty-seven paragraphs the prerequisites for the establishment of a Japanese people's democracy.† To enlist as wide a support as possible, the Party promised all things to all men. A more confused listing of political platitudes and demands can scarcely be imagined. Much of the interpretative literature is equally vague. The following analysis, concerned with the salient features of the Program, represents an effort to bring a degree of order to this confusion.

POLITICAL PROGRAM

Until Japan's surrender in the fall of 1945, the government of the Empire had been technically a constitutional monarchy. Actually, the Emperor, "descended from the Sun Goddess in unbroken line through ages eternal," was the fountainhead of all authority. In his name and only with his approval were decisions made. Domestic and foreign policy did not originate in the Diet but in the rarified atmosphere of the Imperial Palace, and, following Japan's venture onto the continent, only after they first had found favor in the offices of the General Staff. It was the Emperor who on December 8, 1941 declared war upon the United States and Great Britain "in the confident expectation that the sources of evil will be speedily eradicated." Again, when the war situation had developed "not necessarily to Japan's advantage," for the first time in history the

---

*Sanzo Nozaka, *Nihon minshuka no tame ni* (Toward the Democratization of Japan). Tokyo, 1948, pp. 78-79. Nozaka's views on "new democracy" are unquestionably colored by his experience in Communist China. The Chinese Communist leader Mao Tse-tung popularized the term in his widely read work, *China's New Democracy*, which appeared in 1940. The connection is further suggested by Nozaka himself in the columns of a Japanese periodical where he discusses the "new democracies of China and Eastern Europe." ("The Democratic Revolution in Japan," *Chuo Koron*, Jan. 1949.)

†Besides the Party's basic Program of Action, dozens of specific programs exist. These apply to particular fields or to the operations of specified Party organizations. Thus, for example, there is an "Agricultural Program," a "Fertilized Industry Rehabilitation Program," and a "Gumma Prefecture Political Program."

Emperor's voice was heard throughout the nation, announcing: "We have resolved to pave the way for a grand peace for all the generations to come."

The Japanese Emperor's subsequent repudiation of his divine origin and his greatly diminished political importance in the postwar period have not lessened the Communist Party's historic opposition to the existence of the Imperial institution. "The Imperial institution forms a fortress for the reactionary forces in their attempt to crush the freedom and spirit of the people," the Party's official handbook on the program explains.[3]

At the end of World War II, Party leaders relegated the question of the future of the Imperial institution to a less conspicuous position, but this should not be interpreted as a change in basic policy. Despite Japan's defeat, the Emperor continued to command the loyalty and respect of the vast majority of the people. Party strategists were aware of this situation; and as long as popularity with the masses constituted the immediate objective, the issue was played down. The growing radicalization of the Party, which characterized the period after January 1950, produced the inevitable return to a more doctrinaire approach; and abolition of the Imperial institution again became one of the Japanese Communist Party's major political demands.

Exactly what was to take the place of the Imperial institution and the existing form of government is not made clear in the Program of Action beyond mention of what is termed "people's government," a "people's police system," and a "people's democratic constitution." Nozaka's interpellations before the Diet concerning the new (SCAP-inspired) constitution, submitted in 1946 by the Yoshida Government, shed some light on the nature of the Communist Party's proposed "democratic constitution." "A constitution," Nozaka explained, "guarantees legal protection for what has been acquired through revolution. But such can be achieved only after completion of this process of social upheaval."[4] The Party's proposed constitution would thus legalize many of the basic demands contained in the Communist Program of Action.* This is confirmed by Nozaka, who stated before the Diet that a "truly democratic" constitution must include, in addition to the usual guarantees of freedom of speech, assembly, and the like, such specific provisions as the right of the worker to participate in the management of

*The Party published a 100-paragraph draft constitution on June 29, 1946. The full text appeared in *Zen-ei*, July 1, 1946. This draft constitution, in many respects identical with the SCAP-sponsored Japanese government draft constitution, contains a number of specific provisions relative to the rights and duties of citizens, the Diet, governmental structure, administration, and the judiciary branch. The Communist draft constitution does not contain, however, a single significant point not found in the 1947 Japanese constitution or in the Communist Party's Program of Action.

industry and concrete safeguards for the protection of the unemployed, the aged, and the sick.

The details of governmental structure and political organization of the democratic people's republic are conspicuously absent from the Program of Action. Not only is this in line with Marxist theory, which views the state as a mere reflection of the nation's economic arrangements, but it is clear that the Party was not anxious to reveal all of its political plans.

ECONOMIC DEMANDS

In contrast to the cursory treatment accorded governmental structure, the economic aspects of the Communist Program of Action are worked out in more detail. Communist doctrine, in Japan as elsewhere, divides the nation into two groups: the "exploited" and the "exploiters." A dictatorship of the proletariat, it is stated, would eliminate the "exploiting classes" and permit the realization of socialism. Such a dictatorship can be achieved only, the Japanese Communist Party believed, after successful completion of the bourgeois-democratic revolution.

The Communist Party of Japan advocated in several specific fields a variety of economic measures designed to pave the way for the destruction of the existing capitalist system by weakening the power of the "exploiting classes."

FINANCE, COMMERCE, AND INDUSTRY

The Program of Action speaks only in general terms of "government management through people's control of financial institutions, important industries, and commercial enterprises" and of a "development toward nationalization." The official commentary of the Party program, however, deals more concretely with the plan and its implementation. Mines, oil fields, the construction business, maritime transportation, private railways, radio broadcasting corporations, and the electrical, iron, steel, cement, fertilizer, textile, and paper industries are slated specifically for "government management and people's control." National railways and government-controlled communications are also earmarked for "people's control."

"People's control," a term constantly used in postwar Japanese Communist literature, apparently was regarded by the Party as the panacea for all of Japan's ills. The Party's amplification of this concept, as applied in the economic realm, throws some light on the economic policy which would prevail in a people's democracy:

> A supreme economic council will be established under the authority of the National Diet. This council will be made up of representatives of trade-unions, agricultural associations, medium and

small businessmen's associations, civic groups, and democratic political parties. The council will establish an over-all economic plan for Japan, determine economic policy, and supervise its implementation.

Under the authority of this supreme council, a control committee will be established for each of the government-operated industries. This committee will be composed primarily of trade-union representatives. The committee will rehabilitate the particular industry under its jurisdiction. It will plan new projects and determine production output, personnel needs, and financial and material supply requirements. It will work out a plan for the distribution and transportation of material supplies and supervise and check on the implementation of the plan . . .

All financial institutions (big banks, insurance companies, trusts) must be combined into a single national bank under the jurisdiction of a financial control committee. Representatives of trade-unions within these financial institutions as well as representatives from outside unions, farmers, and small and medium businessmen will serve on this committee. The control committee will plan the national budget, determine the national financial requirements, and specify the amount of funds required by the government-operated industries. It further will formulate concrete policy relative to currency circulation, foreign exchange, foreign investments, and government bonds. With the realization of people's control, bank deposits of the average citizen will be transferred intact to the national banking institution . . .

Commerce must also be placed under people's control.[5]

Taxation was viewed as one of the less violent means of weakening the power of the "moneyed interests." Although levies on the laboring masses were to be reduced or entirely eliminated, "highly progressive" taxes were prescribed for the wealthy classes.*

That the Communist blueprint envisages a highly industrialized Japan has been emphasized repeatedly by Nozaka who, as early as the spring of 1945 in a speech before the Seventh Congress of the Chinese Communist Party held at Yenan, stated: "Only a high degree of industrialization, with special emphasis on the electrical, chemical, and precision-machine industries, will enable us to solve Japan's problems of unemployment and overpopulation."[6]

*The question of the "moneyed interests" (*Zaibatsu*, big family trusts) is dealt with by Secretary General Tokuda in "The Dissolution of the *Zaibatsu* and the Future of Industry," *Zen-ei*, July 1, 1946. Tokuda described the *Zaibatsu* as "an important component [of the Japanese economic structure], closely allied with the feudalistic, autocratic Emperor institution" and voiced the Party's dissatisfaction with the Japanese government's policy on the matter.

The small and medium businessman* is assigned a precarious place in the Party's program for the establishment of a democratic people's republic. In a speech before a gathering of Japanese businessmen in the fall of 1948, Nozaka emphasized that this group could hope to survive only by "uniting with the workers and farmers who comprise with them 95 percent of Japan's population."[7] The Party reassured the small and medium businessman that, for the time being, he would be allowed to engage in business free from people's control.[8]

Although the Party hoped to curry favor with various management groups, industrial labor continued to constitute the mainstay of Communist strength in Japan and formed, in the Party's own words, "the vanguard of the revolution." In the past, much of the responsibility for the physical welfare of the worker had been assumed by the family group or by the employer; in the postwar period, the foundation of a social-security system was laid by the Japanese government. But the Japanese Communist Party has expressed dissatisfaction with the nature and scope of the government's program, which consists mainly of an unemployment-insurance system with the cost borne proportionately by the government, employer, and employee. Not only has the Communist Party insisted that the contributions to the insurance fund be the sole responsibility of the employer and the government, but the Communist social-security plan has been worked out in considerably more detail and goes far beyond anything contemplated by the present Japanese government. The Communist program calls for an elaborate system which would accord the worker full protection against unemployment, illness, injury, and disability. This plan also includes provisions for child welfare and old-age care as well as pensions for widows. All workers are guaranteed adequate housing, which the Party proposes to make available through a government-financed housing program and by "liberating" large residences and idle buildings. The major specific demands pertaining to industrial labor have been:

> Complete freedom for the trade-union movement (including the unconditional right to strike);
> An eight-hour working day and forty-hour working week;
> A minimum-wage system;
> A yearly three-week minimum vacation with pay;
> Full employment;
> Immediate adoption and people's control of a social-insurance system;
> Abolition of taxes on labor as well as reduction of or exemption from payment of rent and fees for public utilities;

*A clear line of demarcation between medium and big business is not apparent from the Program of Action.

Guarantee of housing for all homeless workers;
Improved working conditions.

If this program seems to go little beyond similar programs already in force in the United States and Great Britain, it must be reëmphasized that the Japanese Communist Party's Program of Action was designed primarily to hasten the completion of the bourgeois-democratic revolution as a transitional stage on the road to a socialist state.

AGRICULTURE AND FISHING

Approximately half of Japan's population derives all or most of its income from the land. Smaller in area than California but with eight times the population, Japan must feed eighty million people. Since only one-sixth of the total area is considered suitable for cultivation, the Japanese farm, by necessity, is extremely small.

At the time of the surrender, three-fourths of the Japanese farmers were dependent to varying degrees on rented land. Average rent amounted to half of the yield (in rice); thus, the tenant and his family, even in normal times, at best could eke out but a meager living. Leases could be terminated by the landlord at any time. Threatened with loss of the land he tilled and knowing that it would be impossible to find land elsewhere, the tenant was completely at the mercy of the landlord. This situation often was aggravated by indebtedness contracted in years of crop failure. The Japanese tenant farmer was tied to the soil he did not own and unable, because of poverty, to improve his lot. Agrarian unrest was a natural outcome of this situation.

"There is no need for me to point out the importance of the agrarian revolution," Ritsu Ito, the Party's specialist on the subject, reported to the Fifth Party Congress in 1946. "Removal of all traces of feudalism from the farm villages constitutes the most significant social aspect of the democratic revolution."[9] And again in 1949, two years after the SCAP-inspired land reform had been initiated by the Japanese government, Ito wrote: "Under the existing government is it possible to liberate the farm population and to develop agriculture? To this, the farmer answers with an emphatic 'no'."[*]

The Communist solution to the "agrarian problem," as outlined in Party literature, emphasizes two basic measures: redistribution of all farm lands not tilled by the owner and the establishment of collective farms—a system which was calculated to facilitate a rapid transformation from a people's republic to a socialist state.

[*]Ritsu Ito, *Nomin no tatakai* (The Peasant's Struggle). Tokyo, 1949, p. 5. Although the SCAP-inspired land reform eliminated all absentee landowners and resulted in almost complete disappearance of the tenancy system, Party specialist Ito, as well as Secretary General Tokuda, continued to proclaim that the Japanese farmer had by no means been "liberated."

The Party's immediate agrarian program may be summarized as follows:

> Confiscation of all land belonging to the Imperial House, religious organizations, and absentee landowners. Such land will be redistributed to the agrarian proletariat by land-control committees.
>
> Seizure and distribution among the farm population of all idle land, thus doubling the surface under cultivation.
>
> Establishment of coöperatives which will utilize farm machinery supplied by the government.

As to the administration of such a system once it is in operation, the Party further advised:

> All decisions concerning land reform will be made by farmers' committees established along democratic lines in each village and comprised of working farmers. Nonworking landlords will be excluded.
>
> Farmers' committees, in seeking to develop agriculture and to liberate the farmers, will decide the manner in which all farm lands, undeveloped lands, pastures, and forests will be utilized. For the purpose of implementing decisions of the above committees, special committees, designated "land committees" and composed of all farmers directly concerned, will be formed.

Both in its official Program of Action and in other, interpretative literature the Party is intentionally vague on the issue of land ownership. This is consistent with its strategy relative to the more general question of private property. An excerpt from the proceedings of the Fifth Party Congress will serve to illustrate: "Our Party has never advocated an unqualified nonrecognition of private property. There can be no general nonrecognition of private property in any society. Even under a socialist system, private property will continue to exist in accordance with the stage of society."[10]

Apparently recognizing the Japanese farmer's attachment to his land and desire to own the soil he tills, the Party avoided any specific reference to the size of holdings which would be subject to seizure by the government. But the inability to reconcile completely the farmer's desire with the Party's inflexible objective is evident from the official treatment of the subject in the handbook on the Communist program for Japan:

> If the farmer insists on owning land, he may buy it [from the government]. Our Party respects this feeling and will assist the farmer by making land available to him at a reasonable cost. However, small holdings render the development of agriculture and efficient management impossible. The farmer can never escape from poverty by

simply purchasing and owning land . . . Only the nationalization
of land can prevent the ruin of the working farmer and improve his
livelihood. Of course, the nationalization of land will probably be
accomplished only after a democratic government of all working
people has been established.[11]

The Party's program for the fishing industry paralleled its agricultural program. The "exploited" fisherman, who possesses neither net
nor boat, is compared to the landless tenant farmer, while the fishing
company which owns the "tools of production" is likened to the absentee
landlord. "With the aid of the government, monopolistic capital protects
and assists the fishing industry. At the same time it oppresses the common
fisherman," a Party expert on conditions in the fishing industry wrote in
1948.[12] Thus, the Party sees the fisherman at the mercy of his employer.
The Communist program was designed to eliminate this "oppression."
The Party's solution, as in the case of agriculture, lay in the establishment
of fishing coöperatives to replace the large fishing companies. Specifically,
the Party demanded:

> Seizure, without remuneration, of semifeudal fishing rights and
> their transfer to independent fishermen's associations;
> People's control of fishing grounds;
> An end to exploitation of the poor fisherman who owns neither
> net nor boat;
> Establishment of fishing coöperatives;
> Removal of unnatural limitations on areas of operations [that
> is, limitations imposed by Japan's surrender].

A CLASSLESS UTOPIA

The political, social, and economic demands of the Japanese Communist Party's Program of Action, if realized, were to have brought
about what is termed a Japanese people's democracy. Party theorists of
the postwar period have described this end product of the Communist-
sponsored bourgeois-democratic revolution as a short-lived, but necessary,
stage in the creation of a socialist state. That the transformation of the
semisocialist people's democracy into a socialist state would be an extremely rapid process is suggested in the most important Communist
document to come out of postwar Japan, the "1950 Draft Thesis," entitled
"Fundamental Tasks of the Communist Party of Japan in the Coming
Revolution." The pertinent passage reads: "The development of Japanese
capitalism already has reached the imperialist [that is, the final] stage
and now has assumed an extremely monopolistic character . . . Consequently, the revolution must inevitably proceed toward the rapid attain-

ment of a socialist revolution. This coming revolution . . . must be carried through to socialism."[13]

The Japanese socialist state may not be expected to look much different from Soviet Russia today, which the Japanese Party points to as the only example of a "true socialist state." But the ultimate goal lies even beyond: at the end of an indefinite period of regimentation and struggle stands the promise of a classless Communist society and peace. Here "exploitation of man by man will be unknown." The Communist Party of Japan paints a glowing picture of a utopian society where "the benefits of labor, science, and culture will become the property of all."[14]

CHAPTER XIV

The Strategy and Tactics of Peaceful Revolution

T HE surrender of Japan in the fall of 1945 marked the beginning of a new era in the development of the Japanese Communist movement. The prewar Party had been essentially an association of radical intellectuals given to theoretical discussions and conspiratorial scheming. Though efforts had been made to mobilize the urban proletariat and the peasantry, the "mass party of the workers" called for by the Comintern strategy had never materialized. Only after the surrender—or more precisely, after Nozaka's return from China in January 1946—did the Communist Party of Japan show signs of developing into a real threat to the existing order. Largely responsible for this metamorphosis was Nozaka's concept of a "lovable Communist Party" engaged in a "peaceful revolution."

A LOVABLE COMMUNIST PARTY

The brief history of the "lovable Communist Party" may be said to have begun in February 1946 when Tokuda, at the Fifth Party Congress, endorsed the Nozaka plan.

It was in Yenan during the years of "antiwar work" with the Chinese Communist armies that Nozaka formulated a Communist policy for occupied Japan. His approach, which bore strong traces of Mao's "New Democracy," was adopted by the Japanese Communist Party some time after its leader's return to Tokyo. "Mass support is the key to success or failure," Nozaka wrote on several occasions, but the veteran Communist fully realized that to make the Party attractive would not be an easy task, for the prewar Communist organization had, by and large, failed to convince the Japanese people that it was more than a foreign-directed secret society, disrespectful of the Emperor and bent on espionage and violence.

Specifically, how did the Communist leaders go about attempting to remove this stigma? The Party officially and explicitly denied the existence of any ties with the Soviet Union or with the international Communist movement.* The long-suppressed organization, now legal, opened branch offices throughout Japan and invited the public to participate freely in its work. The word "Communism"—in the past a word to be whispered and then only at the risk of arrest—soon became familiar to everyone. Communists and their sympathizers missed no opportunity to appear before the microphone to discuss the Party's program for assisting

*See Chapter XX, p. 230.

the countless victims of the Pacific War. Bookstores featured displays of memoirs of the Communist leaders, and Party literature was sold over the counter. Flanked by red flags and protected by U. S. military police, Communist speakers appealed to crowds in city parks and municipal auditoriums to work together for a new and peace-loving Japan. By introducing a fine distinction between the person of the Emperor and the "odious Emperor system" and by playing down the whole issue, the Japanese Politburo, without abandoning its traditional stand, sought to make the demand for abolition of the monarchy appear less significant. The same process was discernible on the organizational level: no longer was revolutionary experience or extensive study of Marxist doctrine a prerequisite for admittance to membership in the Party; anyone "opposed to exploitation" the Party welcomed into its ranks, and the "working class" was redefined to include even the medium businessman and his counterpart in the countryside. Finally, in contrast to the doctrinaire and often militant tactics employed by the Party in Imperial Japan, Communists in occupied Japan showed unexpected restraint, and spoke, often convincingly, of "achieving social justice and of building a democratic Japan through a process of peaceful revolution."

THE MEANING OF PEACEFUL REVOLUTION

Violence had always seemed to the Japanese Communists inseparably linked to the idea of social change. Certainly, conditions in Imperial Japan held out slight hope for a Communist victory short of insurrection. But in postwar Japan the situation was different: the Communist Party enjoyed full protection of the law and could avail itself of all the facilities and opportunities for political action which a democratic system affords. In such an environment, the red leaders reasoned that much might be accomplished by peaceful means. Emphasis on the use of peaceful methods seemed indicated for still another reason: Nozaka was fully aware of what he termed "the realities of the situation," that is, of the presence of thousands of American soldiers in Japan. "Let us not forget," he cautioned the Party in the fall of 1949, "Japan is still under international control."[1]

It would be a serious mistake, however, to assume—as some observers have done—that the Japanese Communists in publicly advocating peaceful methods had basically altered their thinking on the question of revolution. Nozaka himself pointed out the error in such reasoning. "There are some people who hold the opinion," he wrote in 1948, "that a peaceful revolution represents a new type of revolution which neither Lenin nor Stalin had ever envisaged. This constitutes a social democratic view fraught with grave dangers for the cause of revolution. Although at times the possibility of a peaceful development of revolution may exist, peaceful revolution is no more than a type of tactics. With changing conditions, the approach must also change."[2] Addressing a meeting of Party leaders less than a year later, Nozaka, in defending his policy, clearly defined its ultimate objective: "If pursued skillfully," he said, "this policy will facilitate the development of conditions for direct revolution and make possible the seizure of power."[3]

PARLIAMENTARIAN POLITICS

Parliamentarian politics represents only one of the many aspects of the Communist struggle for power in Japan and, from the Party's point of view, not a very important one. Even at the height of the "peaceful revolution" in the spring of 1949, its protagonist, Nozaka, felt the need to reassure Party members that adoption of his approach did not mean an abandonment of the traditional practice of emphasizing nonparliamentarian activities. "Were we to confine our action to the National Diet," he further advised, "we would be doing just what the ruling class wants. Then the people could never seize power."[4]

In view of the relatively limited role assigned by the Party to parliamentarian politics even during the period of "peaceful revolution," only the broadest outline of Communist activity on the political scene will be presented here, omitting those details which would interest primarily the student of Japanese parliamentarian history.[5]

Japanese governments in occupied Japan generally have been controlled by conservative and ultraconservative parties, successors in spirit, if not in name, to the prewar political organizations which dominated the Japanese Diet prior to the victory of the military over the civilian element. Except for the period from the spring of 1947 to the fall of 1948 when the Katayama Cabinet and its successor, the Ashida Cabinet, were backed by a coalition of socialists and quasi-liberals, the conservatives—first under Baron Shidehara and later under ex-Ambassador Shigeru Yoshida—have constituted the dominant force in postwar Japanese politics. Early in the occupation these elements began to gather around the person of Yoshida, who combines an understanding of the principles of democracy with an old-fashioned conservatism. Whereas shortly after the surrender two conservative organizations, the Liberal Party and the Progressive Party, were vying for political power, in the spring of 1950 the forceful personality of the seventy-year-old Yoshida had succeeded in attracting the bulk of the conservative forces in Japan to the Liberal Party (for a time known as the Democratic-Liberal Party). Except for a conglomerate of conservative and liberal elements, the People's Democratic Party (product of a merger effected early in 1950)—which will probably disintegrate if the world-wide trend toward left-right polarization continues—only the Socialists have constituted a block of sufficient strength to prevent Premier Yoshida from developing a one-party system in Japan. Apart from a multiplicity of negligible political groups, ranging from pro-Communist (such as the Labor-Farmer Party*) to frankly reactionary, the Japanese Communist Party has been confronted in the postwar period with only two serious rivals—the conservatives and the Socialists.

How has the Japanese Communist Party sought to eliminate or neutralize these opponents? Two very different types of tactics have been used: in the case of the conservatives, the policy has been one of frontal attack; for the Socialists, a combination of work from within and pressure from without has been the rule.

Japanese conservative leaders throughout the postwar period have been united in their opposition to any compromise with Communists in Japan. Some men, like Ichiro Hatoyama (a well-known figure in prewar politics and after the war one of the most powerful influences in the conservative camp), have, in fact, built their programs around an anti-Communist theme. Accordingly, a policy of frontal attack was adopted by the Communists in order to undermine the authority of the conservative government and to destroy public confidence in conservative leadership.

As the large number of conservatives purged in 1946 and 1947 on Allied initiative clearly indicated, Japan's postwar conservative parties in the early phase of the occupation were still largely dominated by veterans of Imperial Japanese politics. Many of them, before and during the Pacific War, had been associated in one way or another with ultra-nationalist organizations or activities; and few of them could convincingly disclaim responsibility for the course which led to Japan's defeat.† Though the traditional conservative parties reappeared after the surrender under the names "progressive," or "liberal," their characteristic prewar conservatism could not be so easily dispelled. The Japanese Communists adroitly exploited the vague suspicion which many Japanese harbored toward the recently democratized conservative leaders by accusing them—often unjustly—of being nothing but "reactionaries in disguise" or "fronts for well-known undemocratic elements." By the constant reiteration of such accusations and by the skillful use of the new

*In 1949 Nozaka confirmed this indirectly: "With the exception of two or three cases," he said, "our Party and the Labor-Farmer Party have made common cause." Nozaka, *Senryaku, senjutsu no shomondai*, p. 239. Two years later *Pravda* described the Labor-Farmer Party as an element of the "democratic forces" in Japan. *Pravda*, Aug. 27, 1951.

†Typical is the case of Progressive Party leader Hatoyama, mentioned above, who was removed from public life a few hours before assuming the Premiership when his past endorsement of fascism was brought to the attention of the Allied authorities. Although purged, Hatoyama continued to play an important role behind the scenes. He was depurged in 1951.

invective "undemocratic," the Communist Party succeeded to some extent in engulfing its conservative opponents in an atmosphere of suspicion.

The extensive purges of undemocratic elements (more than one thousand incumbents of and candidates for important positions in the national government had been purged by the summer of 1946) did not in any way calm the Communist propaganda storm: the large number of conservative purgees was merely cited by the Communists as proof of their assertions and further spurred them on to demand a "more thoroughgoing democratic purge." Communist Party leader and Diet member Tokuda, from the floor of the House in the summer of 1946, attacked the conservative Yoshida Cabinet: "The government has a tendency," he shouted, "to protect war criminals. I am convinced that there are among the cabinet members some men who are suspected of being war criminals."[6] As the purges neared completion in 1948 and with an increase in tension between the Soviet bloc and the free world, the Japanese Communist Party shifted its emphasis to "anti-imperialist" propaganda. The word *baikoku,* that is, "selling out the country" (to foreign imperialists), and the description of Japan as a "foreign colony" became the leitmotif of Communist propaganda. Again and again the Japanese government and its members were attacked in the Diet by Nozaka and Tokuda as "traitors," "fascists," and "servants of foreign imperialists."[7] Every proposal submitted by the government—whether the revision of labor laws, a new taxation plan, the dismissal of civil servants to streamline the administration, the import of food and raw materials from the United States, or an economic-stabilization policy— was berated by the Communists within and outside the Diet as a "measure aimed at subjecting Japan to the complete domination by foreign monopolistic capital" and as a prelude to the "transformation of semicolonial occupied Japan into a mere colony of foreign imperialists." By the end of 1949, despite the constant repetition of the nationalist theme, the Party still has not succeeded in convincing the people that the true Japanese patriots were to be found in the Communist camp.

While Communist propaganda was attempting to make the conservatives appear as sinister forces of reaction and partners with "foreign imperialists" in a plot to enslave the Japanese people, different tactics were being employed against the Socialists. The Japanese Communists saw in an alliance with them a convenient means of rapidly gaining mass support. Socialists were traditionally strong within labor and many farmers' unions, and they could count on considerable support from the intelligentsia and the lower middle class. A Socialist-Communist coalition, operating under the slogan "union of all truly democratic forces," would control millions of votes, but, more important, it would dominate the labor scene. Mobilized, the combined Socialist-Communist forces could paralyze transportation, communications, utilities, and key industries. The threat of such action, in itself, might be enough to force the resignation of a weak cabinet, thereby paving the way for a broad "people's government" on the Eastern European pattern.

How did the Communists expect to offset the numerical superiority which the Socialists would undoubtedly have enjoyed in any such arrangement? Nozaka suggested the answer in his 1949 report on Communist Diet activities, in which he described Communist plans for the establishment of a people's government to be formed of representatives of the Communist Party, the pro-Communist Labor-Farmer Party, the Socialist Party, and what he termed "other democratic forces." It is this last group, to be composed of representatives from labor unions, farmers' unions, and similar "mass organizations," that the Communist Party counted on to bring its own strength within the coalition up to and beyond that of the Socialists. This technique of packing the people's committees is familiar to the student of Eastern European politics. Once the desired coalition had been achieved, the superior Communist discipline and determination could be brought into play to eliminate "halfhearted and uncoöperative Socialists," thereby assuring a Communist monopoly of power.

This simple theory the Communist Party found difficult to apply in Japan owing to the complex make-up of the Socialist Party there. The postwar Japanese Socialist movement, although organized into a single political party, split on most vital issues into three factions: the right wing, under the leadership of Suehiro Nishio, Chosaburo Mizutani, and Komakichi Matsuoka, for a while weakened by the purge of its war collaborators, was outspokenly opposed to an alliance with the Communist Party; the moderate, middle-of-the-road Socialists, represented by the Christian leader Tetsu Katayama, preferred to face right but, reluctantly and under special circumstances, might have considered a coalition; and the left wing, comprising the Party's most dynamic figures, veterans of Japan's popular-front movement, Kanju Kato and Mosaburo Suzuki, despite many bitter experiences in the past, was at times attracted to the concept of "people's government." The Communist plan appears to have been to force the right wing out of the Socialist Party and to effect a coalition with the remaining sympathetic elements.

Despite the Socialist Party's decision to act independently in the national elections of April 1946 (in which the Socialists won 92 seats and the Communists 5 in a 466-member Diet),* a Socialist-Communist

*The party alignments in the House of Representatives as a result of the national elections of 1946 were as follows: Progressives, 93; Liberals, 139; Socialists, 92; Coöperatives, 14; Communists, 5; minor parties and vacancies, 40; independents, 83.

coalition seemed almost possible a month later when mounting economic difficulties and the inability of the conservative government to cope with serious food shortages and inflation brought forth outbursts of public dissatisfaction. On May 1 and again on May 19 hundreds of thousands of workers assembled in front of the palace to cheer the Communist and Socialist speakers who were calling for the resignation of the Shidehara Cabinet. A powerful movement for the creation of a "popular" government appeared to be developing—for a government which the Communists agreed should be led by the Socialist Party. On the policy-making level, however, enthusiam for such a coalition was one-sided: in their caucus room the Socialists, isolated from the contagious atmosphere of tumultuous masses, were as unwilling as ever to tie their fate to that of the Communist Party.*

Formation of the Katayama Cabinet in the spring of 1947 marked the end of any thought of Socialist collaboration with the Communists. The Communist Party's failure in the abortive general strike of February 1 (prohibited by Allied headquarters) and the Socialist Party's relative success in the national elections of April (the Socialists won 143 seats in the Diet, the Communists only 4)† convinced even the left-wing Socialist leaders Kato and Suzuki that it would be both impractical and undesirable for the Socialist Party to ally itself with the Communists. The resignation of the Katayama Cabinet in February 1948 and the formation of another Socialist-centrist coalition government under Hitoshi Ashida did not change the Socialist Central Committee's determination to reject collaboration with the Communists. The succession of conservative cabinets under Yoshida after October 1948 (when Ashida resigned because of a series of scandals involving him as well as members of his cabinet) placed the Socialists in the opposition, but neither this fact nor the striking Communist success at the polls in the national elections of 1949 (about 10 percent of the total vote; 35 representatives elected to the Diet)‡ resulted in any fundamental change in the relation between the two parties of the left. Whatever working arrangements the Communist Party succeeded in establishing with the Socialists were on local or an

---

*The Socialists' reluctance to coöperate with the Communists was increased by a number of violent demonstrations spearheaded by Tokuda, who, long after Nozaka's return to Japan, seemed to find it at times difficult to adapt his temperament to the new strategy of "peaceful revolution."

†The composition of the new House of Representatives was as follows (valid votes and percentage of popular vote in parentheses): Socialists, 143 (7,170,484; 26.2 percent); Liberals, 132 (7,260,377; 26.5 percent); Democrats, 126 (7,097,208; 25.9 percent); People's Coöperatives, 31 (1,940,105; 7.1 percent); Communists, 4 (996,507; 3.6 percent); minor parties, 18 (1,562,213; 5.7 percent); independents, 12 (1,362,213; 5.0 percent).

‡The composition of the House of Representatives after the elections of 1949 was as follows: Democratic-Liberals, 264; Democrats, 68; Socialists, 49; Communists, 35; minor parties and independents, 50.

individual basis and clearly in violation of the Socialist Party's policy.

Thus, although the strategy of "peaceful revolution" may have been successful in so far as it helped to broaden the base of the Communist Party, it did not convince the Socialist leaders of the Communists' worth as partners in a coalition and as a result failed to produce any significant Socialist-Communist coöperation.

CHAPTER XV

Mobilization of Workers and Peasants

ACTION ON THE LABOR FRONT

THE SETTING

Uɴᴛɪʟ the fall of 1945, when the Allied Powers inaugurated a series of social, economic, and political reforms aimed at encouraging the growth of a democratic system in Japan, conditions there had been altogether unfavorable for the development of a strong labor movement. Legal restrictions imposed by prewar governments on trade-union activity and a general tendency on the part of the Japanese authorities to equate labor unrest with radicalism and strikes with revolution had circumscribed severely the usefulness of labor unions to the Japanese worker. On the other hand, this situation had permitted the survival of the feudal institution of "labor bosses"* and stimulated the development of company-sponsored or semiofficial labor organizations. When, after the Manchurian Incident (1931), nationalism and militarism began to permeate all phases of Japanese life, legitimate labor unions gradually were forced to disband or were driven underground, a development which could not but accentuate their natural proclivity toward radicalism and encourage a belief among organized labor in the necessity for a socialist revolution as a prerequisite for the betterment of society. Other factors—such as a constant ample supply of workers (resulting from the overpopulation in the countryside) and the continued existence of a quasi-patriarchal pattern of labor-management relations (encouraged by the government)—substantially weakened the bargaining position of the Japanese worker. Stunted in their growth, the Japanese labor unions, even in the peak year of 1936, never succeeded in organizing more than half a million workers. With the outbreak of war in China the following year, the number of organized workers dwindled rapidly as unions, suspected of a lack of enthusiasm for the war, were disbanded and their

*Most labor for construction work and practically all casual labor was supplied in prewar Japan by a small number of labor bosses (oyakata) who ruled their "clients" with an iron hand. These bosses, who in some cases headed organizations of several tens of thousands of workers, kept a certain percentage (up to one-half) of the wages of their men and often lent their influence to wealthy politicians or industrialists. Some of them even specialized in the procurement of votes, in union-busting, strikebreaking, and other similiar activities. Under the occupation these labor bosses lost much of their influence, although SCAP-sponsored measures did not succeed in entirely eradicating their practices.

leaders (among them a number of Communists) sent to prison. By 1940 labor unions had all but ceased to exist in Japan. They had been replaced by the government-sponsored Industrial Patriotic Association *(Sangyo Hokoku-kai* or *Sampo)*, patterned after Germany's national-socialist *Arbeitsfront.*

The growth of Japanese labor unions during the first years of Allied occupation offers a striking contrast to the prewar situation. Within a few months after the surrender, the major obstacles to the development of a strong labor movement were removed: SCAP introduced and established the democratic principles of freedom of assembly, speech, and the press; freed all political prisoners, including many labor leaders; repealed the ordinances which previous governments had issued to regiment labor; and dissolved the Industrial Patriotic Association, barring its officers from positions within the postwar unions.

Labor received direct support from the Supreme Commander himself. On October 11, 1945, General MacArthur told the newly-appointed Prime Minister, Baron Kijuro Shidehara: "I expect you to institute the following reforms in the social order of Japan, as rapidly as they can be assimilated: . . . The encouragement of the unionization of labor —that it may be clothed with such dignity as will permit it an influential voice in safeguarding the working man from exploitation and abuse and raising his living standard to a higher level."[1]

In line with this policy, later confirmed by the Far Eastern Commission in a sixteen-point statement, "Principles for Japanese Trade Unions,"[2] and in its "Basic Post-Surrender Policy for Japan,"[3] two laws were passed by the Japanese Diet upon the recommendation of SCAP. These were the Trade Union Law *(Rodo Kumiai-ho)* and the Labor Adjustment Law *(Rodo Kankei Chosei-ho)* of 1945 and 1946, respectively. The former, similar to the U. S. National Labor Relations Act, guaranteed labor's right to organize and to strike in support of its demands, recognizing also for the first time collective bargaining in Japanese industry. The latter established a comprehensive system of conciliation, mediation, and arbitration for the settlement of labor-management disputes.

Freed from all restrictions and encouraged by the Allied authorities, Japanese labor made rapid progress toward unionization. Although the majority of workers still lacked a clear understanding of the purpose and functions of a trade-union, by the millions they joined the numerous labor organizations which sprang up throughout Japan in 1946. The following table will illustrate the trend:[4]

	June 1945	Dec. 1945	June 1946	Dec. 1946
Number of unions	0	707	11,579	17,265
Number of members	0	378,481	3,748,952	4,849,329

By June 1947, union membership had grown to 5,594,699 workers; and by the winter of 1947 there were 28,013 unions with 6,268,432 members—estimated to represent 48.6 percent of Japan's nonagricultural labor.[5] Further progress was slow as the saturation point apparently had been reached: in June 1949 union membership was listed as 6,655,483.[6] A slight decrease marked the second half of the year, reducing the figure to 6,252,868.[7] This trend continued during 1950—owing in part to political considerations and in part to dismissals from private industry and government agencies.

Soon after General MacArthur's statement encouraging the unionization of labor, trade-unions multiplied throughout the more heavily industrialized districts. In the beginning, organized on a local and only seldom on a regional, national, or industry-wide basis, unions exhibited great variety in their structure and size as well as in their program and leadership. Many had been formed around men with experience in the prewar labor movement; others were created by employers preferring to direct their own union rather than to be forced to recognize an organization over which they would have little or no control. Whether true unions or company-dominated unions, these first labor organizations had come into existence without much planning or coördination. Operating in most cases within a single factory, they rarely constituted an effective weapon in the hands of their leaders. A definite need for combining these isolated unions into larger units was soon to make itself felt. By the end of 1945 a modest beginning had been made toward this goal with the formation of district and prefectural labor federations. The creation of national industrial unions (of newspaper workers, government railway workers, electrical, steel, and communications workers, and coal miners) followed in the spring of 1946. Although the organizational pattern was still confused and of considerable complexity (some unions were affiliated directly or indirectly with several over-all organizations), the crystallization process obviously had set in.

At this point it seems necessary to examine briefly the position of the first postwar unions within the Japanese political scene and especially their relation to the new political parties which had come into existence at about the same time—since this relation had a definite bearing on Communist strategy in Japan and eventually did develop into one of the crucial problems facing SCAP and the Japanese government.

Postwar Japan became in many respects what SCAP had wanted it to be. Policies were laid down in General Headquarters at Tokyo by the Supreme Commander personally or by his subordinates, and the Japanese authorities generally carried out these policies to the best of their ability. If there was at times passive resistance on the part of the Japanese government, this resistance did not prevent the execution of any major measure recommended by the Allied authorities. In occupied Japan a SCAP "recommendation" had the force of law. Labor appears to be one of the few areas in which events did not develop along the lines desired and hoped for by the occupying authority. The pattern remained distinctively Japanese.

It is true that the Far Eastern Commission policy statement, cited earlier, recommended that "trade unions should be allowed to take part in political activities and to support political parties,"[8] but this was hardly intended to encourage a trend toward the domination of labor unions by political parties. Allied policy (or at least United States policy) in Japan viewed labor unions as economic institutions designed to produce better working conditions in the broadest sense of the word. It was expected that, with SCAP guidance, Japanese labor organizations would develop along the lines of the A. F. of L. or the C. I. O., which generally have refused to subordinate the economic interests of their members to those of any political group. The chief of SCAP's Labor Division underlined this point at a convention of Japanese union leaders when, on October 21, 1948, he enunciated the three "basic principles" which would "prevent possible destruction of the country's remarkable union development":

1. Complete autonomy of unions to make possible freedom from domination of political parties, employer control, and government interference;

2. Full democracy to vest union control in the rank and file instead of an officer clique, aided by a vigorous program of labor education, simplification of union structure, and holding of regular union meetings;

3. Real awareness by the union of its responsibility to society as a whole leading to regulation of its activities to protect public interest to the fullest degree consistent with its own aims and objectives.[9]

Despite these warnings, Japanese labor unions from the beginning have exhibited a distinctly political character. The reasons for such a development, which was not desired—and possibly not anticipated—by the occupation authorities, must be sought in the nature of Japanese politics.

Even under so-called "liberal" cabinets, the Japanese worker, until 1945, never had been considered by his government a factor to be reckoned with in determining the nation's social and economic policy. As industrialization progressed, the number of factory workers grew; but their political influence did not. In a militarist Japan, dominated by a clique of bureaucrats, industrialists, landowners, and professional soldiers, labor had no voice. Attempts on the part of unions to improve the economic condition of the industrial proletariat almost invariably ended in failure, since power was concentrated heavily in the hands of management, which, in turn, enjoyed the backing of the government. This situation gave rise to the so-called "proletarian parties," established with the objective of gaining for the workers and for the tenant farmers —termed the "proletarians of the countryside"—a political and economic influence commensurate with their number. That these parties were short-lived and were unable to exert a decisive influence served to confirm the labor leaders' belief that economic improvement could be achieved only through political action. Hence, we find in the labor organizations of prewar Japan a degree of political orientation unknown in a country like the United States, where labor has enjoyed for decades the right to participate in state and local politics and has possessed the machinery for making its weight felt in the formulation of national policy.

To the traditional political impotency of Japanese labor organizations must be added another, by no means less notable, trait: the feudalistic master-retainer, master-disciple, or patron-client pattern was as predominant in Japanese trade-unions as it was in political parties or in the business world. Direction of organized labor tended to remain in the hands of a small number of men who, for the most part, were not workers but intellectuals. What is perhaps more significant is that these intellectuals were predominantly Marxist—though not necessarily Communist— in orientation, a fact which increased the Japanese government's fear of an active labor movement and led it to adopt a policy of systematic suppression.

When, after the surrender of Imperial Japan, the prewar union leaders emerged from prisons or hideouts, from army barracks and navy yards, and from "retirement," many of them went back to the task of organizing the workers, if anything, more convinced than before that the solution for labor lay in political reform along Marxist lines. The continued hegemony in Japanese politics of the conservative elements further encouraged such reasoning. Thus, organized labor in postwar Japan continued to be led by a relatively small number of politically minded intellectuals, the majority of them favoring the Marxist solution or at least the system of social reforms which generally is designated by the term socialism. As in prewar times, these men in the main belong to one of two factions—the Socialists or the Communists. The recurrent cycles of splits and mergers which are characteristic of the labor movement in postwar Japan may be explained by the fact that these two factions, while attempting to preserve a solid front of all trade-unions against management, are at the same time engaged in a bitter fight for supremacy.

As hundreds of unions were formed in Japan during the last months of 1945, it is only natural that Socialists (social democrats) and Communists should have vied with each other in their campaigns to combine all labor organizations in a single federation. The original Communist plan appears to have been to work toward a merger of Communist-dominated and Socialist unions. To win control from within was considered a relatively simple matter compared to the task of taking over a strongly organized Socialist trade-union federation from the outside.* However, Communist efforts failed to bring about the desired result, mostly because of the strong opposition of such Socialist leaders as Komakichi Matsuoka, a veteran labor organizer. The Communist Party's shift to a somewhat more moderate policy after Sanzo Nozaka's return from Communist China in 1946 created a more favorable atmosphere for collaboration between the two groups. But despite determined efforts on the part of the Socialist left wing to enter into an alliance with the Communists, the unity movement was rejected by a majority of the Socialist labor leaders. Socialist fear of the consequences of a merger with Communist-dominated unions could not be overcome. Reluctantly, Communists and Communist sympathizers established their own organization. In August of 1946 two separate national federations of labor unions emerged: the All Japan General Federation of Trade Unions *(Zen-Nihon Rodo Kumiai Sodomei)* or JFL—generally referred to as *Sodomei*—was clearly controlled by the Socialists; its rival, the National Congress of Industrial Unions *(Zenkoku Sangyo-betsu Rodo Kumiai Kaigi)* or NCIU—known as *Sanbetsu*—although denying any connection with the Communist Party, from the outset exhibited partiality for the Communist cause. Two of its leaders, Katsumi Kikunami and Kazuyoshi Dobashi, eventually made public their affiliation with the Japanese Communist Party.

THE PLACE OF LABOR UNIONS IN THE OVER-ALL PLAN

True to the Marxist-Leninist axiom that the industrial worker forms the "vanguard of the socialist revolution," the Japanese Communists consistently have directed their main propagandistic and organizational effort toward this segment of the population. Even at the time when Nozaka's policy of a broad popular front encompassing also farmers, white-collar workers and even the "petty bourgeois" was being faithfully implemented, there could be no question as to the prime objective of Party work. In 1948 Kikunami stated without qualification:

> The worker is the real builder of socialism. The other classes of society can under no circumstances fulfill this role. Only when fighting together with the worker and under the workers' direction

*On December 1, 1945, Kyuichi Tokuda addressed the Fourth Party Congress on this matter. "We must not forget," he stated, "that among those who are not under the influence of corrupt Socialists, there are many who are interested in our Party . . . With a somewhat more intensified propaganda campaign, we can make them join forces with us." Kyuichi Tokuda, *Naigai josei to Nippon kyosanto no nimmu* (The Domestic and Foreign Situation and the Tasks of the JCP). Tokyo, 1949, p. 263.

can they participate in the task of establishing socialism. By their own strength they can never achieve this objective.[10]

Why is the farmer, who outnumbers the worker even in the relatively industrialized Japan of the postwar period, considered by the Communists congenitally incapable of leading a revolution? Why does even the tenant farmer—although termed by the Party "the proletarian of the countryside"—require the guidance of the worker at all times? Perhaps the most illuminating exposition of the Party's views on this issue is contained in an official Communist handbook on trade-unions.[11] The Communist line of reasoning runs as follows: Farmers and small businessmen attend to their own little plot of land or their small store; they have a tendency to think in terms of individual effort. Because of this, they generally fail to realize the need for solidarity among the working people and find it difficult to comprehend the tenets of socialism. "Numerous though they are," the Communist author comments, "these groups are unable to recognize a clear objective in their [economic] struggle and hence vacillate somewhere between the worker and the capitalist."[12] This limited political consciousness and the relative impotence of the farmer and the petty bourgeois are contrasted with the outlook and potential of the industrial worker. A "direct victim of capitalist exploitation"— who, moreover, has experienced community life and collective action to a degree unknown to other social groups—the Japanese worker, in the Communist view, possesses the combination of strength, cohesion, and purposefulness necessary to effect the overthrow of the capitalist system. It is pointed out further that even the starving tenant farmer conceives a solution to his economic problems only in terms of redistribution of large landholdings, whereas the worker—owning neither property nor tools of production—seeks and by necessity must seek a solution to his problems in the establishment of some sort of coöperative management. Thus, as a direct result of their function in capitalist society, the workers are believed more apt than any other social class to comprehend the principles of Marxian theory and practice.

As a logical outcome of this analysis, the Japanese Communist Party considers successful mobilization of the workers a prerequisite for any movement aimed at the establishment of a socialist state. But the mobilization of the worker can be accomplished only by harnessing this vast potential· of revolutionary force—in other words, through the unionization of labor. Unions, however, cannot constitute effective revolutionary weapons until they have been combined under a single authority, able to coördinate and to exert a measure of control over all labor action. Communist policy, therefore, works for a total mobilization of labor, to be accomplished through the welding together of all unions into a single organization.[13] As to the structure of such an organization, the Communist Party clearly favors the "one union per industry" principle of the Congress of Industrial Organizations.[14] Accordingly, in contradistinction to the Socialists, who long favored a regional pattern of unionization—valuable in obtaining votes, but less effective in large-scale strikes[15]—the Japanese Communist Party, from the beginning of its organizational drive among labor, emphasized the necessity for national industrial unions.* That particular attention was given to the creation of national unions in the fields of transportation, communications, and power industries is not surprising in view of the Communist Party's stated objective: the seizure of power through general strikes and revolutionary action.†

Within the Communist over-all plan, labor unions constitute "schools in which the worker learns class struggle and Communism."[16] Again and again Party doctrine emphasizes this point: that unions can fulfill the role assigned to them in the struggle for political power only if they are converted into a training ground where the worker is given the opportunity to acquire a high degree of political consciousness.[17] Made up of heterogeneous elements, varying among each other in the extent of their understanding of the nature of capitalism and of the best "solution to the problems posed by the capitalist system," these mass organizations are in constant need of "guidance" and of "enlightenment." Responsibility for this task rests with the Communist union members. "Enlightenment"—indoctrination of the worker—forms then an essential part of Communist union leadership; a gradual initiation of the worker into Marx-Leninism—"the scientific theory of the liberation of the working class"[18]—prepares the union member for his "historic role" as one of the "vanguard of the revolution."

Labor unions, then, are not mere economic institutions but, instead, constitute instruments of Party policy. Their function within the Communist plan, as well as their peculiar relation to the Party itself, was summed up by Central Committee member Shoichi Kasuga in the following terms:

> Revolution cannot be achieved by reliance on the Party's strength alone. It must be carried out by the people grouped around the workers. The labor unions thus perform the function of a belt linking the Communist Party to the masses.[19]

*The first truly national industrial union came into being on February 9, 1946 under the name All Japan News and Radio Workers' Union. Its leader was the ex-journalist Katsumi Kikunami. Supreme Commander for the Allied Powers, *Summation of Non-military Activities in Japan.* Tokyo, Feb. 1946, p. 192.

†As early as November 1945, Yoshio Shiga, in a report to the Party National Consultative Conference, pointed out that the communications and transportation industries were "the nerves of the nation." *Akahata,* Nov. 22, 1945.

METHODS AND EXTENT OF PENETRATION

Unquestionably the most effective means employed by the Japanese Communist Party in its attempt to penetrate non-Communist labor organizations was the establishment and operation of the so-called "fractions" or "Party member groups."* In view of their importance in terms of Communist strategy, the official Party regulations pertaining to the organization and function of these Communist units, adopted in December 1947 by the Sixth Congress of the Japanese Communist Party, are quoted here in full:

Article 49. *When there are more than three Party members within a mass organization,* such as a labor union, a farmers' organization, a youth association, a coöperative or cultural organization, these members shall form *a Party member group.* Party member groups within a mass organization, while acting within the limits set by the rules and regulations of the particular organization, *must strengthen the Party's influence* by gaining the confidence of the organization's members through positive and exemplary conduct. The Party member group elects a directorate to attend to daily activities.

Article 50. Party member groups belonging to the same organization may have central, regional, metropolitan, and prefectural or district group directorates, in accordance with the territorial breakdown of the particular organization. These directorates form a chain of command running from top to bottom; *but they are all subordinate to the Party's Central, Regional, Metropolitan, Prefectural and District Committees,* respectively, and they are *bound by the decisions of these Party Committees.*

Article 51. Party member group directorates shall be composed of:

(1) *Party members in executive positions* on the various levels within a mass organization;

(2) Representatives of Party member group directorates or of Cells within the lower executive echelons of the said organization; and

(3) *Representatives from Party organs* which direct the Party member groups at each level.

*The term "fraction" was replaced in 1947 by the phrase "Party member group." This rectification of names was decided upon at the Sixth Party Congress, apparently in an attempt to mitigate the violent criticism being directed against the Party by non-Communists because of Communist "fractional" activity. The Party had been accused of setting up a government within the mass organizations and of plotting to take over the control of all Japanese labor unions through a process of subversion. The term "group" with its more "democratic" connotation has since been used in official documents, although the word "fraction" has by no means disappeared from the everyday vocabulary of the Party member.

Article 52. *Joint meetings of the group directorates and of the Party organs* at the central, regional, metropolitan, prefectural, and district levels shall be held for the purpose of (*a*) coördinating activities of the groups within each of the various mass organizations; (*b*) *coördinating the activities of these groups with the activities of the Party itself;* and (*c*) *coördinating all group activities with Party policy.*[20]

It is evident from these regulations that fractions, although technically not components of the Communist Party's organizational structure, are allowed but little freedom of action. The Party's insistence on the exercise of absolute control over all fractional activity, as reflected in the detailed regulations governing the relation between fractions and Party, can be understood only in the light of the position of the Communist worker within the non-Communist labor union.

As a result of the relative numerical weakness of the Communist Party during the first year after Japan's surrender and for a variety of other reasons—mostly tactical considerations—Party policy from the beginning had rejected the concept of exclusively Communist trade-unions. Rather than establish an organization of its own in the field of labor, the Communist Party preferred to rely on organized infiltration. Accordingly, Communists were directed to join a union and to strengthen the Party's influence by gaining the confidence of their co-workers "through positive and exemplary action."[21] In line with these recommendations, the Communist worker actively participated in the economic struggle of his union. He appeared at the forefront of those who were fighting vigorously for higher wages, better working conditions, shorter working hours, and greater job security—all essentially economic demands. Often, as a result, he began to exhibit a tendency to identify himself with his union rather than with the Communist Party; and gradually he came to lose interest in Party affairs. As a consequence of such an attitude on the part of the Communist worker—condemned officially as "trade-unionism" or "syndicalism"—the Party risked losing its most valuable supporters to the unions and felt itself in danger of becoming a mere appendage of the labor movement.

This emphasis on the role of fractions as representatives and agents of the Communist Party produced another danger of a different nature. Undue stress on political action, as was likely to result from subordination of fractional to Party activities, easily could lead to intraunion strife between Communist and non-Communist workers. Whatever the outcome of such a struggle, splits, secessions, and isolation of the militant Communist union members were bound to occur. To prevent such a development, which would destroy any hope for a united front of organized labor, a delicate balance between political and nonpolitical fractional activity had to be maintained. Although theoretically the differentiation between the Communist Cell, a Party organization, and the fraction operating under Party supervision—but within the framework of the particular union's regulations—should have been sufficient to accomplish this difficult task, in practice it was often found impossible to avoid the conflict arising from the Communist Cell member's dual loyalty to Party and union. The directorates of Communist fractions were obliged to steer a precarious course between the Scylla of "trade-unionism" and the Charybdis of "political sectarianism," and they were not always successful.

Much of the Communist Party's success in mobilizing labor for political purposes must be attributed to the effective work of Communist fractions within the labor unions. On the other hand, there is little doubt that the appearance after 1947 of a militant anti-Communist element within the majority of Japanese labor organizations was equally the result of Communist fractional activity. Faced with the choice between indirectly strengthening the anti-Communist wing through provoking resentment by Party interference in union affairs or abolishing altogether the Communist hierarchical arrangement within the labor unions, the Party never hesitated. The Communist concept of "democratic centralism" vested all authority in the policy-making body of the Party. There was no room for even a limited degree of autonomy. Dissolution of fractions and relaxation of Party control over the individual Communist union member would have been contrary to all Communist practice. Moreover, Communist successes in Western Europe generally were interpreted by the Japanese Party as proof of the importance of establishing factory Cells and of conducting fractional activity.* Though anxious to keep anti-Communist feeling to a minimum, the Party, nevertheless, continued to pursue its traditional policy of organized infiltration by means of strictly supervised Communist fractions. A statement by labor leader Kikunami in 1948 confirms this point. When attacked for his connection with Communist fractions, he replied:

> The activity of Party members within the trade-unions strengthens the class character of these organizations. This, in turn, stimulates their development. Such activity, therefore, must be considered absolutely indispensable [for a healthy development of Japanese unions] . . . There are those who proclaim that they have no objec-

---

*A book recommended by the Communist Party and composed in the main of articles taken from *Akahata* contains the following pertinent comment: "The Italian and French Communist Parties are able to direct a very large mass movement because they possess vigorous factory cells everywhere." Kentaro Yamabe (ed.), *To-seikatsu* (Party Life). Tokyo, 1950, p. 18.

tion to our being members of the Communist Party but that they object only to our fractional activity. This is like telling a man that he may continue to live as a human being but that he must absolutely refrain from walking.[22]

Although Communists at no time have constituted more than a small minority even in the so-called "Communist unions" of the NCIU, they have been able to exert, through skillful operation of fractional units, a degree of influence out of proportion to their numerical strength. Representing often less than 10 percent of the total membership of an organization, they actually succeeded in gaining complete control.* The gradual process of Communist penetration, although never quite uniform because of varying local conditions, generally followed a distinct and discernible pattern. Communist workers—few in number but always in the forefront of the union's struggle with the employer—would organize Communist fractions as prescribed by a resolution of the Central Committee, adopted in May 1946 at a time when it had become clear that the Communist unification drive, at least temporarily, had failed.† Once the fraction had been formed with the active assistance and under the supervision of the appropriate Party agency, a suitable individual would be selected among the Communist union members for a position of leadership. Thereupon, the fraction could initiate an organized campaign to send its leader into the policy-making body of the union. Backed by a well-disciplined team of supporters, trained in psychological warfare, and armed with a clear-cut answer to any and all political and economic problems, the candidate—who, during the early period, seldom admitted to membership in the Party—from the outset commanded a decisive advantage over his generally inexperienced opponents. Even when he faced a Socialist candidate, the Communist union leader was apt to find himself in the more favorable situation, for his competitor's camp was likely to be split into left-wing, centrist, and right-wing factions, engaged in a permanent feud with one another. Moreover, the Communist candidate could count on unorganized, but nevertheless vital, support among the nonpolitical minority of union membership, for, as a vigorous fighter for the union's demands, he usually was popular among the rank and file. Superior training in practical politics, accompanied by an acute awareness of audience reaction and—in many cases—augmented by a flair for public speaking, further favored the Commu-

*According to SCAP, this fact was openly admitted by the Communist leaders themselves. Satomi Hakamada, a veteran of the prewar Communist movement and in the postwar period a member of the Central Committee, commenting on the question, reportedly boasted in 1946: "A handful of Communist members hold the actual leadership." *Summation of Non-military Activities in Japan*, Feb. 1947, p. 36.

†The pertinent portion of the resolution read: "Whenever there are three or more Party members [within a union], a fraction *must* be formed."

nist candidate when the union membership proceeded to select its representatives. Thus, although outnumbered many times by the non-Communists, the Communist fraction very often succeeded in placing its candidate on the union's policy-making board. Once elected—and this constitutes the beginning of the next phase—the Party representative would attempt to strengthen Communist influence through the judicious use of a variety of techniques.

Advocacy of direct action and the calling of political strikes were among the methods most frequently employed. If successful, they increased the prestige of the Communist Party—which invariably supported such action—and even when unsuccessful, they tended to advance the Communist cause. Unrest, turmoil, and resentment thus fostered against the employers and the government seldom failed to produce an atmosphere conducive to the propagation of Communist views. While attacking political opponents as "lackeys of the bourgeoisie," Communists often entered into alliances with sympathetic left-wing Socialists. Such coalitions took the form of "democratic fronts," intended to bolster the Communist position. This approach was used during the first year of the occupation when a process of polarization of Communist and non-Communist forces had not yet split the left-wing labor organizations.

A vociferous advocacy of higher wages and better working conditions, this coupled with a relentless campaign for direct action against the conservative authorities and for the mirage of a "people's government," further tended to enhance the popularity of the Communist candidate, at the same time rendering more difficult the position of moderate elements within the labor unions. In this manner, a single seat on a union's directorate frequently was parlayed into a Communist majority. The same technique applied on a larger scale in turn brought whole national unions under Communist control.

Although Communist operations seldom deviated from this pattern, the infinite number of variations on the general theme and the real extent of Communist success or failure can be shown only in proper perspective within the framework of the postwar labor situation.

THE PLAN IN OPERATION

As the economic position of wage earners steadily deteriorated throughout 1946, owing to food shortages, inflation, and anemic production, labor resorted to its newly won weapon—the strike. During the first half of the year, in the absence of strong national unions, strikes were limited to single factories or smaller areas. They generally were quickly settled, with employers accepting the workers' demands; but labor derived little real benefit from these agreements, as inflation was rampant and wages never quite caught up with the steady rise in prices. By this time the Party's influence on labor had begun to make itself felt in various ways. Perhaps the most interesting tactic was the introduction of a new type of strike termed "production control." Workers, instead of deserting their factory, seized and operated the plant until the day when management agreed to offer a satisfactory settlement. This novel technique of securing labor's demands, if not actually invented by the Party, received its vigorous support.[23] Undoubtedly, it did much to strengthen Communist influence among labor, as it inspired the workers with confidence in their ability to produce without the help of "capitalists" and created before their eyes a small-scale model of a "proletarian" economy. In conjunction with a number of short-lived strikes during that first year, the Communist Party launched a series of mass rallies and popular demonstrations in support of its central slogan, "Immediate formation of a people's government."[24] Workers formed the nucleus of this growing antigovernment movement.

With the inauguration of the NCIU in the summer of 1946, the strike waves suddenly assumed major proportions. Encouraged by an official NCIU resolution referring to the possibility of a general strike to prevent the dismissal of 130,000 railway workers as proposed by the government,[25] the first big nation-wide work stoppages occurred. The movement gained rapid momentum, led by the Communist elements and their sympathizers but sweeping along also the moderate elements within the major federations. On October 13, the Communist newspaper proclaimed: "The capitalist camp directed by the Yoshida Cabinet, frightened by the intensification of the labor offensive, already has begun to weaken."[26] Strikes now assumed an increasingly political character, and ominous articles began to appear in the Party press discussing the relation between "peaceful revolution and general strikes."[27] As the labor offensive sponsored by the NCIU was pressed forward, virtually all labor groups agreed that a change in government would be necessary to produce any improvement in what was termed an "intolerable economic situation." The time for a merger appeared to be drawing near. On January 15, 1947, when a National Union Joint Struggle Committee came into being—a merger again had been rejected by the JFL—more than three million organized workers, having agreed on a uniform set of demands, were poised against the Yoshida government.[28] All major federations and national unions, whether Communist, Socialist, or neutral, had joined in the snowballing movement for the overthrow of the conservative cabinet. Although there was much hesitation and not a little confusion among the heterogeneous labor groups as to the tactics which should be pursued, the Communist Party and all other radical elements within the NCIU followed a clearly delineated course. On

New Year's Day 1947 Nozaka had stated: "1947 will bring the high point in Japan's crisis . . . Only a people's government can overcome it."[29] A few days later, the Party organ proclaimed: "The decisive battle is approaching! A general strike is now inevitable!"[30] A last-minute minor concession by the Japanese government failed to impress the government workers, who formed the main body of the Struggle Committee. The militant elements succeeded in carrying along the moderates on a wave of popular enthusiasm for a general strike. When, on January 30, negotiations broke down completely, the general strike planned for February 1 seemed unavoidable. Economic pressures, a reluctance on the part of the conservative government to grant justified claims in time, and the strong desire of left-wing parties to share more fully in the government—these three factors had created an explosive situation which was being skillfully exploited by the Communist Party. On January 31, on the eve of the projected general strike, the Japanese Communists seemed close to a large share of political power. A few hours later the situation had changed radically. A direct order from General MacArthur to the leaders of the strike movement made it clear that the occupation authorities would not permit what was called "the use of so deadly a social weapon."[31] The head of the strike committee was forced to call off the general strike by means of a nation-wide broadcast. Although discouraged, he hinted at future action, commenting, "One step back, two steps forward."[32]

There could be no doubt but that the Japanese labor movement, and especially its radical wing, had suffered a serious setback. Little wonder then that long-repressed voices rose to accuse the Communists of having made of labor an instrument of political struggle. There was some truth in this accusation, since the radical elements in the NCIU had seized the initiative in the fall of 1946 and had carried the moderate forces along— often against the latter's will. But if they all had followed the line advanced by the militant Communist labor leaders, it was because they had reached the conclusion that the government was showing neither a particular desire nor great ability to improve the condition of the rapidly disintegrating Japanese economy. Statistics showing the rise in retail prices during 1946 will illustrate the point:[33]

(July 1914 = 100)

January	1,057.2	July	3,291.8
February	1,276.9	August	3,229.7
March	1,851.5	September	3,432.5
April	2,455.3	October	3,854.5
May	2,761.4	November	4,016.9
June	3,154.9	December	4,352.1

If the abortive general strike did not result in anything even approximating the conditions the Communist Party had hoped to create by paralyzing what little remained of Japanese economy, it was at least successful in forcing the withdrawal of the government, which, by that time, was thoroughly unpopular. The subsequent elections of April 1947 offer a convenient yardstick for measuring the degree of Communist influence in Japanese labor unions. The JFL, true to its traditional policy, endorsed exclusively Socialist candidates. Its rival, the NCIU (counting then about a million and a half members), was about evenly split between left-wing Socialists and Communists, since, of fifteen candidates endorsed by the organization, eight ran on the Socialist and seven on the Communist ticket.[34] Communist influence in the Railway Workers Union (approximately 550,000 members) appears to have been still greater, as among its six official candidates five claimed Communist affiliation.[35]

The election results, however, showed no corresponding gains in general popular support. The Communist fraction in the Diet remained of negligible strength, whereas the Socialist Party, polling seven times as many votes as the Communists, advanced to the leading position. The "people's government," for which the Communist Party had been agitating, did not materialize. Instead, a coalition cabinet was installed under the anti-Communist Socialist leader, Tetsu Katayama, who was careful to exclude Communists and Communist sympathizers from his cabinet list.

This new situation produced a certain adjustment in the Communist Party's labor tactics. A comparative lull in Communist-sponsored strikes marked the first months of the Katayama Cabinet. Communist labor leaders publicly indulged in a modest amount of "self-criticism" of their past militant tactics. Though they clearly were on the defensive and despite a good deal of opposition, Communist labor leaders succeeded in retaining their positions in the left-wing unions. A proposal to exclude Communists in order to remove the main obstacle to a merger with the JFL, which was eager to align labor behind the Socialist cabinet, was voted down by a NCIU convention.[36] Attesting to the strength of Communist influence within its ranks, the NCIU also refused to follow the JFL in its unconditional support of the Katayama Cabinet, preferring to "judge each issue on its individual merits."[37] A renewed attempt on the part of the NCIU to prepare the ground for a gradual merger of all unions finally was successful in the spring of 1947.

An invitation was issued to all Japanese labor unions to join in establishing an informal liaison organ which would represent the interests of labor and eventually, in this capacity, would participate in the work of the World Federation of Trade Unions, which, at that time, included practically all non-Communist and Communist trade-unions from the United States to the Soviet Union. The JFL—main obstacle to previous attempts at unification—decided to accept the invitation, but only after having been assured that the new organization—to be called the National Liaison Council of Japanese Trade Unions *(Zenkoku Rodo Kumiai Ren-raku Kyogikai* or simply *Zenroren)*—would be merely a consultative and not a policy-making body.

The economic deterioration which had been the inevitable aftermath of total defeat continued on its seemingly relentless course under the Socialist coalition cabinet. The possibility of mass starvation in Japan appeared very real in the summer of 1947. Only large-scale distribution of food from the United States averted a serious loss of life.[38] Communist labor leaders took the occasion to revert to more aggressive tactics. They apparently believed that the Katayama Cabinet had lost all support among labor and that the time had come to invite the Socialist left wing to desert the Party which had failed so conspicuously to make good its promises to labor. But the Communist Party, as later events showed, had grossly underestimated Socialist strength as well as Socialist resentment against Communist tactics.

Forced to abandon large-scale strikes for fear of SCAP intervention, Communist labor leaders during the second half of 1947 devised and applied new techniques: the staging of regional strikes, temporary work stoppages, demonstrations for food, and increasing absenteeism, attributed by the Party to "malnutrition." The Katayama Cabinet, unable to control the progress of inflation, the pressure of unions for higher wages, and the too-often contradictory desires and programs of the coalition parties, finally resigned in the spring of 1948.

Continuing to overestimate the effect of Katayama's failure upon the political alignment of labor, the Party pursued a policy aimed at splitting the Socialist Party and its peripheral organizations. In line with this policy, Makoto Kan, chairman of the NCIU, immediately after the resignation of the cabinet, asserted that Katayama had "betrayed" the people and had been overthrown by the counterattack of the "suffering masses." Simultaneously, the NCIU issued a statement urging formation of a "democratic front" including left-wing Socialists and Communists.[39] Contrary to Communist hopes, a new coalition cabinet was inaugurated, comprising this time even the left-wing Socialists.

The over-all picture of union activity during the following months was complex and disturbing. Government-workers' unions were fighting their employers over the issue of higher wages. The government was attempting to placate labor and to control inflation at the same time. SCAP reluctantly was quelling strikes which, although provoked or led by Communist union leaders, were in many cases understandable, for the position of the workers had, if anything, deteriorated even further. The Communist Party was engaged in an all-out drive to bring the

NCIU under its complete control, to split rival unions, and to absorb the left-wing Socialists; but it in turn found itself under fierce attack from newly organized anti-Communist labor groups. While the Communists had been attempting to monopolize the initiative on the labor front, by calling "piston strikes" (brief work stoppages repeated in rapid succession) and by inciting workers to mass absenteeism and other types of "guerilla warfare," SCAP and Japanese government pressure hampered Communist action at every turn. As a result, there were no large strikes comparable to those of the previous year but, instead, a rash of minor but disturbing outbreaks of labor unrest throughout the country and particularly in the strategic Tokyo area.

Communist action timed to coincide with the disappointing performance of Socialist coalition cabinets had accomplished a marked radicalization of labor and had dealt a blow to Socialist prestige. On the other side of the ledger, Communist fractional activity was beginning to produce the inevitable reaction. In August 1947 the JFL had withdrawn from participation in the pro-Communist *Zenroren*.[40] A few months later, the JFL followed up this action by sending out invitations to other unions to join together in an anti-Communist drive.[41] At about the same time several local unions decided to secede from the All Japan Newspaper and Radio Workers' Union, accusing it of being Communist-dominated.[42] But this was only the beginning: even within the NCIU, and especially in those affiliated unions where Communist influence was strongest and militant tactics predominated, the long-smoldering feud between non-Communists and Communists flared up. This anti-Communist movement crystallized in the form of "Democratization Leagues" (*Minshuka Domei*).[43] Members of the new Leagues were determined to eliminate Communist influence within their unions in order to pave the way for a united front of all labor. Although by the spring of 1948 these Leagues had not made any significant impression on the labor movement as a whole, their following was increasing steadily.[44]

THE BALANCE SHEET

July 22, 1948 marked the turning point in the development of Communist influence on labor. Until that date Communist propaganda work had been particularly intensive among the more than two and a half million government workers and especially in the key railroad and communications unions. Much of the labor unrest during 1947 and the first half of 1948 centered about the government-workers' unions, partly because civil servants were so poorly paid but largely also because of strong Communist infiltration. These unions had formed the core of the abortive 1947 general strike. Now again, in the summer of 1948, they appeared to be preparing for a full-scale offensive, this time designed to embrace also farmers and other groups.[45] Faced with the prospect of a total strike of all government workers, supported by the NCIU unions and by large segments of the population—a situation which might throw Japan into turmoil and endanger the mission of the occupation—General Mac-Arthur sent an open letter to Prime Minister Ashida stating that in his view "no person holding a position by appointment or employment in the public service of Japan or in any instrumentality thereof should resort to strike."[46] Immediately, pending the formal revision of the National Public Service Law, the Japanese government promulgated an anti-strike ordinance.*

The Communists made attempts to circumvent these anti-strike orders by the use of a variety of subterfuges, aimed at achieving the effect of strikes without actually involving what might be termed "strike action." Even so, government workers gradually came to lose the predominant position they had held in Communist labor strategy. During the remainder of 1948, the emphasis of Communist labor activity was shifted to private industry. Private railroad workers—reinforced by electrical workers—were preparing for nation-wide work stoppages toward the end of the year, when again SCAP intervened and "advised" the union leaders to call off the walkout. Reluctantly, the unions complied with the order.[47]

Despite these reverses, Communist influence in the Japanese trade-unions was stronger in 1948 than it had been the previous year. Although few of the more than a million and a third members of the NCIU[48] were actually connected with the Party apparatus, Communists had forced themselves to the top of the organization. The directorate of the NCIU generally looked to the Communist fraction leaders for advice. The Communist position perhaps was even stronger among the public-workers' unions which had been the main target of Communist propaganda until the middle of 1948. Although no accurate figures can be compiled because of the nature of the issue, it is estimated that in 1948 about half of organized labor was under varying degrees of Communist control. This was reflected in the results of the January 1949 elections, which witnessed an increase of the Communist share in the total national vote from less than 4 percent to about 10 percent—with much larger percentages in the industrial areas.

While Communist control over Japanese labor continued strong throughout 1948—despite determined efforts on the part of the Ashida (and later the Yoshida) governments to break the hold of left-wing elements—a marked rise in anti-Communist feeling among labor was noticeable from about the beginning of 1949, becoming more pronounced toward the end of the year. The Democratization Leagues already have

*The revised National Public Service Law was adopted by the Diet toward the end of the year.

been mentioned as groups of anti-Communist workers and union organizers established with the objective of ridding Communist-dominated unions of outside influences. They scored their first real success during the spring of 1949: on April 26, newspapers reported that the leader of the Democratization League within the Government Railway Workers Union had been elected chairman of the central executive committee of the organization. Among twenty-three seats on the central excutive committee, the Democratization League secured nine—as against seven for the Communists and seven for the left-wing, but non-Communist, Renovationists.[49] A few weeks later one of the strongest left-wing unions, the All Japan Electrical Workers' Union *(Densan)*, adopted the League's policy statement by a vote of 290 to 281 but rejected by a margin of thirty-six votes a proposal to disaffiliate from the Communist-dominated NCIU.[50] Thus, it would be a mistake to interpret such victories of the Democratization League as having spelled the end of Communist control over the particular organization. In these and similar cases the two camps were almost evenly balanced; and any minor change in government policy or in economic conditions could, and actually did, upset this precarious balance of power.

The sudden emergence of vigorous anti-Communist forces, after more than a year of rather unsuccessful attempts to break the Communist hold over many of the key unions, apart from the growing anti-Communist feeling engendered by the international situation, may be attributed to the impact of the economic-stabilization program in Japan which was then being carried out upon United States recommendation. This program, known as the "Dodge Plan," was designed to alleviate the critical situation produced by three years of continuous inflation and economic atrophy when only the production of bank notes reached any sizable volume. Calling for a balanced budget, limited credits, wage stabilization, maximum exports, and increased production, the program was frankly deflationary in character. Although it demanded heavy sacrifices by all segments of the population, it was evident from the beginning that its effect on labor would be particularly strong. Deflationary policy and dismissals of surplus workers, coupled with the already existing severe restrictions on strikes and other types of labor action, must necessarily have resulted in a decrease in the importance of labor.

The Economic Stabilization Program had the full backing of the occupation authorities. In April 1949, shortly after the first steps to implement the plan had been taken, representatives of the NCIU were asked to visit General Headquarters to familiarize themselves with the implications of the new program. The labor delegates were warned that "politically inspired strikes against revision of the labor-union laws would not be tolerated" and were informed that "Japan must implement the nine-point Economic Stabilization Program and that, therefore, no political strikes or activities by the Japanese workers will be tolerated."[51]

Almost without exception, labor deplored the implied wage freeze and the added restrictions, but was divided in its opinion as to how to protect its interests. On one side were the Communist-controlled unions and their sympathizers mainly in the NCIU, who advocated resistance and the overthrow of the Yoshida government through the exercise of concerted pressure; on the other side were the "moderates" of the JFL and all those who were beginning to reconcile themselves to the idea of a strategic retreat. The Communist Party spoke of the "road to fascism," of "capitalist offensive" and "foreign monopolies," of the government's policy amounting to a "selling out of the country," and of Japan's future under a "semicolonial regime." Throughout 1949 the Party strove to arouse workers, farmers, women, and young people under the slogan "Peace and Independence" in an attempt to prevent implementation of the plan. The anti-Communists—frequently as much opposed to the "Dodge Plan" as the Communists—accused the Party of being responsible for the situation and for the antilabor measures recommended by the Supreme Commander and adopted by the government. The feeling was widespread that without the militant and reckless action of the Communists, who obviously were more interested in perpetuating strikes than in settling them, labor would not have been deprived of the many privileges it had enjoyed in the earlier phase of the occupation.

During 1949 the process of polarization, which had begun much earlier, was intensified; throughout the year two factions of about equal strength faced each other in almost every one of the once clearly Communist-dominated unions.

As the Communist Party showed signs of taking its stand more positively alongside the other components of the international Communist movement, the attitude of SCAP and of the Japanese government toward the radical left wing stiffened. Pro-Communist labor delegates were refused permission to attend the convention of the World Federation of Trade Unions in Moscow,[52] although their anti-Communist colleagues were allowed to go to London for the first convention of the International Confederation of Free Trade Unions.[53] SCAP and the Japanese authorities did everything in their power to encourage the anti-Communist labor groups.[54] The economic-retrenchment program further weakened the Communist position, as private industry and government showed an increasing tendency to utilize the program as a convenient excuse for dismissing militant unionists.

As a result, many Communist-dominated unions lost their leaders. Other unions split into two camps, or were taken over by the Democratization Leagues. Membership in the NCIU and in the *Zenroren*-affiliated unions steadily declined during the year as one secession after another

occurred.* By the beginning of 1950, the prospects for a successful unification of non-Communist forces were favorable: Communist influence
had been curbed by the developments of the previous year, while the
effect of the new militant strategy ordered by Moscow and endorsed by
the Communist Party was to hamper further Communist endeavors to
form alignments with other labor groups.†

WORK AMONG FARMERS AND FISHERMEN

Despite determined efforts on the part of the Communist Party to
enlist the support of Japan's vast farming and fishing population, Communist influence in the countryside was at no time comparable to that in
the city. Several factors account for this situation: the traditional conservatism and comparative political apathy of the Japanese farmer; the
effect of the SCAP-inspired land-reform program which, in a single blow,
destroyed the economic bondage that hitherto had enslaved the tenant
farmer and thereby eliminated a source of permanent unrest from which
the Party had hoped to derive strength;‡ the relative economic well-
being prevailing throughout the farming districts (due mainly to the
temporary inflation and the black market in food) in contrast to the
continuous food shortages in the cities;§ the relatively weak impact of
the Pacific War on the farmer's pattern of life (there was hardly any war
damage outside the urban centers);‖ and the Communist Party's inability

*In September 1949 there were 769,813 dues-paying members in the NCIU. This
represents only slightly more than half the number of members claimed by the union
at its peak. *Rodo Hyoron,* Feb. 1950.

†For developments in 1950 and 1951, see "Anti-Communist Labor Offensive,"
Chapter XXI.

‡The Party's slogan, "Land for the Toiling Farmer," used for example in the
national elections of 1946 by Communist propagandists (see *Akahata,* Jan. 1, 1946),
became almost meaningless after the implementation of the SCAP-initiated land-reform
program. Nevertheless, Communists insisted that the problem of redistributing the
land had by no means been solved. As more than four and a half million acres pur-
chased by the government from the landowners were involved in the transfer to tenants
and small farmers, the redistribution of farm land required considerable time. The
Ministry of Agriculture and Forestry announced in October 1949, however, that all but
2 percent of the land had been sold by July of the same year, almost all of it to the
former tenants. Tenancy thus was reduced from almost 50 percent to a little more than
10 percent. No large landholdings remained.

§SCAP, as well as the Economic Stabilization Board, estimated that agriculture in
1949 received about 30 percent of the national income, as against approximately 10
percent before the war.

‖The release of figures after the surrender concerning the number of air-raid
casualties suffered by the inhabitants of Japan Proper shows clearly the remarkable
contrast in the intensity of Allied air attacks against highly industrialized areas on the
one hand and predominantly rural areas on the other. Whereas the Tokyo Metropolitan
District suffered 216,988 casualties, the Osaka Metropolitan District, 39,988, and Hyogo
Prefecture (containing the city of Kobe), 32,865, the almost wholly agricultural prefectures of Iwate, Shimane, and Nara suffered only 184, 24, and 190 casualties respectively. Figures from *Nihon tokei nenkan* (Statistical Yearbook of Japan). Tokyo,
1949, p. 639.

to reach the more remote districts in its propaganda drives—due mainly to a lack of trained personnel, but partly to a natural tendency to concentrate on the area of least resistance, in this case the larger population centers.

It would be a mistake, however, to conclude that the Communist Party had failed to recognize the importance of farmers and fishermen— who, in 1947, together made up about half of Japan's total working population (as compared to about one fifth in the United States).* Soon after the surrender, the first Party workers began to tour the country in an attempt to build a network of agrarian Cells. In accordance with Party policy, their main effort was directed toward propaganda among tenant farmers, the "proletarians of the countryside." Figures released in 1948 for the information of Party members, however, strongly suggest that Communist work in the village was encountering numerous difficulties. Indicative of the nature of these obstacles is the fact that in November 1947, out of a reported total of 844 agrarian Cells scattered throughout Japan, only 53 percent dared engage openly in Party work; 94.1 percent of these Cells did not maintain offices; and only one Cell in twenty published a Cell newspaper.[55] Party authorities attributed this "deplorable" lack of activity in the main to an inclination on the part of members to "hide behind farmers' unions."[56] It is hardly necessary to point out that this tendency was not so much the result of a lack of "political consciousness" among new Party members as the product of a desire to avoid retaliation by the firmly entrenched conservative forces.

That consistent propaganda work, however, was beginning to bear fruit by the fall of 1948 is clear from the appearance of so-called "red villages." The case of Sakuragi in Shizuoka Prefecture is a striking example.† There the Party had fully succeeded in bringing the local chapter of the principal farmers' union under its domination. Six hundred fifty out of a total of seven hundred young people had joined the union's youth section, which was equally under Communist control. Through the five Communist and nine Farmers' Union *(Nichino)* township commissioners, the Communist Party controlled all fiscal and administrative positions. Upon the suggestion of the Communist Cell members, the village had instituted a "Women's Liberation Day," and women were assembled every month for lectures dealing with the "improvement of their social position." High school students had been organized into a federation and a "cultural coöperative" had succeeded in enrolling seven

*According to the Japanese official census of 1947, out of a total of 33,880,000 individuals then gainfully employed, 17,100,000 were in agriculture and forestry and 710,000 in fishing. Office of the Prime Minister, Bureau of Statistics, Population Census of Japan. Tokyo, 1949, p. 206.

†According to the national census of 1947, the rural community of Sakuragi in Shizuoka Prefecture had a total population of 5,570.

hundred members (that is, an average of one per family). The Party further had taken the first steps toward the implementation of the Communist Party's agrarian program by organizing an agricultural coöperative. Through an actively conducted "enlightenment movement," in the form of lectures, discussion groups, debating clubs, and study circles, the Party sought to consolidate its gains and to strengthen its position. All civic activities were supervised by the local Communist Cells, as was the newly established Social Science Library.[57] All these measures were in accordance with the Party's three-pronged policy which proposed to combat the "traditional conservative-reactionary elements" in the Japanese village by "propelling the revolutionary front through an agricultural, a political, and a cultural revolution."[58]

Such isolated successes were due principally to the work of "Party activists" who began to visit the rural areas after 1947. Under the able leadership of the Chief of the Party's Agrarian Section, Ritsu Ito (himself the son of a small farmer), training courses were organized in 1948 throughout Japan to produce experienced and versatile Party workers. It is characteristic of the Party's makeup that the personnel selected for this purpose generally included few farmers. For example, a report (published in 1949) on the training of rural Communist cadres in western Japan described the composition of one such thirty-man group as follows: workers, fifteen (mainly unemployed railway and metal workers); Party officials from various levels of the Party structure, five; repatriates, four; students, three; farmers, one; others, two. The age of the trainees ranged from nineteen to forty-two, with the majority in their early twenties.[59] The scarcity of suitable personnel is evident from the fact that the members of this group—and this seems to have been true for the entire Communist training program—were predominantly Party members of only one year's standing.* The course itself normally was divided into three phases. The first, lasting three days, was devoted to a discussion of Communist agrarian policy and of the specific problems arising from the postwar situation. The second phase emphasized practical training within —and in coöperation with—already existing Party Cells. At this stage, the activists, in groups of two or three, were sent into villages to study local conditions and to participate in and guide Party activities in the particular area. The third and final phase would then consist of a discussion of the experiences gathered in working within the agrarian com-

*The Japanese Communist Party possessed, however, a core of trained and experienced Party workers from the days of the prewar underground movement. These were but seldom committed for propaganda work on the lower level. Nozaka indirectly confirms this in an article dated June 1946, dealing with the importance of Party workers. "We must always," he said, "preserve a certain number of workers in the rear." Sanzo Nozaka, *Nihon minshuka no tame ni* (Toward the Democratization of Japan). Tokyo, 1948, p. 158.

munity, closing with an exchange of views, suggestions, and "self-criticism." [60]

Parallel with the strengthening of the Party apparatus in the rural areas went a concerted drive aimed at gaining control of the farmers' unions. Communist success was greatest within the powerful left-wing Japanese Farmers' Union *(Nippon Nomin Kumiai)*, commonly known as *Nichino*. The *Nichino* unions, established a few months after Japan's surrender to represent the interests of the landless tenant and small farmer and to counterbalance the influence of conservative forces in the countryside, almost immediately became the scene of a violent struggle between two factions. Although the Japanese Farmers' Union had not committed itself to the support of any one political group, members of the Socialist and Communist Parties occupied from the outset the key positions within the organization. At the second convention of *Nichino* —a meeting in February 1947 marked by unusual turbulence—left-wing members carried the day; and their opponents, under the right-wing Socialist leader Rikizo Hirano, seceded and set up their own organization. For a while Communist influence seemed to be on the increase, even though few of the local units of *Nichino* were ever dominated by the Party. Only a small percentage of the Union's estimated one and a half million members in 1948 were actually Communist Party members. By the end of 1948, the Communists had succeeded neither in revolutionizing the millions of small farmers nor in gaining a firm hold in the countryside. This fact strongly influenced their subsequent strategy in the rural areas. Conscious of the weakness of their position, Party leaders called for a "united front of all farmers and small landowners" and declared their readiness to include in this front even the anti-Communists—as long as the latter were prepared to join in a fight against the "reactionary" Yoshida government.[61] Efforts to create an antigovernment united front, however, ended in failure since, by 1949, the antagonism between the Communist and anti-Communist left wing—so conspicuous then in the trade-unions—had also become apparent in the countryside. Rival unions, under the Christian leader Toyohiko Kagawa, had grown in strength; and even within *Nichino* an anti-Communist faction had begun to crystallize. Throughout 1949 and 1950 the situation within this organization continued to present a picture of utter confusion: while the Central Committee of *Nichino* had split neatly into two feuding groups—each claiming to constitute the legitimate leadership—the largely autonomous local unions ranged from aggressively anti-Communist to clearly pro-Communist in political outlook.

More than in the urban areas, Communist strategy in the countryside depended heavily on political alliances. Even among tenant farmers, distrust of Communism as an alien doctrine and of Communists as advo-

cates of bloodshed and revolution was slow to disappear despite the
Party's emphasis on the use of "peaceful methods" in pursuing its stated
objective. Numerically the Communists were substantially weaker than
their left-wing opponents, the Socialists. This became evident in the
national elections of 1947: whereas in the highly industrialized Tokyo
and Osaka districts, the Communists polled one-fifth of the number of
votes polled by the Socialists, the proportion in the rural areas was only
about one-fifteenth. Before the national elections of 1949, therefore, the
Party made determined efforts to swing the support of the left-wing
farmers' unions, coöperatives, and agricultural associations behind popular-front candidates with Communist sympathies. Once the various groups
which formed the basis of Socialist strength in the countryside had agreed
on a united-front ticket for a particular area, the Communists spared no
effort to draw their candidate into the Party organization. Although the
Socialist Party discouraged its local units and all Socialist-dominated
organizations from entering into such alliances, the Communists in many
cases successfully pursued their objective. For example, Central Committee member Yojiro Konno reported in December 1948 with satisfac-
tion that the Party had succeeded in Iwate Prefecture (northern Japan)
in "producing a red and mature apple where only a green apple existed
before" and that, although the local Communist organization had been
singularly weak and lacking in initiative, energetic efforts of a few Party
workers from Tokyo headquarters had convinced the left-wing Socialists
of the necessity for a popular-front ticket and of the "unselfish spirit of
the Communist Party."[62] The prospective candidate, the same account
reveals, subsequently joined the Communist Party.

Communist propaganda in the village had one immediate goal: to
create the necessary conditions for the establishment of a people's government by weakening the position of the progovernment conservative
forces. While in highly industrialized Tokyo and Osaka, in the 1949
elections, about half of the successful candidates were Communists and
Socialists, such was not the case in the countryside, where the dominant
position of the conservative and independent elements supporting the
Yoshida Cabinet remained virtually unimpaired. As long as this situation prevailed, there was clearly no hope for the establishment of a
popular-front government. How could the position of the conservatives
be undermined?

Communist propaganda tactics in the villages, designed in Tokyo
headquarters and constantly adapted to the needs of the hour, shifted
in rapid succession from propaganda drives against compulsory rice
deliveries, "fair prices for agricultural products," and "higher taxation
against the rich" to the organization of tax strikes and subsequently—
when food shortages in the cities became less critical owing to the import

of American grain—to attacks against the government's reliance on foreign support. What all these slogans had in common was their usefulness in pitting farmers of every political complexion against the "upper classes," their government, and the Allied authorities. An excerpt from a speech by Politburo member and Party spokesman Ritsu Ito illustrates the technique used: "We are now importing tremendously expensive wheat from abroad," he said in the fall of 1949. "I would not be surprised," he continued, "if [Prime Minister] Yoshida soon stated: 'We Japanese should be ashamed to eat rice. We must eat wheat; and this, of course, must be foreign wheat. How can we Japanese understand democracy as long as we don't eat [foreign] wheat?' "[63]

Communist propaganda in the fishing village has been part of the same pattern: by a relentless attack upon the government for imposing restrictions on fishing, for not furnishing sufficient equipment, for "favoring the big companies and crushing the small fisherman, who owns neither boat nor net," the Party has sought to incorporate also the fishing population into a united front against the government.

To evaluate Communist strength in the nonindustrial areas of Japan is a difficult task. Not even Party leaders venture any guess as to the extent of their influence in the countryside. As in the past, the Japanese farmer or fisherman takes a less active part in politics than does the industrial worker. Although even in the village a gradual change undoubtedly is taking place, the Japanese farmer still is largely willing to move in the direction in which the acknowledged leader of his community—and this, in most cases, means the wealthier landowner—wants him to move. The result is a marked trend toward conservatism, against which Communist propaganda has made but little headway. This conclusion is confirmed by a comparison of the number of successful Communist candidates in the national elections of 1949 with the number of representatives elected by Prime Minister Yoshida's Democratic-Liberal Party: in the six electoral districts which comprise the major industrial centers of Japan the ratio of Communists to Democratic-Liberals was one to two and a half, whereas in the forty predominantly agricultural districts the ratio averaged one to thirteen. Thus, despite a number of "red villages" and several Communist-dominated local chapters of farmers' and fishermen's unions and coöperatives, Communist influence in rural postwar Japan has remained surprisingly small.

CHAPTER XVI

Mobilization of Auxiliary Forces

ENROLLMENT OF STUDENTS, ARTISTS AND INTELLECTUALS

CONTRARY to Marxian doctrine, which characterizes the industrial proletariat as the vanguard of the revolution, reason and experience dictate assignment of this role in Japan to the student and the intellectual. Not only were the latter largely responsible for such success as the Party could claim in Imperial Japan, but, from the dawn of the new era in 1945 until early in 1950, students, teachers, university professors, actors, artists, writers, lawyers, and professional men, came forward in ever-increasing numbers as converts to Communism and ardent supporters of the Party's "peaceful revolution."

For five postwar years the Japanese Communist Party carried on intensive propaganda work in these several spheres: within professional groups of writers, artists, actors, and so forth; in elementary and secondary schools; and on university and college campuses. With the conversion of the articulate members of Japanese society, the Communist leaders reasoned, a long step will have been taken toward the Party's final goal, the seizure of political power.

Early in the occupation the Communists launched a sustained cultural offensive. At the Fourth Party Congress, in 1945, Secretary General Tokuda saw Communist influence reaching into every intellectual corner of Japan: "Throughout the nation," he said, "we are developing democratic journalists' guilds, progressive doctors' associations, etc."[1] To support this cultural drive, the Party arranged for the publication of a wide range of literature tailored to the needs of every conceivable professional group. For the members of the Communist-sponsored Japan Democratic Cultural League, there were four publications: *Cultural Times, Cultural Revolution, Friend of the Masses,* and *The Working Woman.* Five publications appeared bearing the imprint of the Communist-inclined Association of Democratic Scientists: *Our Science, Democratic Science, Social Science, Theory,* and *Historical Review.* Literally dozens of such periodicals served as mouthpieces for the many new "democratic" organizations which appeared during the postwar period. No group was considered insignificant; no organization too small. Thus the red-tinged Japan Art Society published *The Art Movement,* and even an obscure poetry society, the left-wing New Haiku League, had its own publication, not devoted purely to poetry.

To coördinate and strengthen these many groups and their activities, the Party maintained a Cultural Section. This special department functioned in close coöperation with four other divisions of the Secretariat: the Scientific, Women's, Propaganda and Education, and Publications' Sections. Chief of the Cultural Section has been Central Committee member Koreto Kurahara, well-known writer and veteran of the prewar cultural movement.

The effectiveness of the Party's cultural offensive may be judged by the large number of groups which, by 1949, had pledged their wholehearted support to the Communist program. The case of the *Zenshinza* troupe of actors, one of Japan's leading theatrical groups, is typical. In March 1949, thirty members of the troupe and their families joined the Communist Party en masse. The presence of the Party Secretary General and of the second-ranking Party official, Sanzo Nozaka, at the initiation ceremony suggests the importance attached by the Japanese Communists to such "cultural victories."

The progress made by the Communist Party in elementary and secondary schools is more difficult to trace. There can be no doubt, however, that Communists have been very active among Japan's six hundred thousand teachers. In the schools, as elsewhere, the pattern is a familiar one. The Party early made a strong bid for leadership within the newly organized All Japan Conference of Teacher's Unions, which, in 1947, claimed a membership of five hundred thousand. That its efforts were not without success is evident from the fact that Communist sympathizer Masao Iwama (who later joined the Party) became head of the Conference's important "struggle committee." In addition to teachers' Cells discovered from time to time in elementary and secondary schools, cases of teacher-propagandists expounding the Party line in the classroom and thousands of Communist handbills scattered systematically on school grounds and campuses throughout Japan, there have been other disturbing signs. Just prior to the national elections of 1949, more than one hundred fifty Tokyo school teachers visited the homes of their pupils to deposit a leaflet entitled "Toward the Rehabilitation of Education and National Independence—Statement Made on Joining the Party." Several of the teachers, upon investigation by the occupation authorities, admitted that the Communist Party had assigned them this task.[2]

The distressing state of life in postwar Japan, coupled with the ideological vacuum resulting from Japan's renunciation of her traditional values, produced among university students and professors a state of mind peculiarly suited to the purposes of the Communist Party. Though the Japanese student, like the student in China, had never been well off by Western standards, he had never been so plagued by inflation, want, and outright hunger as in the postsurrender situation. Gone was all the charm, much of the pride and the sense of mission once associated with student life. As a consequence, the university student, having rejected the past and dissatisfied with the present, longed for a cause and a better life. Some found fulfillment in working for a democratic, peace-loving Japan and for world brotherhood; but an alarming number sought salvation in Communism, which seemed to offer greater promise of an immediate and definitive solution to the world's problems in general and to the needs of Japan in particular.

Largely responsible for carrying out the Party's propaganda campaign within the universities and colleges of Japan was the National Federation of Self-governing Student Associations *(Zengakuren)*. Formed by left-wing students in 1948 and with branches on virtually every campus in Japan, the organization came more and more to be dominated by the Communist Party. The first major undertaking of the Federation was a student strike centering in Tokyo, early in 1948, against the government's plan to triple tuition fees. The highly political character of the strike can be seen from the slogan under which it was conducted. The Federation called upon all students to sign protests against "the reactionary cultural and financial policy of the antidemocratic Ashida government." Though failing to enlist a very large number of students, the demonstration was the beginning of a series of increasingly widespread and serious disturbances, directed by the Communist campus Cells. By the end of 1949, perhaps 40 percent of all university and college students in Japan supported the Communist Party's program.*

RECRUITMENT OF WOMEN

Japanese women went to the polls for the first time in history on April 10, 1946. Contrary to the election forecasts, they voted heavily; thirteen million out of an eligible total of twenty million took advantage of their newly acquired suffrage and, to the surprise of everyone—including the Japanese suffragettes—38 of the 79 women candidates were elected to the 466-member Diet.[3] The new SCAP-approved constitution, promulgated a few months later (November 3, 1946), completely altered the legal, economic, political, and social position of Japanese women, who for centuries had been thoroughly subordinate to the authority of their husbands or fathers. "All the people are equal under the law," the constitution stipulated, and "there shall be no discrimination in political, economic, or social relations because of race, creed, *sex,* social status, or family origin." The Japanese woman suddenly became a major factor in politics.

*The student movement in Japan will be treated more fully in Mr. Langer's study, currently in progress at the Russian Institute, Columbia University.

Communists in Japan had always advocated the "liberation of women from their feudalistic bondage," but until 1945—owing to the social status of Japanese women and because of the militant revolutionary character of the Japanese Communist Party—the percentage of women Communists had remained small. No woman had ever sat with the Central Committee or otherwise exerted direct influence on the formulation of Communist policy. This situation may in part explain why the Communist Party remained essentially a man's party during the first year after Japan's surrender. Yet another factor retarded Communist work among women: until the time when it became clear—even to those who opposed Nozaka's policy of gradualism—that the establishment of a revolutionary government could not be accomplished in the immediate future, Party workers and Party funds were applied almost exclusively to the penetration and conquest of workers' and farmers' unions. Only after 1947 did the Central Committee, in line with the Nozaka strategy, begin to direct its attention to the "strengthening of Party work" among women. The new policy was slow in making itself felt; a resolution of the Central Committee as late as May 1948 expressed regret that the Party's "neglectful attitude" toward women had "not yet been fully overcome."[4] Despite a continuing tendency on the part of the lower echelons of the Communist Party to neglect the utilization of women, it was reported that a fairly large number of female sympathizers was inducted during the spring of 1948, raising the total number of women Party members from less than 5 percent to almost 10 percent.[5]

Work among women was directed by a special division of the Party apparatus, the Central Committee's Women's Section, headed by Nozaka's wife Ryo, who had returned to Japan in 1946 after fifteen years in Moscow. This appointment appears to have been motivated rather by Ryo's Russian background and by her husband's preëminent position within the Party than by any special organizational ability. The only woman representative on the Central Committee of the Japanese Communist Party, Mrs. Nozaka has left the formulation of policy to the male Committee members, especially to Tokuda, who has always shown particular interest in the activities of women and young people. She has further delegated much of her authority to assistants, such as Hamako Matsuzaki and Yuriko Miyamoto, and often has enlisted the aid of Tokuda's wife and daughter.*

Yuriko Miyamoto, wife of the prominent Communist Kenji Miyamoto, until her death early in 1951, held a unique position with the Party. Although she did not occupy any major post in the Communist organization, her great popularity as a writer made many friends for the Party,

*Tokuda's daughter, Suya, is married to Ryuji Nishizawa, member of the Control Commission of the JCP.

especially among intellectuals. Mrs. Miyamoto's name appeared regularly among those of the sponsors of the many Communist-front organizations aimed at rallying women, young people, and intellectuals behind the idea of a Japanese people's democracy.

While no accurate figures on the number of women Communists in Japan are available, a distinct trend toward a gradual proportionate increase in women Party members was noticeable throughout the period of "peaceful revolution." Mrs. Nozaka confirms this in the official Party organ, *Vanguard,* in which she reported in January 1949 that women Party members then accounted for "almost 20 percent" against 10 percent half a year earlier.[6] All evidence points to the fact that this development continued throughout 1949. The 1950 policy shift, which resulted in a return to stronger emphasis on underground activity, reversed this trend, creating a situation reminiscent of prewar times.

Little distinguishes Party work among the more than eleven million working women from similar activity among male workers.[7] The policy has been to encourage the establishment of women's departments within the already existing unions rather than to create separate organizations for them. It is in the mobilization of the Japanese housewife that the Communists have developed most interesting—and, at times, very effective—methods of familiarizing millions of Japanese women, and their children, with Communism.

In a situation where, as in postwar Japan, food shortages* and the low level of real wages[8] affected adversely almost every urban home, a community of interest among housewives was readily established. The Japanese Communists, therefore, did not find it difficult to enlist the support of large numbers of women for their "Give us rice" campaigns or for concerted drives to detect "hoarded and concealed goods" (that is, illegally acquired and not reported goods) in the homes of the wealthy or in government warehouses.† For the same reason, demonstrations for "popular management" of food distribution found immediate response. The main difficulty lay, however, in channeling this expression of temporary dissatisfaction with existing economic conditions into organized

---

*Food shortages were particularly acute during the first year after the surrender. Mrs. Shizue Kato, Socialist member of the Diet, could say in 1946 to General MacArthur without fear of being contradicted: "We are all hungry in Japan now." Supreme Commander for the Allied Powers, *Political Reorientation of Japan,* p. 752.

†The Tokyo Military Government team reported, for example, in August 1948 that "Communist-led demonstrations of large groups of housewives have been staged in Shinagawa, Adachi, Hongo, Katsushika, Chuo, and Shibuya Wards and at Shinagawa Ward in particular." Ward officials "were intimidated into releasing a supply of relief rations . . ." "Tokyo MG Hits Communists' Tactics," General Headquarters, Far East Command, Public Information Press Release, Aug. 31, 1948. The same release mentions also that the Communist Party put up posters in Tokyo, spreading rumors that local ward offices had accumulated a large supply of relief rice rations which was being withheld from the people.

political action, that is, in converting the inactive, grumbling housewife into a Communist housewife. During 1948, when increasing attention was given to the mobilization of these millions of unorganized women, the Party believed itself to have found an answer to the problem. In a dual process of indoctrination, the Party brought Communists and non-Communists together in undertakings of common interest on the one hand, while on the other it induced the housewife to join in mass rallies and political demonstrations aimed at creating an atmosphere of revolution.

The technique was simple and effective: the Communist daily newspaper *Red Flag* reported in June 1949 that a Cell in the Katsushika District of Tokyo had organized a group of Party and non-Party members, all housewives, to supplement their husbands' income through work at home. The group met regularly, adding members as it went along. Originally, the majority of the housewives had been attracted by the hope of making a few extra yen; but "as they worked together with Party members and discussed life's difficulties with one another, these non-Party members came more and more to support the Party."[9] In this way, the Cell added to its campaign fund and gained the sympathy of many who otherwise might have refused to listen to Communist propaganda. Often, women Cell members were encouraged to tour the neighborhood, peddling soap, towels, and other household items. On the second or third call, the peddler-propagandist would strike up a conversation, leading it unobtrusively along political lines. *Vanguard* reported that, in the industrial community of Kawasaki (located between Tokyo and Yokohama), this approach had resulted in a number of housewives promising to vote the Communist ticket while others had even volunteered to visit friends and neighbors to enlist support for the Communist cause.[10]

The establishment of social and legal counseling services, of nurseries, reading circles, and courses in home economics all contributed to the desired broadening of the Party's contact with women. In this way, the memories of violence, bloodshed, and revolution, which had been associated with the Japanese Communist movement, became fainter. The Party appeared on the way toward endearing itself to the millions of housewives who, confronted with unwonted economic difficulties and somewhat dazed by their newly-won freedom, were obviously in need of guidance.

While the Party encouraged activities on an individual basis, it also consistently attempted to incorporate women into large-scale mass movements, rallies, and demonstrations against the government. Whereas, early in the occupation of Japan, the Party mobilized women mainly for rallies centering around economic issues, food imports from the United States coupled with the recovery of an economic equilibrium between town and country made a shift in emphasis imperative. After 1948 Party propaganda took up the world-wide Communist call "for peace and against the rearmament of Germany and Japan." One of the major vehicles for this propaganda was the Communist-dominated, Japanese Democratic Women's Conference *(Nippon Minshu Fujin Kyogikai),* established in 1948 and said to have—with its affiliates—close to half a million members.[11] Among its outstanding activities was the celebration of Women's Day (March 8) in 1949. On that day about fifteen thousand women and an unspecified number of men, young people, and children assembled in the center of Tokyo to listen to speeches in favor of peace and against "warmongers." Although the participants were by no means all Communists, the character of the meeting may be judged from the following: delegates of the Korean Democratic Women's League marched in procession, carrying a picture of the Korean Communist leader Kim Il Sung together with a likeness of Tokuda, while a Soviet delegate through her interpreter (Mrs. Nozaka) spoke to the meeting on the "liberation of women in the Soviet Union."[12] By exchanging messages with women's organizations in the Soviet orbit and by publicizing the various Soviet-sponsored women's conferences and peace rallies, such as the Asian Women's Congress—convened in the winter of 1949·in Peking—the Communist-dominated Japanese women's organizations have pursued a policy aimed at the identification in the Japanese woman's mind of the Communist Party with the universal longing for world peace.

ENLISTMENT OF YOUNG PEOPLE

Even before a plenary session of the Central Committee on August 26, 1948, when Secretary General Tokuda pointed out that "women's organizations must not necessarily be run by women, but should rather be guided by young men,"[13] Communist youth groups had closely collaborated with the organizational and propaganda work of Communist women's organizations. This peculiar relation stems from the Communist Party's view of the structure of Japanese society. The Communists hold that the "democratic revolution," already carried out in the industrialized countries of Europe and America, in 1949 had not yet been completed in Japan.[14] Thus, certain "feudalistic remnants" were said to exist in Japanese society, remnants which, the Party insisted, would have to be eliminated before the working masses could embark on a socialist revolution.

In this view, young people and women suffer double oppression: the oppression which Marxism regards as an inevitable concomitant of the capitalist system is aggravated by the pressure—in the postwar period somewhat mitigated—exerted by a semipaternalistic society. Both groups are victims of the same oppression; both are fighting for common objectives: absolute equality with the rest of the working population as expressed in equal wages for equal work and equal treatment in employment practice.* Party work among women and young people is conditioned by this theory of a community of interest between these two segments of the population and aimed at their "liberation from semi-feudal bondage."[15] Hence, we find a concerted effort to link all activities of one group to those of the other. Time and again Party resolutions or reports put "work among women and young people" into one and the same category, and policy outlined for one group generally applies to the other.

The principal organization through which Communist proselytizing has been carried on among the young people (men and women) is the Japan Young Communist League *(Nippon Seinen Kyosan Domei)*, generally referred to as *Seikyo*. The League, established shortly after Japan's surrender as the successor to its illegal prewar namesake—smashed by the police in the early thirties—is organized along the lines of the Russian *Komsomol*. In many respects it constitutes a Party in miniature, although only a minority of its members belong to the Communist Party. As in the Russian organization, the League leaders are ultimately responsible to the Party itself. Policy is mapped out by the parent organization, the Communist Party, and executed through the various echelons from the Central Committee down to the smallest unit, the "squad" or *han*, organized in factories, villages, and schools. The League numbered 2,300 members at the time of its first convention in February 1946. By March 28, 1947, when the organization held its second convention, membership was reported to have reached twenty-five thousand, of which women constituted 10 to 15 percent.[16] Meanwhile, the League had established three youth schools for specialized training and had begun to publish its own paper, the *Flag of Youth (Seinen no hata)*. After 1947 membership increased only slowly, and probably, even in the peak year of 1949, never topped fifty thousand. With the growing radicalization of the Party after January 1950, the League lost much of its numerical strength, though it may have gained in revolutionary zeal.

From its inception in 1945 the Young Communist League had posed a problem to the Communist Party. A recurrence of "deviationist" or "sectarian" tendencies within the League prompted the Central Committee of the Party to remind the youth group and its members from time to time that they were not to consider themselves a "young Communist Party."[17] While the independent attitude of *Seikyo* may be attributed in the main to the youthful spirit of its members, a measure of

---

*The younger worker does not have the same degree of job security the older worker has, and he is generally the first to be dismissed in times of retrenchment.

responsibility rests with the Party itself. As in the case of women's organizations, the lower echelons of the Party did not always give sufficient attention to the special problems faced by youth and thus precipitated a situation where the League members felt impelled to resort to independent action.

The Party defined the mission of the Young Communist League for the first time at the Fourth Party Congress (December 1945): the League was to be a mass organization of young people, welcoming anyone who opposed militarism and exhibited interest in the objectives of the Communist Party.[18] It was to fulfill the role of a "primary school" in Communist education. The Fifth Party Congress, a few months later, elaborated on the previous instructions: since the Japanese youth movement was already split into numerous separate entities, the Young Communist League was to consider the unification of all youth organizations—right- and left-wing—its main task. The common denominator was to be the "realization of democracy in Japan."

In the meantime the leaders of the Young Communist League, for the most part industrial workers, apparently had begun to set up their own Cells (termed "fractions") within labor unions. As early as the summer of 1946, the Central Committee of the Japanese Communist Party had reprimanded the League leaders for organizing fractions—a right reserved to the Party—and ordered them to concentrate on the penetration of right-wing youth groups but without abandoning the long-range unification plan.[19] A resolution adopted by the Central Committee in May 1948 called for the appointment of a Party official in charge of youth affairs on every level of the Party structure. This measure greatly relieved the strain and contributed to closer coöperation between the two organizations.[20] A month later a conference of Party organizers reëmphasized the importance of youth and proposed the establishment of a "youth organizer corps" which was to specialize in propaganda work among young people and women.[21] This step was in line with the decision of the Sixth Party Congress to encourage the creation of so-called "action corps" *(kodotai)*.[22]

Although "youth action corps" had been in operation as early as 1947 within a number of factories, they did not reach full effectiveness until 1948. Formed around a nucleus of League members and bolstered by radical young workers, army veterans, and often augmented by hoodlums, ready to join any organization which promised action, the action corps developed into somewhat unruly, but effective, shock troops of the Communist Party. Although the various units were by no means of uniform composition or fighting quality, their role in strengthening the Communist position should not be underestimated. In many cases these action corps succeeded in breaking up union meetings (when the non-Communists had the majority), in preventing strikebreakers from entering factories, in instituting "production control" in struck plants, or in seizing hoarded foodstuffs. Government measures to suppress the corps were rarely successful, since these shock troops could be as easily re-assembled as they were dispersed.

A special committee established by the Sixth Party Congress (December 1947) defined the role to be played by Japanese youth as "the central and propelling force behind the now developing people's struggle [for political power]."[23] It also prescribed the proper psychological approach to be used in enlisting the support of young people: Communist propaganda was to appeal to the "strongly emotional character and to the patriotism of youth."[24] Application of these suggestions during 1948 and 1949 facilitated the establishment of popular fronts composed of Communist and non-Communist youth associations. Through work from within, alliances with youth sections of left-wing labor unions, and through mergers, the League achieved a degree of success in its campaign for a united youth front. While Communists were seldom able to control any of the groups affiliated with the conservative five-million-member Japanese Youth Corps *(Nippon Seinendan)*,[25] an over-all organization of left-wing and centrist youth groups, including the Young Communist League, emerged in 1949 under the name Japanese Democratic Youth Corps *(Nippon Minshu Seinendan)*.[26] Although its potential value to the Communist movement was considerable, its effectiveness in propagating Communist views was limited by outside factors. The process which was in 1950 to isolate Communist and Communist-dominated groups had already begun. The subsequent acceleration of this process destroyed any hope the Party may have entertained of unifying under the banner of "people's democracy" the millions of politically conscious young people of Japan.

THE TRAINING OF CHILDREN

Unlike other Japanese parties, the Communist Party of Japan does not confine its activities to those of voting or near-voting age. The Japanese Communists follow a long-range plan. The seizure of power through the parliamentarian process, although not entirely ruled out as a possibility by some Party members, is certainly not the only means envisaged to bring about the desired social and political upheaval. In preparing the ground for a Communist revolution—whether of the "peaceful" or the "violent" variety—no less important than the indoctrination of the adult population is the training of children. With the exception of the leaders, the majority of Party members are in their early or late twenties, and the percentage of those who have come up through the Communist youth organizations has been increasing steadily. If the Party should succeed in inculcating a firm belief in Communism in the minds of those who will in a few years be the workers, the farmers, the government officials, and the teachers of Japan, seizure of power could be merely a matter of time. The organized and well-planned attempts by the Communist Party to become popular with Japan's children is perhaps its most distinguishing, if disturbing, feature.

Party work among children—though severely curtailed after the spring of 1950—has been carried out mainly through a host of children's clubs (*kodomokai*). Most of these clubs are organized and managed by Communist Cells or individual members of either the Communist Party or the Young Communist League, often teachers, young workers, or housewives. Such a club may include anywhere from ten to several hundred children. In the latter case the children's club is generally subdivided into smaller groups on the basis of age. These organizations bear such names as "Smiling Children's Club," "Friendly Children's Club," and "Happy Children's Club." They fulfill a number of important functions: they create a feeling of unity among the children, who tend no longer to act and react as individuals but as a group; they implant certain sympathies and antipathies in the child's mind, thereby helping to shape his or her outlook on society along the desired lines; they create in the child a feeling of class consciousness; and they form—and this is one of their principal objectives—a tie between the parents and the Communist Party, a relation which often results in the parents' joining the Party.

The children's club in the town of Akama, Kyushu (population about six thousand) was established in February 1949 to spread Communist ideas among children and parents. Beyond this, it was part of a nationwide campaign against the organization of Boy and Girl Scout troops which the Communists branded "tools of imperialism" and insisted were "imposed" upon Japan "from high quarters."* At the first club meeting there were about eighty children; by the time the fourth of the weekly gatherings was held, their number had increased to three hundred. Club activities, though guided by Party members, left ample room for the child's initiative. Rather than bore or confuse the child with stories about "social justice," about "reactionaries" and "fascism," the club offered a variety of amusing games and entertainment: puppet plays, community sings, narratives illustrated by pictures (*kamishibai*) or colored slides. After a while the children had come to look forward to these weekly gatherings where they could enjoy themselves in an atmosphere of unwonted freedom. They took this atmosphere home, and even parents who at first had only reluctantly permitted their children to participate

---

*The Boy Scouts are extremely unpopular with the Japanese Communist Party. Their number is actually very small, probably not more than 12,000.

in club activities came to feel grateful to Party members who seemed to be so devoted to the community. From here it was only a step to parent participation in Communist-sponsored community enterprises. As time went by and the club grew in popularity among children and parents alike, a committee made up of children was elected. Dues were then collected for the expansion of recreational facilities: the addition of a small library with comic magazines and children's books. Even a baseball team was selected. Through the medium of puppet plays and colored slides, the children were familiarized, in language they could understand, with "simple sociology," that is, with the concept of "classes," with the meaning of "capital" and "capitalist exploitation." Within a few months the children's club had grown into the center of social activity for many hundreds of youngsters and their parents. It had become a permanent recreational institution and, at the same time, a center of Communist propaganda.*

Hundreds of such clubs were similarly formed throughout Japan. Others originated as nurseries, school libraries, sport clubs, or supervised study groups and eventually branched out into other fields. The Party even distributed an official guide, entitled "How to Set Up a Children's Club."[27] These community centers must be presumed to have strong and lasting effects upon the children of Japan, but their usefulness to the Party does not end here. "Once we have the children," Tokuda said in 1949, "the mothers and the young people can be gathered around them in surprisingly little time. Children mature very fast. Let us not make the mistake," he concluded, "of underestimating their potential role as organizers and propagandists."[28]

THE CAPTURE OF MINORITY GROUPS

Communism's minority policy constitutes one of its most potent selling points. Whether the Communist Party is genuinely concerned about the welfare of minorities or whether its sympathetic pronouncements must be regarded merely as a means of enlisting support for its cause is another question. In any case, Communists the world over pursue such groups assiduously. In Japan, the scant number and comparatively small size of minority groups does reduce the potential of this fertile field for revolutionary agitation and propaganda. Even so, the Japanese Communist Party, in postwar as in prewar times, has spared no effort to exploit this relatively limited area. Of the several minority groups in Japan, only two have figured in the Communist problem

---

*This brief description of the Communist children's club in Akama is based in the main on an official report submitted by the Fukuoka Prefectural Committee of the JCP to the Tokyo headquarters. It was published in *Akahata* and subsequently republished by Control Commission member Kentaro Yamabe.

actively enough or in sufficient numerical strength to warrant consideration here. They are the Koreans and the members of Segregated Communities.

By far the most significant racial minority in Japan is the sizable Korean population, which numbered in 1950 more than six hundred thousand.* Though the Korean war served to focus attention on Korean residents in Japan and to intensify the issues involved, Communist interest in the question was manifest throughout the period of Allied occupation. At the time of the surrender there were about two million Koreans in Japan. Almost half a million of them independently made their way back to Korea in fishing vessels and other small craft in the period of confusion following Japan's defeat. During the first year of occupation, another nine hundred thousand Koreans availed themselves of the opportunity offered by SCAP's alien repatriation program to return to their original homes; the rest chose to remain in Japan. It has been the position of the government of the Republic of Korea that Overseas Koreans should be accorded the rights, privileges, and immunities of United Nations nationals. The Korean residents themselves have been adamant on this point. SCAP and the Japanese authorities, on the other hand, held the view that Koreans in Japan must remain subject to Japanese jurisdiction until their status could be regularized after conclusion of a peace treaty. It was perhaps inevitable that this situation should produce friction.

There was trouble from the beginning. Korean schools established soon after the surrender refused to acknowledge that they were subject to Japanese education laws. Clashes between irate Korean residents and local police were reported from time to time. The first incident of real magnitude occurred in Tokyo during December 1946 when thousands of Koreans, charging discrimination, marched on Premier Yoshida's residence, smashed in the doors, and broke the windows before they could be dispersed by the police. During 1947 incidents involving Koreans became more numerous, and Korean riots took place in the large centers of population throughout Japan. By the spring of 1948 the situation had become so serious that the United States Army found it necessary to declare the occupation's first "state of limited emergency," as a mob of fifteen hundred Koreans stormed the Hyogo Prefectural headquarters in western Japan in protest against an ordinance closing Korean schools.

Growing Korean unrest was accompanied by increased speculation as to the degree to which the Japanese Communist Party should be held responsible for the explosive situation. The branding of these incidents

*In 1950 there were only about 40,000 Chinese residing in Japan, the majority of whom were, at that time, considered sympathetic to the Nationalist government on Formosa.

and riots as Communist-inspired evoked from time to time the charge "red herring" leveled against SCAP and the Japanese government. While both SCAP and the Japanese government have been criticized on their handling of the problem* and although the Koreans' legitimate complaints and a certain spontaneity of some of their outbursts should not be omitted from any analysis of the minority question in Japan, it would be a serious mistake to underestimate Communist responsibility in the matter.

Communist policy on Korean residents in Japan was stated in clear terms in the March 1947 issue of *Vanguard*. The Korean Kim Tu Yang wrote: "The direction in which the six hundred thousand Koreans in Japan are moving, that is to say, whether or not they will constitute a strong wing in the struggle of Japan's revolutionary forces, is becoming of supreme importance. The significance of the issue is not so much a matter of sheer numbers but stems from the fact that these Koreans constitute an exploited, racial minority which has developed an intense hatred for Japanese imperialism. In other words, their resistance and revolutionary fighting strength must be properly organized as part of Japan's democratic revolution. To consolidate the fighting power of these individuals and to guarantee that, ideologically and politically, they come under the influence of the [Japanese Communist] Party is the fundamental task of Korean Communists."[29]

The Japanese Communist Party's evaluation of the Korean minority's role in the "coming revolution in Japan," Kin defined two months later: "If we look at the role and importance of the Korean movement within the larger scheme," he said, "we find that the movement's nature is such that it cannot be considered on a par with the labor movement or the agrarian movement, both of which are central forces in the revolutionary movement. Rather, the Koreans must be included among those diversified antigovernment elements—city dwellers, victims of the war, repatriates, and small and medium businessmen—which can be mobilized around the labor-farmer forces."[30]

How has the Japanese Communist Party gone about mobilizing this minority, and how effective has it been? The first step was to place a Korean, Kin Ten Kai (Kim Chôn Hae), on the highest level of the Party organization, the Central Committee and the Politburo. He and his assistants immediately set about the task of organizing Korean residents in order to bring them into the Communist fold. Japanese Communist propaganda directed to Korean residents in Japan has taken up such issues as Korean rights, tax exemptions, and discrimination, while the

---

*The Korean minority problem is treated by David Conde in an article highly critical of the Japanese government and of the occupation authorities entitled "The Korean Minority in Japan," *Far Eastern Survey*, Feb. 26, 1947.

tactical principle has been to identify the welfare of Koreans in Japan with the strengthening of the Japanese Communist Party and to emphasize that work for a "democratic Japan" and work for a "democratic Korea" are really but aspects of a single task.

Returning now to the "limited emergency" of 1948, we are in a better position to evaluate the fragments of contradictory and speculative information relating to Communist influence over Korean residents and to Communist responsibility for the specific incident. An official of the Korean Residents' League (in Japan) denied that the riots in Hyogo had been Communist-inspired. "It was an explosion of dissatisfaction of the masses against Japanese imperialism," he said. On the other hand, eight Japanese Communists were among those arrested at the time; and, upon questioning, they admitted that the outbreaks had been planned by Party headquarters in Tokyo. A Communist spokesman in Tokyo was even reported to have acknowledged that the Party was supporting the Korean outbreaks.[31] Further, Col. George A. Jones, Eighth Army Intelligence Chief, added: "I am convinced that Communists are behind these disorders, just as they are in South Korea."[32] Finally, National Police Headquarters in Tokyo revealed that the Communists had been instructed to step up demonstrations in Japan to culminate in a large rally in that city, scheduled for May 10, simultaneous with the elections in Korea.[33]

Similar, if less spectacular, incidents resulted in mounting tension during the remainder of 1948 and much of the following year. The situation reached its climax in September 1949 when the Japanese government ordered the dissolution of four Korean leftist groups, branding them antidemocratic and terroristic associations that resisted orders of the Allied occupation. Organizations affected were the Korean Residents' League, the Democratic League of Korean Youths in Japan, and two local organizations of radical Koreans. The order did not apply to the conservative Association of Korean Residents, which had been a rival of the Korean League.

Of the four organizations, the three-hundred-fifty-thousand-member Korean League was by far the most important, numerically and otherwise. Apart from numerous Japanese government reports linking the League to the Japanese Communist Party, it is not difficult to establish such a relation in general terms by reading the Japanese Communist press, drawing the obvious conclusion from the fact that the Korean member of the Central Committee and the Politburo of the Japanese Communist Party was, concurrently, leader of the Korean Residents' League.

The League's political complexion was highlighted during its last hours, when its leaders had announced that they would refuse to heed the government order to disband. Tokyo police threw a cordon of two hundred fifty men around the organization's headquarters in downtown Tokyo, cutting off traffic from the area. The flag of the Korean Communist Party flew from the roof of the five-story concrete building throughout the day, and banners calling for the overthrow of President Syngman Rhee's Korean government appeared. After an all-day siege, the police, by what they termed "peaceful negotiations," finally persuaded the last few die-hards to leave the building.

With the North Korean push southward in the late spring of 1950, Korean "unrest" in Japan increased in scope and violence, parallel with the radicalization of the Japanese Communist Party.*

The second important minority group in Japan, which the Communist Party has been actively wooing, is of an entirely different character: the members of the Segregated Communities, formerly known in Japan as *Eta* or Outcasts. They are the children of centuries of discrimination against those engaging in trades which were traditionally taboo—principally slaughtering, the tanning of hides, and the making of leather goods and footwear. Their history remains somewhat obscure, although the origin of their inferior social status usually is traced back to early Buddhist influence. Actual segregation dates only from the Tokugawa period (1600-1867). Today, perhaps as many as three million of them are scattered throughout Japan. In cities they live in "ghettos"; in rural areas they exist segregated from "respectable members" of society. The name by which they were known, *Eta*—literally, "filth galore"— offers sufficient comment upon their unhappy plight. One might think that Communism would find them receptive. A glance at the prewar record of Communist influence upon the group confirms this assumption.

Although the Outcasts were legally emancipated by Imperial decree in 1871, the discrimination and prejudice associated with certain occupations could not be so easily removed. They continued to be treated as outcasts and to live in segregated communities as before.

Then, amid the social awakening which followed World War I, these individuals, ostracized by society, began to take an active interest in improving their situation. In 1922, two thousand of the Outcasts gathered in Kyoto to inaugurate the Horizon Movement *(Suihei Undo)*. The manifesto which that conference issued set forth the new organization's general principles: "We mean to secure our emancipation by self-help; we mean to win absolute economic freedom, including freedom of choice of occupation; awakening to human truth, we mean to attain the highest goal of humanity."

At first a spontaneous movement embracing all kinds of political

*This phase of the problem will be discussed in Chapter XX, which deals in part with the relation between the Japanese Communist Party and Korea.

thought, as well as a few Marxists and anarchists, the Horizon Movement steadily drifted—or was pushed—toward the left. By the organization's fourth convention in Osaka in 1925, a Communist-dominated radical faction had come into control, and a year later at the fifth convention in Fukuoka the third of the general principles was revised to read: "Since we understand the reason for the existence of prejudice, we shall develop our movement along lines of definite class consciousness."

But Communist influence with its emphasis upon class struggle had a twofold detrimental effect upon the movement. First, almost immediately, it produced schisms within the organization. One faction, the National Suihei-sha Free Youth's League, took form, advocating the exclusion of the Communist element from the organization and a return to the "pure" character of the movement. Another group, the Japan Suihei-sha, was organized early in 1927 by those who were dissatisfied with the radical faction's alliance with the proletarian political parties. Secondly, Communist influence served to increase public antipathy and to crystallize government apprehension over the direction in which the movement was progressing. Consequently, when members of the Japanese Communist Party were rounded up in March 1928, not only did the Suihei-sha group lose its radical leadership, but a vigorous suppression of the organization itself was begun. Within a few years, the movement had come to a virtual standstill. It did not regain its momentum until after Japan's surrender in 1945.

The movement was revived in Kyoto in 1946 by the All Japan Committee for the Emancipation of Segregated Communities. Seventy-two delegates appeared from local groups throughout the country. The chairman of the new organization was Jiichiro Matsumoto, a Socialist, and later member of the House of Councillors.* How far the Outcasts have come in politics since the early twenties may be judged from the results of the 1947 elections: two of them won seats in the House of Councillors, seven were elected to the House of Representatives; twenty-seven gained seats in prefectural assemblies; and sixteen were elected to prefectural land commissions.

The extent to which the Communist Party has been able to penetrate the postwar movement is difficult to determine, although there is evidence that Communism has made considerable headway within the segregated communities. A study of one such community in Nara (near Kyoto), for example, showed that out of a population of eighteen hundred there were one hundred Communist members. The headman of the village

*Matsumoto was born June 18, 1887 in Fukuoka City, Kyushu. He spent his life working for the emancipation of the Outcasts and serving the cause of socialism in Japan. Matsumoto was elected member and vice-president of the House of Councilors in 1947 but was purged from that position in 1949 for membership in a wartime political organization. The purge order, however, was rescinded in 1951.

was a young intellectual and Communist, who had earlier worked in Tokyo with the All Japan Committee for the Emancipation of the Segregated Communities. Though the case may not be typical, the presence of a relatively large number of Communists within a single segregated community would seem to substantiate the thesis that Party workers pursue minority groups in Japan assiduously and to confirm the fear that their efforts have not been without success.

CHAPTER XVII

Converts to Communism—Case Studies

Aɴʏ account of a Communist movement would be incomplete without a consideration of the reasons which prompt an individual to join a Communist organization. To understand why an impoverished tenant farmer in China or an underpaid industrial worker in Japan may find irresistible the Communist Party's promises of social justice and of a better world requires little insight. Communism's appeal to certain other segments of the population, however, is more difficult to explain.

Five case studies of Japanese who are neither workers nor farmers, and must by any standard be considered above average, are presented here in the belief that they contribute to a better understanding of this important question. The brief sketches included have been translated from two books published in occupied Japan.* There can be no doubt that these accounts were intended to serve the interests of the Japanese Communist Party; yet their value to us is not primarily as material for the study of Communist propaganda. Despite an obvious bias, they do help to explain Communism's appeal to members of various occupational groups and to illustrate the specific ideological progression by which a number of individuals, of varied family background, interests, and education, have found their way into the Communist Party. Rather than attempt to analyze the convert's personal history and to speculate upon his probable motives for turning to Communism, we have chosen to let the Party member speak for himself.

A GOVERNMENT EMPLOYEE

Biographical data: Name—Kazuyoshi Dobashi; born—Shimane Prefecture (southwestern Japan), 1908; graduated from Law School, Meiji University (Tokyo); employed at Central Post Office, Tokyo, and later at Communications Ministry; after Japan's surrender, chairman of the Central Executive Committee of newly founded All Japan Communications Workers' Union; reëlected six times to same position; elected to House of Representatives in January 1949.

---

*Rono Kyuen-kai (Labor-Farmer Assistance Association) *Jiyu no hata no moto ni—Watakushi wa naze kyosantoin ni natta ka* (Under the Flag of Freedom—Why I Became a Communist Party Member). Kyoto, 1949. Masao Iwama (ed.) *Watakushi wa naze kyosanto ni haitta ka* (Why I Entered the Communist Party). Tokyo, 1949. Owing to space limitations and in order to avoid unnecessary repetition, the accounts have been abridged; but the original wording and intent have not been altered.

"Before and during the Pacific War, I was one of the Communications Ministry's typical bureaucratic employees. I had neither contact with nor personal experience in the social, political, or labor movements, nor did I feel any desire to study such problems. But during the war life became very difficult and, to add a little flavor to my drab existence and to the tedious routine work in communications, I took up the study of history. In this way I learned a good deal about the destruction of social systems through revolutionary action, about revolution in general, and about the sacrifices of revolutionists throughout the ages.

"After the war I realized that in the interest of developing defeated Japan along democratic lines it would be necessary to do something about the government employees' traditional timidity. As a first step in this direction, we decided in November 1945 to form a labor union in the Tokyo Central Post Office. I advanced preparations among the one hundred seventy employees of the Foreign Mail Division to which I belonged. It was amusing to see how the workers were afraid to affix their seal to my petition recommending union affiliation. They were afraid that they might be dismissed, reduced in salary, or that they would incur the displeasure of the Bureau Chief. I walked around, explaining to them the basic principles of democracy and the meaning of paragraph ten of the Potsdam Declaration guaranteeing freedom of speech, assembly, and association. As a result, the Central Post Office, on December 6, 1945, was the first in the country to have a labor union. I became chief of the union's planning section and in this capacity dealt with planning, organization, operations, and propaganda.

"At the time I was firmly convinced that at least the highest union officials should not favor any one political party. On this basis [of political neutrality] we were able to build up a comprehensive organization of some four hundred thousand communications workers. This policy remained in force for about a year, although I fully realized that we had adopted what might be termed a 'syndicalist' stand. I was not even sure which political party I personally should support.

"On December 6, 1948, however, I made up my mind to join the Communist Party. This decision was the result of my numerous experiences as a union leader; it was not a decision made on the basis of theoretical analysis or scientific examination. To the experiences which influenced my decision must be added a second factor, the impression made upon me by the earnest and conscientious attitude which the comrades of the Communist Party exhibited whenever they discussed politics, an attitude totally lacking in other political parties or, for that matter, in trade-unions. As to the third reason which prompted me to join the Party ranks: the great task before us—a goal toward which we must all work together, men and women, young and old—consists of fostering democracy and of setting up a government of the working people, who comprise 95 percent of the nation. It is generally agreed that a defective social system, mistaken national policies, and improper education have driven society into a state of extreme contradiction. Today those who cleverly compromise are 'social successes' and those who are earnest in their endeavors are 'honest fools'! But the dishonest individual who skillfully slips through the loopholes of the law and perpetrates crimes so evil as to be inconceivable to the average man—this is the type of man who becomes a big capitalist or a great politician. These are the gentlemen whom society considers exemplary figures. How cleverly they conceal their crimes! One finds them in all [but the Communist] parties, these 'skilled technicians of crime.' These are the men who in the Diet interpret and discuss vital questions affecting the future of our nation."

A SCHOOLTEACHER

Biographical data: Name—Masao Iwama; born—Miyagi Prefecture (northeastern Japan), 1905; graduated from Miyagi Normal School; taught for twenty years in various schools in his native prefecture and in Tokyo; after the surrender, chairman of the Tokyo Metropolitan District Teachers' Union; chairman of the Central Executive Committee of the Japanese Teachers' Union; chairman of the Struggle Committee of the All Japan Teachers' Union Conference; elected to the House of Councilors in 1947; also known as a poet.

"With my own eyes I have seen it. I have seen how rotten Japanese politics are. I have seen the Socialist Party, posing as a party of the working masses, abandon the interests of labor by compromising with the parties backed by finance-capital. I have seen other things too! I have seen the enemy skillfully exploiting the lack of unity on the political and labor front, thereby harming the interests of the working masses and bringing about the inevitable retreat we witness today. This and more! I have noted how the Katayama, Ashida, and Yoshida Cabinets all have displayed a conspicuous lack of enthusiasm toward education for the people, a lack of sincerity and nothing but idle promises and deceit. Though I fought as best I could, the results, I fear, were meager in terms of the people's expectations.

"We are all witnesses to the birth of a powerful conservative-reactionary regime which, by mass dismissals, the sanctioning of poor working conditions, and the adoption of bad labor legislation, points a dagger at our throats. For two years I found how difficult it was to fight without the backing of an organization. It became increasingly clear to me that only a heavy concentration of democratic forces could offer hope of successfully countering the onslaught of the capitalists. The Japanese

Communist Party represents the new hope of these democratic forces. It is their emblem and their leader.

"As one of the independent members of the House of Councilors, I consistently had worked for unity [among the masses]. With full realization of the importance of this mission, I finally resolved to join the Communist Party. I did not make this decision without experiencing considerable emotional conflict. From our home in the country my aged mother sent me a message and some rice cakes, ten days before I took the final step. 'Join any political party except the Communist Party,' she pleaded. My elder brother also wrote me numerous letters advising against becoming a Communist. But stronger than any of these warnings was an awareness of political danger, an awareness which weighed heavily upon my heart. I was deeply concerned with the fate of the working masses. In a sense I was a weapon of the masses. I felt that I must advance. I felt impelled to step forward into battle."

A CIVIL ENGINEER

Biographical data: Name—Denichi Kaneiwa; born—Aichi Prefecture (central Japan), 1899; graduated from Tokyo Imperial University, 1925; entered civil service; occupied a number of important positions in his native prefecture and in Tokyo (Home Ministry); elected in 1946 to chairmanship of the All Japan Construction Association; elected to the House of Councilors in 1947.

"Born in 1899, some ten miles north of Nagoya in the heart of one of Japan's silk-producing areas, I was one of eight children. My father owned a silk mill, employing sixty women and seven or eight male workers. As a child I had to help in the mill. I entered the Gifu Commercial School in 1913, just at the time when the economic crisis was at its worst. The position of our enterprise, which had been producing high-quality silk thread for export to the United States, became precarious; but when war broke out in Europe the following year, the United States experienced a tremendous boom, and my family's business recuperated quickly. These events left an indelible mark upon me. How was it possible, I asked myself, that there could be so many ups and downs? Would this sort of thing continue, and was it possible to build a stable society? Earnestly, I began to examine these questions.

"I read avidly and listened to the sermons of Gumpei Yamamuro of the Salvation Army. His eloquence—when he spoke of divine providence —held a mysterious attraction for me. Still the world around me became more and more incomprehensible.

"In the fall of 1917 Lenin formed his revolutionary government. When I read the extra reporting that event, I felt that Lenin must be a remarkable man, a hero like our Takamori Saigo [one of the leaders of the Meiji Restoration]. It did not occur to me, however, that developments in Russia bore any relation to the problems with which I was so deeply concerned. About this time Darwin's theory of evolution was introduced into Japan. When I became acquainted with it, for the first time I thought I understood the world we live in. I developed a feeling of great respect for the natural sciences and decided thereupon that I must, somehow, acquire a university education. In 1919 I began my studies in the Department of Science of the Eighth College Preparatory School and three years later entered the Department of Engineering at Tokyo Imperial University.

"The great and unexpected harvest of my higher education was the realization that Japan had nothing to teach us in the field of science. During six years, we studied only science and technology developed in the United States, Germany, France, and England. I had not realized until that time how poor my country was in the field of science and technical skills.

"In the university I sought salvation in religion. I took a room at the Tokyo Imperial University YMCA, but the more sermons I heard the more I moved away from religion. It was during my second year of university that the Great Earthquake (1923) turned most of the capital into a smoking wilderness and severely shook Japan's economy. Again my family went through difficult times and had trouble sending me a monthly check. Though my interest in Christianity remained small, I became increasingly concerned with social problems. At the YMCA I began to study *Das Kapital* concurrently with the Bible. Yoshio Shiga must then have been active in the Communist movement; but though we were in the same year of university, I did not know his name. I had not even heard of the existence of such a movement.

"In 1925 I graduated from the Department of Engineering. With the idea of helping with the reconstruction of the capital, I served on the government's Reconstruction Board. My assignment was to build the foundation for the Kiyosu Bridge. The job was extremely dangerous [for the workers]. Wages ranged from one yen twenty sen for a common laborer to two yen eighty sen for a carpenter. Under my supervision the workers were continuously risking their lives. Out of a feeling of responsibility, I began to work alongside them."

[Kaneiwa then did his military service, after which he worked in various capacities, being finally appointed prefectural town-planning engineer in the large industrial city of Nagoya.]

"I was deeply absorbed in my work and developed an ambition to discover the laws which govern the growth of cities. Little by little, I approached the social sciences. I learned that our cities are cities of a capitalist society. This made me realize the necessity of understanding the laws of capitalism. As a result I began research into Marxian economic theory. At the same time I took up the study of Soviet town planning.

"The failure of my family's business did much to stimulate my studies of economics. The general economic crisis which had followed the American crash of 1929 also had affected Japan. Its impact ruined the silk mills which, until that time, had managed to exist precariously on bank loans. Among the victims was my family. Complex problems weighed on my shoulders.

"Then the Manchurian Incident took place in 1931. I witnessed the rise of the militarists and the restrictions on thinking and on the labor movement. On May Day workers were marching peacefully along the main street of Nagoya when suddenly the police pounced on them. It was the first time I had witnessed such inhuman treatment. Within me surged a deep and irrepressible feeling of indignation.

"On December 6, 1941, the Pacific War began. I hardly could believe that it had happened. With no original scientific foundation, how could Japan face the United States—the same Japan that had needed the technical skill of America in order to build even a bridge over the Sumida River; Japan that possessed not a tenth—or even a twentieth—of the iron, coal, or oil resources of America. Could there be any doubt about the outcome of such an unequal struggle!

"As I had anticipated, the war ended in Japan's total defeat. I now understood one thing quite clearly: politics decide the life of a nation. It is a basic mistake to leave politics to certain people under the pretext that one is a scientist or a technician and, therefore, not concerned with such problems. That attitude leads directly to the destruction of a nation and to the destruction of science itself. There can be no hope for a rehabilitation of the cities which have been burned to the ground nor for a country which has become a wilderness. We must rise and wipe out all that is feudalistic and militaristic; we must construct a democratic and peace-loving Japan. I made a resolution that I would devote my life to the task of reforming the feudalistic, self-righteous, clannish government offices by appealing to civil engineers throughout the country.

"As a result my efforts there was formed in November 1946 a democratic cultural organization known as the All Japan Construction Association, comprising fifteen thousand specialists in the fields of civil engineering, architecture, and town planning. I was elected to the position of president; and the organization began an active program to carry out its plans, which called for the rehabilitation of the country, the democratization of the government structure, and freedom for science and technology. In April 1947 I was sent to the House of Councilors as representative of my professional organization.

"From the days of Japan's first general elections [1928] I had been sympathetic to the Socialist Party, but the Socialist Party betrayed my confidence in it. Instead of drawing a line between itself and the bourgeois parties, as it should have done, it drew a line between itself and the proletarian parties—a line which never should have been drawn.

"In the House of Councilors, as in the House of Representatives, the Communists had only four members. Even we seventeen independents felt keenly our numerical weakness. How much more must this have been true of the Communists! But their attitude really was splendid. Courageously, they opposed all bills and budget plans. Though 246 representatives would stand signifying agreement, the four Communists would not budge. At first their attitude struck me as rather peculiar since I thought that, after all, a four-man opposition did not make much sense. But in two years of parliamentary life I learned that my view had been entirely mistaken. At first a party always is small. If simply for this reason a party begins to compromise, it will never grow.

"I was impressed particularly by the Communist faction in the House of Representatives. Whenever I found time, I went to listen from the gallery to the discussions since I was interested in knowing the reaction of each party to the bills which I had initiated in the House of Councilors. Here again, the battle which the four Communist members put up was impressive. It was an inspiring feeling to watch the figures of the two great politicians, Tokuda and Nozaka. When I viewed these noble men who were fighting for the people, I felt that I—who was five or seven years their junior—no longer could tarry. I realized more and more clearly that my hopes for the Socialist Party would have to be abandoned. I came to the conclusion that it would be better to strengthen the Communist Party and to build around it a coalition with the Socialists, the Labor-Farmer Party, and other labor and farmers' organizations, a democratic people's government. The Communist Party had to be strengthened.

"Clearly Japan's rehabilitation may proceed along one of two paths. The first is a capitalistic one—a colonial one—the road to war. It is a road characterized by overpopulation and suicides of whole families, by malnutrition and degeneration, and by a few privileged ones who eat well and live in luxury. It is the road toward a world where the strong prey on the weak. I oppose such a way; but there is a second road. It is that which leads toward the establishment of a people's government and toward Japan's rehabilitation achieved through a grouping of the Socialists, the labor and farmer groups, and all the members of the working masses around the Communist Party. It is based upon the philosophy that those who do not work shall not eat, that suffering must be shared by all; and it leads toward the establishment of a prosperous and peaceful socialist state on friendly terms with all the world's peace-loving states of the working people. To bring this about, we must strengthen the Communist Party. Should we fail, only national ruin can be the fate of our eighty million. This is my firm conviction.

"The establishment of a democratic people's government—based on a democratic people's front demanded by the Communists—is the way to salvation for our nation and the only road which will lead to a rehabilitation of our country. I have considered this matter thoroughly, and in January of 1949 I decided to abandon my neutral attitude as a representative of a professional organization. I decided to enter the Communist Party and, in doing so, to come forward as a simple soldier of the democratic revolution."

A PROFESSOR OF GREEK PHILOSOPHY

Biographical data: Name—Takashi Ide; born—Okayama Prefecture (southwestern Japan), 1892; graduated from Tokyo Imperial University, 1924; visited England, France, and Germany in 1926, appointed full professor at Tokyo Imperial University, 1935; still a professor at the same institution (now called Tokyo University) in 1948 when he joined the Japanese Communist Party.

"I am a child of a poor family of samurai lineage. My father was a primary-school teacher, and we lived in near poverty. Though I knew what it was to be poor, deep within me burned 'the spirit of the warrior class.' Unlike the sons of merchant families, I was possessed of a strong pride and even when hungry—like others of similar background—I refused to complain. I grew up steeped in a feudalistic, militaristic, and aristocratic tradition, yet I detested the wealthy and the capitalists. From Kotoku's *The Essence of Socialism*, which I read during my high-school days, I gained the impression that socialism was a wonderful theory designed to create an ideal free and equal world where the distinction between poor and rich would disappear. At the same time I came to the conclusion that only Christianity was free from the many superstitions which had pervaded my youth and that Christian faith was the most ethical of all religions. Subsequently, I began to attend church. It seems to me that I must have been deeply interested in a vaguely Christian and idealistic type of socialism."

[At the age of twenty-one, Ide entered Tokyo Imperial University where he studied philosophy. As a student and later as a professor he had little contact with Marxism; but, during his many years of teaching and especially during World War II, he came to doubt the worth of philosophy as taught in the university and even began to question the value of his own course in ancient Greek philosophy.]

"Such philosophy merely facilitates domination and exploitation by the ruling classes through teaching the poor the art of resigning themselves to poverty. And when they refuse to resign themselves any longer, 'God' appears on the scene and the poor are told that after death they alone will enter the 'Kingdom of Heaven.' The philosophy of Christianity in this way sanctions and even defends the tyranny of the ruling classes. Such was my feeling toward Greek philosophy (and Christianity) all through the war, but it was in no way related to Marxism. Although it was clear to me that true philosophy must prove its worth in practice, I had little opportunity to supplement this conviction during the war years."

[In such a frame of mind, after the surrender, Ide even considered for a time resigning his university position. Rumors to this effect spread through Tokyo and appeared in the press.]

"In April 1948 a Communist Party member residing in my neighborhood called upon me and suggested that I join the Party. Without hesitation, I consented. It would be wrong to say that this step was a very serious one for me or that I had given it very much thought. It was rather with a desire to rid myself of half-baked, opportunistic ideas that I joined. I did not act with a full knowledge of materialism or Marx-Leninism, though, of course, I was not completely ignorant of the subject. I joined the Communist Party because it seemed to me that only this organization could eliminate inconsistent, half-way ideologies and opportunism. Moreover, in my judgment, of all philosophies the Communist Party's Marx-Leninism most closely approximates absolute truth. Materialism is not something which one understands by examining it intellectually within the quiet atmosphere of the study. It is rather a weapon, the strength of which the Party member gradually comes to understand while fighting with his class for victory."

AN ARTIST

Biographical data: Name—Iwao Uchida; born—Tokyo, 1900, son of a well-known writer; studied Western painting at the Tokyo Fine Arts School; visited Paris in 1930 to acquaint himself with French painting; presently member of the Japan Fine Arts Association.

"A number of people have expressed their surprise at my action and have speculated on the reasons which prompted me to join the Communist Party. Some wondered why one who after all is not exactly badly off should become a Communist. Others felt that it was a very dangerous thing for an artist to participate in a political movement. That I, who had been until now a bourgeois artist, should join the Communist Party without even studying Marxian theory was interpreted by some as a symptom of insecurity stemming from the sentimentality of an intellectual. There were, too, those who worried about me, evidencing their surprise at the rash action of one who is, after all, not young, has three children, and must be aware that his step might result in tragedy for all concerned, especially for his family.

"I am not quite sure whether I can answer all these questions and doubts satisfactorily. I have had my personal experiences and have worked hard in my own field, painting. By past standards, a man of fifty has reached the point where he should seek quietude. Why did I have to step out in front and act and think from such an advanced position? In a broad sense this may be attributed to the spirit of the times. Someone is supposed to have said that it was not a question of his entering the Communist Party, the Party came to him and he absorbed it. The same may be said of me.

"I am anything but a proletarian. From childhood I enjoyed a peaceful home in which I grew up under the best conditions a middle-class family can offer. I went to the Gyosei Primary School which was then an aristocratic institution. The students were children of high government officials, well-known industrialists, cultured aristocrats, and otherwise famous people. Parents apparently were attracted to this school by its reputation for progressive education, for the refined educational methods practiced by the Catholic staff, and by the international, aristocratic flavor provided by the teaching of the French language. A characteristic feature of this school was the fact that those in my age bracket after graduation from high school split neatly into a left and a right wing. This trend became more accentuated as the students progressed toward university. In other words, the students found two possible answers: either to develop their parents' ideology beyond the point where their parents stood or else to be satisfied with their ideological heritage.

"It was probably because I grew up in such an aristocratic school that, as a child, I constantly reacted against the atmosphere of formalistic emptiness which surrounded the children of the aristocracy, against the special lessons in etiquette, modeled after those of Europe, and against the Catholic, aristocratic refinement of ethics as taught by Professor Humbertclaude. But my father's Darwinism and my mother's Christian faith seem to have provided the initial stimulus for my interest in Communism. Darwinism and Christianity were the two forces which, toward the turn of the century, influenced young people the most in the direction of progressive thinking. My father acted as interpreter for Mr. Eastlake at the Tsukiji church in 1897, but he apparently found it impossible to accept the Christian faith fully and without reservation. He believed in the scientific character of Darwinism. On the other hand, he developed a great fondness for Russian literature through the reading of an English translation of Tolstoy's *My Religion,* while *Crime and Punishment* produced in him an artistic awakening of a sense of social consciousness.

"My mother became a Christian about the turn of the century. At that time Christians were suffering the brand of social oppression which the Communists are suffering now.

"I must have been in my fourth or fifth year of high school when the Kotoku Incident took place. As the younger sister of one of the accused was serving in a relative's home as maid, my family was sympathetic and even we children felt that they were not criminals. About that time, people with radical leanings began to visit my father's home. For this reason I grew up in an atmosphere quite different from that prevailing in most other families.

"From childhood my family spoiled me, while the two things which shaped my character and gave me strength were my father's Darwinism and my mother's Christian faith. Up to my third year of high school I was an ardent Christian. Books such as Naoe Kinoshita's *A Husband's Confession* or his *Pillar of Fire,* which I found in my father's library, were responsible for turning my Christian humanism toward an extreme awareness of social problems. In my fourth year a school strike took place, and I became one of the most active leaders—this with my father's permission! Because of the affair, I quit Gyosei and transferred to Waseda High School. Soon my single-minded Christian way of thinking gave way to that of a young man who, in the midst of the decadent world surrounding him, wanders aimlessly in search of truth.

"Finally, I decided to take up painting. For two years I attended art school where I participated in left-wing art movements. I lived among passionate young people with vague ideas, in the realm of anarchists, bolsheviks, Christians, and radical liberals.

"Why, then, at the age of fifty do I join the Communist Party? I do so because I cannot help but be on the side of justice but also because there is in me now, as in the past, a desire to examine things and to understand their true nature. I am not one who can play a great role in the revolution. But I certainly do not want to be an obstacle in its path. To join the Party has above all the purpose of advancing the cause of revolution. I am not sure how much I shall be able to contribute to this cause; nevertheless, joining the Party means at least that one does not join the enemy. At the present critical stage, neutrality should not be permitted. I say this particularly to the Party's sympathizers.

"From now on I must work and learn. I must concentrate on what is after all my profession, painting. By producing good paintings, I will coöperate with the Party and participate in the revolution. Only in this way can I grow as a human being.

'Within the ranks
Of comrades on the march,
I take my place.' "

CHAPTER XVIII

A New Stage in the Struggle for Power

COMINFORM CRITICISM—THE TURNING POINT

THE concept of a "lovable Communist Party" as the guiding principle of Communist policy in Japan was exchanged for a more radical view early in 1950, shortly after the Cominform* turned its attention unexpectedly from Europe to the Far East. The first tangible evidence of Soviet dissatisfaction with the Japanese Party appeared on January 6. On that day, an anonymous editorial in the official Cominform organ, published in Bucharest, bitterly assailed Nozaka for attempting "the naturalization of Marxism-Leninism in Japanese conditions." Nozaka's approach was described as "nothing more than a Japanese variation of the anti-Marxist and anti-Socialist 'theory' of the peaceful growing over of reaction to democracy, of imperialism into socialism, a 'theory' which was exposed long ago and which is alien to the working class." After continuing at some length in this vein, the Cominform editorial concluded: "Nozaka's 'theory' has nothing whatever in common with Marxism-Leninism. Actually . . . [it] is an antidemocratic, antisocialist theory . . . [which] serves only the imperialist occupiers in Japan and the enemies of independence . . . Consequently . . . [it] is simultaneously an anti-patriotic, anti-Japanese 'theory.' "[1]

What was behind this sudden attack upon one of Asia's most active Communist parties?

Despite a growing Soviet inclination after 1947 to substitute force for negotiation—as evidenced by Soviet coercion in Eastern Europe, a world-wide radicalization of the Communist Party line, and an intensification of the Communist military effort on the Asian continent—up to the end of 1949, the Japanese Communist Party, apparently with the tacit approval of Moscow, continued to pursue a policy of "peaceful revolution." This policy was tolerated, if not encouraged, for the Kremlin was apparently willing to admit Japan's special position as an American-occupied area where an indiscreet move by the Communist Party might easily provoke the Allied authorities and result in drastic anti-

---

*An organization of nine European Communist Parties, formed at Belgrade in October 1947 by the parties of the U. S. S. R., Bulgaria, Czechoslovakia, France, Hungary, Italy, Poland, Rumania, and Yugoslavia to "coördinate the activities of the Communist Parties on the basis of mutual agreement." The organization, though apparently somewhat more limited in scope than its predecessor, functions much as did the Comintern and is generally regarded to be under the direct control of the Kremlin.

Communist measures which could have a lasting detrimental effect upon the Party. At the same time, growing uneasiness appears to have developed in the Soviet Union over the future of Communism in Japan.

Although in the winter of 1949 membership in the Japanese Communist Party (about one hundred thousand registered members) had reached an all-time high, there were apparently grave misgivings in Cominform circles that this numerical strength had been achieved at the expense of quality, that in an attempt to build toward a mass party Nozaka had sacrificed the very principles considered indispensable to ultimate success: thorough training in Marxist theory and a "true understanding of the nature of Communist revolution." In short, the "lovable Party" was seen drifting into the arms of the social democrats, losing its revolutionary character.

The whole matter of Soviet-Asian relations may well have been involved. In light of the acknowledged debt owed by Nozaka to Mao in the realm of revolutionary theory, such phrases in the Cominform editorial as the "naturalization of Marxism-Leninism" might be interpreted as a warning to Asiatic parties in general not to overstress the "originality" of Mao's contribution to Communist theory and practice nor to go too far on their own, in "adapting" (naturalizing) Marxist-Leninist principles to the local conditions. Further, Stalin—still smarting from the Tito affair—was perhaps apprehensive regarding the ultimate effect in Japan of Nozaka's subtle tactics. Some of the Japanese Communist's statements could easily have aroused fear and suspicion in the Russian Politburo. Consider Nozaka's remarks at a public round-table discussion in 1949 on the topic "Reconsideration of the Democratic Revolution in Japan." He told participants: "There are those who say that in case of war the Communist Party [of Japan] will support the Soviet Union, but we clearly state: we will not take part in any war under any circumstances. Our foreign policy is one of equal friendship toward all democratic, friendly nations."[2]

With China in the Soviet orbit and with hopes for an over-all peace treaty and the withdrawal of American troops from Japan steadily growing dimmer, the world situation, as the Cominform viewed it toward the end of 1949, called for more dynamic action from the Japanese Party—if not immediate victory, then at least more active work toward it by increased underground preparations for war and intensified propaganda for peace designed to weaken the position of the United States in the Far East, cause dissension within Japan, and place the Japanese Communists in a better position to play the role assigned them in the "coming revolution." The decision to strike in Korea perhaps provided the conclusive argument in favor of an immediate reorientation of the Japanese Party.

The criticism from abroad seems to have come as a surprise to Nozaka. Certainly, it came as a severe shock to the Party in general. A Party spokesman characterized the first United Press report of the editorial as "an attempt by the enemy to disrupt Party unity."[3] The manner in which the criticism was conveyed to Japan might appear to have unnecessarily shaken the confidence of Party members in their leader and to have unduly exposed the inner workings of the international Communist movement to public scrutiny. Why then did the Cominform publicly air its grievances against the Japanese Party without, it seems, consulting the Communist leader concerned? The answer which at once comes to mind involves the issue of Soviet-Japanese Communist liasion or the lack thereof. It can be demonstrated, however, that facilities for transmitting secret information and advice from Moscow to the Japanese Party existed almost from the time of the surrender and that this was not, therefore, the determining factor. The paramount consideration appears to have been the feeling of urgency with which the Soviet leaders viewed the Japanese issue. Because of the laxity of Party discipline in Japan, as well as a tendency of Central Committee members to question decisions of the Japanese Politburo and to seek full explanation of their basis, a locally initiated recommendation for a drastic policy shift would almost certainly have resulted in a prolonged and involved intra-Party debate. In order to effect the desired readjustment of the Party line immediately at all levels of the Party structure and in order to integrate swiftly Communist action in Japan with over-all offensive plans on the Asian continent, the full weight of an authoritative pronouncement seemed necessary. Why Bucharest was chosen over Peking in administering the shock treatment is difficult to explain without giving some credence to recurrent rumors and speculation that the Stalin-Mao conference in the Russian capital in the winter of 1949 resulted in, among other things, an "understanding" as to the direction of and jurisdiction over Communist movements in Asia. Despite the rise of Mao and the considerable influence exerted throughout Asia by the Chinese People's Republic, it was to be clearly recognized by Communist leaders everywhere—especially in Peking—that the supreme direction of Communist Parties in Asia and, above all in the key areas of India and Japan, remained in Moscow.

In spite of the Japanese Party's initial reluctance to accept the criticism from abroad, when authenticity of the Cominform editorial had been established by a Tass dispatch quoting *Pravda,* the Japanese Party after some debate and discussion issued a long statement which at once praised Nozaka, admitted that mistakes had been made, and accepted the Cominform's "advice." This was followed by a statement of self-criticism in which Nozaka admitted that his theory had indeed exhibited

202 Communism in Postwar Japan

"rightist opportunist tendencies, exercising an adverse influence on Party activities," but insisted that, owing to the corrective influence of other Party members, the Japanese Communist Party had "generally advanced along a basically correct line."[4] Nozaka, nevertheless, concluded:

> I hope from the bottom of my heart that the above self-criticism of my erroneous diagnosis, which made me err and inflict harm on the Party, will educate and discipline not only myself but the Party and further contribute to the fostering of true leaders through severe and trying practice. We must, thereby, fulfill the important mission assigned to the Communist Party of Japan as a link in the international revolutionary movement.[5]

THE 1950 THESIS

The first substantial evidence that the Japanese Communists were in the process of overhauling their strategy and tactics, because of the Cominform's severe criticism of Party policy, came to light in a document commonly referred to as the "1950 Draft Thesis."

Theoretically, up to 1950, the Japanese Communist Party had been guided in its over-all strategy for the conquest of Japan by the Moscow Thesis of 1932, a policy memorandum defining the mission assigned to the Japanese Communists. Actually, the document appears to have had little direct bearing on the conduct of Communist policy in occupied Japan. Until the day of the Cominform censure, Nozaka's interpretation of the thesis he had helped draft in Moscow more than a decade earlier had emphasized the tactics of "peaceful revolution." His speeches and writings on the subject of "correct" strategy and tactics constituted the official Party line. With the Cominform's violent attack on Nozaka came the necessity for a reconsideration of Party policy.

Twelve days after publication of the criticism, the Central Committee and a number of other important Party officials met at Yoyogi headquarters (Tokyo) in secret session to discuss domestic strategy in the light of the new development. After "passionate discussions"[6] which lasted three days, the Committee endorsed the Secretary General's report and a brief statement which recognized the "past mistakes" and promised "to make efforts to meet the expectations of the international proletariat."[7] But the commotion caused among Party members by the sudden attack did not soon subside. Since Party headquarters had announced no clear policy, lower echelons were at a loss as to the course to be followed. The first signs of splits and schisms appeared shortly after the January session of the Central Committee. Communist leaders recognized the need for a written statement of Party policy, and Secretary General Tokuda was charged by the Politburo with the task of preparing the initial draft of such a document.

On May 18, 1950, after four months of debate, a 52-page memorandum, bearing the stamp of approval of the Politburo and of the Central Committee, was made available to Party members who were invited to examine the document carefully and to submit suggested amendments to the Central Committee. A Party congress, slated for the fall of 1950 (but not held as scheduled), was to approve the Politburo Thesis.

The document, entitled "On the Basic Tasks of the JCP in the Coming Revolution: A Draft," is of more than passing interest since it constitutes the sole organized presentation of the postwar Japanese Party's views on the domestic and foreign situation and because it reveals the Party's new approach to the question of revolution. More than any other document, the 1950 Thesis thus permits a full view of Marxist theory as applied to Japan by the Communists.

The lengthy text, crammed with references to the Marxist classics, deals primarily with strategy and tactics; but since such problems are held to be soluble only when viewed in a wider setting, an analysis of the domestic and international situation is given prominent treatment. The Thesis is divided into seven sections: Capitalism and the Tasks of the Communist Party; Special Features of the World Situation after the Second World War; The Danger of a Third World War and the Tasks of the Japanese Communist Party; Analysis of the Relative Strength of Social Classes in the Postwar Period; Colonization, Militarization, and the Development of the Class Struggle; On the Role of the Right-wing Social Democrats; The Character of the Coming Revolution and the Basic Tasks of the Japanese Communist Party.

Before taking up the specific problems which confront the Japanese Communist Party, the 1950 Thesis draws a picture of the world situation as seen through the eyes of the Marxist. This may be summarized as follows: a world-wide trend toward economic polarization is discernible in the development of capitalism throughout the world. The world is divided into two camps: big capital on one hand, the proletariat (and "semiproletariat") on the other. These two blocks are engaged in a struggle for domination. There are, therefore, basically only two alternatives: the dictatorship of capitalists or the dictatorship of the proletariat. The outcome of this struggle (and the final victory is never really in doubt) will mean the difference between false and true democracy, between war and peace, between poverty and ever-increasing prosperity.

Capitalism, the analysis continues, has entered the final stage, that of imperialism. Characteristic of this developmental stage is the fact that monopoly capital seizes complete control of the economic and political apparatus and aims at the ultimate goal, world domination. But here again a process of elimination is going on. While subjugating and colonizing weaker nations, the powerful capitalist countries vie with one another for markets and resources. This struggle inevitably leads to war. Only a proletarian revolution can eliminate the causes of such a development and produce a peaceful world.

In this two-pronged fight against competing capitalist countries on one hand and the working masses on the other, the Thesis points out, capitalist governments advance along the road to fascism which seems their only hope. But they are waging a losing battle. Soviet Russia, covering a sixth of the globe, has forever abolished capitalist exploitation. The nations of Eastern Europe are following the Soviet example, and the working masses of Asia are rapidly nearing victory in their revolutionary struggle.

Referring to recent world developments, the Thesis states: "Not only has the victory of the Chinese People's Republic substantially strengthened the cause of the (revolutionary) masses; but it has shifted the balance of power between the two camps, giving *the people* an overwhelming superiority."[8] Despite this world-wide trend, the Party cautions that final victory can be won in Asia as well as in other parts of the world only after a number of serious obstacles have been removed. Selected for special comment are the "right-wing socialists." These "servants of the capitalists," these "hateful enemies of the people" must be isolated and their "treasonable acts" exposed. Leaders of the American A. F. of L. and C. I. O. as well as Mr. Attlee and the late Mr. Bevin of Great Britain are listed among those who, by their support of the Marshall Plan—"basis of a policy of colonization, enslavement, and militarization"—have proved their "subservience to the interests of monopoly capital." "In this world, which is developing in an atmosphere of struggle between two camps," the analysis of the international situation concludes, "the way toward salvation for the Japanese nation, which has been forced to subordinate itself to international monopoly capital, is clear. It lies in becoming a part of the world people's forces under the leadership of socialism and people's democracy, in fighting by their side against world imperialism so as to win independence, socialism, and world peace."[9] This particular passage was inserted, the authors of the Thesis point out, to "strike a blow against silly talk about a policy of neutrality."[10]

With this statement concerning the alignment of the Party in any future conflict involving the two blocs, the Thesis proceeds to an examination of Japan's position. The result of this analysis may be summed up in a few words: geographically, politically, and economically, Japan constitutes an important base of operations for the forces which attempt to bring the Far East under the domination of monopoly capital. To prevent this, by rallying the Japanese nation in the deadly fight against war and for peace, is the primary duty of the Japanese Communists.

The Party must realize the heavy responsibility, for success or failure of the Party in its fight against imperialism will have a decisive influence on the outcome of the world struggle. To be as effective as possible, the Japanese Communist Party must adapt its strategy and tactics to the domestic situation. At this point the Thesis enters into a detailed examination of conditions in Japan.

By 1950, the Thesis contends, Japan had been almost five years under the complete domination of international monopoly capital. Three elements had formed the foundation of capitalist domination in prewar Japan: the Emperor institution, the landowners, and monopoly capital. In five years of Allied occupation these basic constituents had undergone certain changes. An examination of these changes furnishes an insight into postwar trends in Japan, constituting at the same time the *sine qua non* for any formulation of Party strategy. The conclusion: the Emperor's position has been weakened in the postwar period by a series of political reforms. He continues, however, to enjoy important privileges and considerable authority, especially because of the close ties between the Imperial institution and the Japanese bureaucracy. Although responsible for attempts to use bacteriological warfare against the Allies—as evidence introduced by Soviet Russia proves irrefutably—the Thesis asserts, the Emperor continues to exert considerable authority since he is considered by the reactionaries throughout the world a valuable tool for the remilitarization of Japan.

The power of the landowners may seem to have been broken by the land-reform program carried out after the surrender. Actually, the Thesis contends, this group still controls 16 percent of the total area under cultivation. Conditions in the countryside, therefore, are characterized by what may be termed "semifeudalistic class relations." These produce a situation favorable for converting Japan into a base for the auxiliary troops needed by international monopoly capital. But other advantages accrue from such a situation: Japan's industry, now as in prewar times, concentrates on textiles rather than on heavy industry. In an atmosphere of feudalism the countryside continues to furnish the capitalist and landowner an ample supply of cheap colonial labor, enabling them to profit at the expense of the worker and farmer.

The third constituent of authority in postsurrender Japan, Japanese monopoly capital, the Thesis argues, has gradually increased its importance at the expense of that of the landowners and of the Imperial institution. Although Japanese monopoly capital has thus come to supplant the two other members of the triad in terms of leadership, it by no means represents the dominant force. During the initial phase of the occupation, international monopoly capital, under the pretext of democratizing Japan, sanctioned the smashing of the *Zaibatsu*. Once this had been accomplished and the subservience of Japanese capital to international monopoly capital had been assured, a period of collaboration ensued— a period which is still continuing in 1950. Accordingly, American-occupied Japan is compared to the Russian troika, the carriage drawn by three horses. The horses—the Imperial Institution, Landowners, and National Monopoly Capital—are pulling abreast, spurred on by International Monopoly Capital, which is in the driver's seat. "It is not advisable," the Thesis warns, "to watch only the driver. On the other hand, we should not look only at the horses. While closely watching their relations one with the other, we must adapt our tactics according to time and place."[11]

Out of this situation, the Thesis emphasizes, arises the urgent need for a revolution. Basically, such a revolution would fulfill two missions: it would free the Japanese people from the tight grip of the international capitalists who exploit Japan and are turning it into a colony and military base; simultaneously this revolution would wipe out the remnants of feudalism and with them the power of Japanese capitalism.

To achieve the first objective and to render possible Japan's participation in the world revolution against imperialist capitalism, the Japanese Communist Party advances seven demands: (1) an over-all peace in accordance with the Potsdam Declaration and the recovery of Japan's independence; (2) withdrawal of all occupation forces from Japan after conclusion of the peace treaty; (3) opposition to a militaristic policy, to a policy tending to convert Japan into a colony and military base of a foreign power; (4) support of a policy of peace and friendly relations with all peace-loving nations; (5) world disarmament and prohibition of atomic weapons; (6) support of the Soviet-Chinese Friendship Pact, of the liberation struggle of the Asian peoples; prohibition of domestic armament production and opposition to the shipment of arms abroad; (7) support of the World Federation of Trade Unions and of the World Peace Congress and similar democratic conferences.

The second mission of the Communist revolution in Japan, that is, the elimination of "feudal remnants" and of national monopoly capital, is embodied in twenty-seven separate demands, which are virtually identical with the Communist Program of Action adopted by the Sixth Party Congress. The slight modification felt necessary as a result of the Cominform criticism was along the lines of more outspoken support of the Communist movements abroad and of a stiffening of opposition to American influence in Japan.

The objectives of the Communist Party of Japan were thus clarified and redefined. How were they to be achieved? The Thesis continues in substance:

There can be no elimination of foreign (mainly American) influence without a thorough domestic revolution, and vice versa. But there are obvious obstacles in the path of such a revolution, obstacles which are greater than those the Eastern European nations faced since those nations possessed armed revolutionary forces and were backed and supported by Soviet might. Conditions in Japan are considered less favorable, and a modified strategy is recommended. To carry out a democratic revolution (which is to be carried over into socialist revolution), mass support is absolutely indispensable. Consequently, a mass organization in the form of a democratic people's front must be formed. Such a people's front should rally, in addition to the large number of workers and farmers, the intellectuals, the small businessmen, and, if possible, even those members of the middle class who, strictly speaking, cannot be classified among the noncapitalists, but whose opposition may hurt the cause of the revolution. The Communist Party must lead and direct these millions toward the coming revolution. It should, however, be careful not to press certain issues at a time when the masses are not yet ready since such action would result in intra-Party splits and isolation from the masses. While being true to its own program, the Party must fully support the more moderate program of a popular front, without, however, losing the initiative. On the other hand, support and guidance of the popular movement must never result in abandonment of Communist principles or in the dissolution of the Communist Party. Always in touch with the masses and always the driving power behind their justified demands and actions, the Japanese Communist Party, the Thesis concludes, must not lose its substance and must never for a moment forget that the democratic revolution is but an intermediate stage. Socialism remains the final goal.

MILITANT OBSTRUCTIONISM

Publication of the 1950 Thesis on May 18 constituted the last rites for the "lovable Communist Party," though there was a sharp disagreement within the Central Committee over the question of timing, that is, the speed with which the more radical and internationally oriented policy should be implemented. If the Japanese Communist press contained only the usual amount of indirect antioccupation propaganda for the next week or ten days, a new line of militant obstructionism was detected by some observers during the ensuing weeks. On May 30, four American military personnel were stoned and mauled by Communist-inspired demonstrators in Tokyo. Eight Japanese were arrested in connection with the incident and were quickly brought to trial by the Allied authorities.* It was the first instance of such violence in more than four years

---

*The June 4 issue of *Akahata* carried a photograph of the defendants and a story bearing the caption: "Eight Patriots Sentenced—Up to Ten Years at Hard Labor." The

of occupation. As significant as the incident itself was the rally at which it occurred.

An American Memorial Day program and a Japanese Communist rally had been scheduled for the same place at the same time. The Communist meeting ostensibly was to honor a Japanese union member who had died during a labor demonstration in Tokyo on the same day of the previous year. The rally was sponsored by a Communist group calling itself the Tokyo People's Front Preparatory Committee. A possible clash was thought to have been averted by barring all Japanese from the Imperial Plaza during the United States Army's ceremonies. Nevertheless, when the day of the memorial ceremonies arrived, about five thousand Communists and sympathizers gathered in the vicinity to cheer Nozaka as he shouted from an improvised platform: "This isn't a parade ground; it's the people's plaza, and we must keep it that way. This can be done only by taking over the government." A growing radicalization of the Party and a determination to stir the masses into action is suggested by the manifesto adopted at the Communist rally. Entitled "The May 30 Rally for the Protection of the [Japanese] Communist Party, Protection of Peace, the Fulfillment of Our Demands, and the Establishment of a United Fatherland (Korean) Front," the document reads:

> We must smash the new capitalist offensive. . . We must (in the coming elections for the House of Councilors) through a general strike of workers and through waves of demonstrations of the patriotic forces, strike a death blow against the imperialist Yoshida Cabinet. Let us not be misled by the mouthings of the Democratic and Socialist Parties' opposition to the transformation of Japan into a military base nor by their "support" of an over-all peace treaty. We must expose their anti-Soviet, anti-Communist, antipeople's nature. Only in this way can we achieve our objectives: over-all peace, the withdrawal of the occupation forces, the overthrow of the imperialist Yoshida Cabinet, the smashing of the warmongers' attempts to repress the Communist Party, the establishment of a democratic people's front government, national independence, and world peace.
>
> Therefore, we must eliminate from labor unions and from the democratic camp in general the plots of warmongers who are aiming at the Soviet Union and new China and the leaders of the Democratization Leagues who are their representatives among the

---

Chinese Communists in the meanwhile encouraged their Japanese comrades in their anti-American actions. The Peking *People's China* of June 16, 1950, in an editorial entitled "Japan's People Rise in Anger," exclaimed gleefully: "The Japanese people have risen openly to fight U. S. imperialism!" and concluded: "Unite, people of Japan! Unity is strength!"

working masses. If we are to achieve independence and peace, we must realize a common program based on the protection of independence and peace, the right to livelihood, and democracy, and we must coördinate our action in the form of a democratic people's front.[12]

Three days later, at Mito, seventy-five miles north of Tokyo, armed police had to be called out to suppress a demonstration by six hundred Communists waving red flags and shouting, "Down with the Yoshida government." The crowd was waiting at the railroad station when the Premier alighted from a train on his way to deliver a political speech. Student demonstrations, Korean riots, trouble at railway terminals, shipyards, and factories throughout Japan—these and similar symptoms of a growing Communist militancy could be observed during the spring of 1950. On the basis of such empirical evidence, it would be difficult to avoid the conclusion that the Party had effected a swift and thorough radicalization in the wake of the Cominform criticism.

Actually, it is now clear from a study of the handling of the entire situation within the Central Committee and from an investigation of the factional struggle which engulfed the Party during much of 1950 that what appeared to be a more radical Party policy of action during that year must be attributed primarily to the extremist elements within the organization (later identified as Internationalists) and that such radical activity was, in fact, in distinct violation of instructions from Party headquarters—anxious to attract as little attention as possible until the bulk of its apparatus and important personnel could be transferred underground.

SCAP INTERVENTION

SCAP's initial policy of releasing political prisoners (including the Communists), legalizing the Communist Party, permitting the domination of many labor unions by Communists, and allowing the publication of volumes of Communist literature highly critical of the Japanese government, understandably gave rise to questions in the minds of the average Japanese unaccustomed to the ways of democracy.

To clarify the U. S. position on the issue, as early as May 1946, the American representative on the Allied Council for Japan, George Atcheson, Jr., felt called upon to state that his government "does not favor Communism at home or in Japan."[13] This point of view was confirmed as SCAP policy by General MacArthur's numerous subsequent pronouncements which pointed out the basic incompatibility of communism and democracy. Nevertheless, SCAP was very careful to make a distinction between this official opinion that communism was regarded as undesirable for Japan and the constitutional right of every Japanese to the political philosophy of his own choosing. For almost five years, the Communist Party of Japan operated with surprisingly little interference from either the Allied authorities or the Japanese government, although the intent of many of its actions may have been open to serious doubt.*

The question of whether the Japanese Communist Party should continue to enjoy legal protection despite its announced purposes was raised by General MacArthur in the summer of 1949. By May 1950 SCAP thinking on the issue apparently had crystallized, for on the third anniversary of the Japanese constitution (May 2), the Supreme Commander stated:

> More latterly its [the Japanese Communist Party's] shattered remnants . . . have cast off the mantle of pretended legitimacy and assumed instead the role of an avowed satellite of an international predatory force and a Japanese pawn of alien power policy, imperialistic purpose, and subversive propaganda. That it has done so at once brings into question its right to the further benefits and protection of the country and laws it would subvert and raises doubt as to whether it should longer be regarded as a constitutionally recognized political movement. Such doubt should, of course, be resolved calmly, justly, and dispassionately with the same consideration and safeguards extended to any antisocial force in a peaceful and law-abiding community.

Not until the summer of the same year, however, did SCAP find it necessary to intervene directly and place a check upon the activities of Communists in Japan. Even then, action was confined to the Party's leaders, while the organization and its members continued to enjoy political freedom under the law.

On June 6, 1950 General MacArthur addressed a directive in the form of a letter to Prime Minister Yoshida, ordering the Japanese government to "remove and exclude from public service" the twenty-four members of the Central Committee of the Japanese Communist Party. In clarifying the basis of his action, General MacArthur said in part:

*A series of violent incidents involving Communist Party members or elements sympathetic to the Party were reported during the summer of 1949. The major incidents were the following: the Taira Incident of June 1949 (Communists seized the police station of the city of Taira in northeastern Japan and held it for the better part of a day); the Shimoyama incident of July (the mutilated body of President Shimoyama of the National Railway Company of Japan was found near a railway track the day after he had dismissed large numbers of workers, a move which had been violently opposed by Communist union members); the Mitaka Incident of July (shortly after dismissals of railway employees, a train ran away in Mitaka, near Tokyo, killing six people and injuring thirteen others); and the Matsukawa Incident of August 1949 (a locomotive overturned near Matsukawa in northeastern Japan, killing or injuring three people, an accident which was widely attributed to Communist workers acting on Party instructions).

The guiding philosophy of this phase of the Occupation has been protective, not punitive. Its purpose and effect has been to provide assurance that the aims of Allied policy in the democratization of Japan would not be thwarted by the influence and pressure of anti-democratic elements. The area of its application for the most part has embraced those persons who because of position and influence bear responsibility for Japan's totalitarian policies which led to adventure in conquest and exploitation. Recently, however, a new and no less sinister groupment has injected itself into the Japanese political scene which has sought through perversion of truth and incitation to mass violence to transform this peaceful land into an arena of disorder and strife as the means of stemming Japan's notable progress along the road of representative democracy and to subvert the rapidly growing democratic tendencies among the Japanese people.

Acting in common accord, they have hurled defiance at constituted authority, shown contempt for the processes of law and order, and contrived by false and inflammatory statements and other subversive means to arouse through resulting public confusion that degree of social unrest which would set the stage for the eventual overthrow of constitutional government in Japan by force. Their coercive methods bear striking parallel to those by which the militaristic leaders of the past deceived and misled the Japanese people, and their aims, if achieved would surely lead Japan to an even worse disaster. To permit this incitation to lawlessness to continue unchecked, however embryonic it may at present appear, would be to risk ultimate suppression of Japan's democratic institutions in direct negation to the purpose and intent of Allied policy pronouncements, forfeiture of her chance for political independence, and destruction of the Japanese race.

The following day a second letter from General MacArthur to the Japanese Prime Minister ordered seventeen leading editors of the Party organ, *Red Flag,* to be added to the purge list of June 6. Referring to the paper as a "mouthpiece for the most violent of lawless elements within the Communist Party," and speaking of "licentious, false, inflammatory, and seditious appeals to irresponsible sentiment," the General charged its editors with attempting to "provoke defiance of constitutional authority, disrupt the progress of economic revival, and create social unrest and mass violence." In calling for prompt corrective action to safeguard public peace, the General significantly rejected the idea of prohibiting publication of the Party newspaper and the concept of precensorship as being inimical to the broad philosophy which had guided the development of press freedom in Japan. Such a solution, he stated, should be imposed only if other measures fail.

PROPAGANDA FOR PEACE AND PREPARATIONS FOR WAR

Communist operations in Japan after January 1950 assumed an increasingly dualistic character, with stronger emphasis on underground activity. On one hand, the Party sought to maintain in operation as much of its legal machinery as circumstances would permit in order to conduct an intensive peace campaign as part of the world-wide Soviet "peace drive"; on the other hand, Party leaders quietly and systematically reoriented and streamlined the organization in anticipation of increased government pressure and in preparation for underground war.

"It seems to me," the younger brother of the Japanese Emperor told Miss Muriel Lester, the well-known British pacifist, in October 1951, "that use of the term 'peace' is becoming taboo in this country."[14] This was a strange statement for a member of the Imperial family of a country which had so recently paid the price for aggression and had in its new constitution renounced war forever; but the majority of the Japanese people, after having been subjected to months of intensive Communist propaganda for peace, probably shared the Prince's view. In response to the Stockholm and Prague peace appeals, Communists in Japan had conducted a series of nation-wide signature campaigns. If reports are true that six and a half million votes were collected for the Stockholm Appeal, the reason for this apparent success stems partly from the fact that all children "able to understand the peace drive to a degree" were invited to sign and that even the names of very young children were secured by having their parents sign for them.[15] Communists mobilized all existing front organizations and even created a number of special peace councils—which they instructed to conceal any ties with the Party —while other genuine peace groups as well as a number of well-meaning liberals unintentionally furthered the Communist cause by their activities and writings. As the day for signing the Japanese peace treaty approached, the Communists called upon the people of Japan to reject what was termed a "one-sided, American-dictated peace treaty," and to join with "all democratic nations everywhere in a truly democratic treaty which would include the Soviet Union and the Chinese People's Republic." Despite numerous student demonstrations against the peace treaty and the United States–Japan Security Pact and claims in *Pravda* and *Izvestiya* in the fall of 1951 that almost five million Japanese had in a few months signed the appeal for an over-all peace treaty for Japan,[16] public-opinion polls conducted throughout the nation the same year revealed that, by and large, the Japanese public had not been taken in by the Soviet technique of talking of peace while preparing for war.

Any serious discussion of the Communist underground preparations for war in occupied Japan is necessarily limited by the nature of the available source material. The problem of locating and maintaining reliable sources of information on this particular aspect of an altogether difficult subject goes without saying.* While the bulk of the obtainable data does not lend itself readily to documentation, enough evidence can be assembled to permit presentation of the characteristic features of the Communist underground as it developed in Japan after 1950.

Tangible evidence that the Japanese Communist Party was in the process of moving underground appeared in June 1950 when, after the purge of the Central Committe, no attempt was made to reconstitute a regular Central Committee, but instead an Interim Central Directorate was set up in Tokyo as official overt Party headquarters. By the time the North Korean Communists were ready to launch their southern offensive, underground facilities in Japan were sufficiently complete to accommodate a select number of Party officials. Tokuda was discovered missing on June 4, 1950. Nozaka, after sarcastically declaring that with so much free time on his hands he intended to open a candy shop, disappeared a few weeks later. Within a month most of Japan's top Communists had vanished.

Communist underground activities in Japan detected since the beginning of the Korean War have included the formation and training of guerrilla units, the systematic gathering of intelligence information (including the mapping of certain strategic areas), the infiltration of Japanese security agencies† and of U. S. occupation offices and establishments, and the distribution of clandestine literature printed in Japan and abroad.‡

*During the course of their research, the writers were frequently impressed with this fact. For instance, one of the writers' researchers disappeared in Japan early in 1950 under mysterious circumstances and at this writing remains unaccounted for.

†While the Japanese government has understandably preferred not to release figures on the degree of the Communist infiltration of its security forces, the situation is believed to be more serious than is generally realized. It has been reported that the Party issued specific instructions to hundreds of its members to apply for positions with the National Police Reserve, the National Rural Police, and the Special Investigation Bureau of the Attorney General's office. This was confirmed in general terms by the chief of the Special Investigation Bureau, Mitsusada Yoshikawa, in a conversation with one of the writers in Washington, D. C. during the summer of 1951. The escape of Communist leader Etsuro Shiino in September 1951, when after elaborate preparations the Japanese police attempted to arrest the members of the Central Directorate, was attributed by Communist Diet member Itaru Yonehara to the fact that Party headquarters had been tipped off by Communist sympathizers in the Special Investigation Bureau.

‡The Attorney General's Office disclosed in May 1951 that the number of illegal Japanese Communist publications (without exception strongly anti-American in character) was on the increase despite repressive measures taken by the government. The Party had generally succeeded in keeping secret the location of its printing plants and details of its distribution network.

The size of the Communist underground in Japan (referred to in most Japanese sources as the "second apparatus") cannot easily be established. It may consist of as many as twenty-five thousand men. Its ranks include Communists in hiding (like Nozaka and Tokuda) and secret Party members. The distinction is important. A secret Party member is an individual whose Communist affiliation is unknown. He is essentially an espionage agent and hence usually expresses little interest in Communism or Party affairs. He may seem to be a politically disinterested scientist, a loyal government employee, or even an anti-Communist. While secret members have served the Communist cause since the Party became a legal organization in 1945, the ratio of secret to acknowledged members appears to have increased markedly during 1950 and 1951. Registered membership, as reported by the Communist Party to the Attorney General's Office, dropped from 108,692 in March 1950 to about 69,000 by the end of the year and continued to decline until in September of 1951 it had reached a low of 56,000. Although this substantial loss in registered strength must be attributed in part to the voluntary withdrawal of lukewarm Communists and to social and economic pressure exerted by the increasingly anti-Communist attitude of the Japanese authorities, there can be no doubt that the Party's policy of transferring members to the secret category has been at least as important a factor. This interpretation is supported by a Japanese government report released in the summer of 1951 which indicatd that the Party leadership during 1950 had ordered its lower echelons to have one-third of their membership make sham defections from the Party.[17]

The first documentary evidence of Communist origin indicating that the Japanese Party was indeed undergoing a reorganization to ready it for any contingency became available to the writers in 1951. A Fourth Consultative Conference was held secretly in Japan during February. A new set of Party Rules and Regulations adopted at that time reads like the field manual of the Imperial Japanese army.[18] This first postwar revision of the Party's standard operating procedure sets up absolute norms of discipline and security. Characteristic of the development is an entirely new introductory section, dealing with the "aggression of the imperialists in Asia and their plans for a third world war," and Article 7, which stipulates that a Communist is duty-bound to protect vital Party secrets even at the risk of his life and that in case of arrest a member must under no circumstances divulge information concerning the Party structure. Discussions of the Party's "military policy" and instructions on the infiltration and subversion of the police force and on guerrilla activity were included regularly during 1951 in the Communists' principal underground publication, *Foreign and Domestic Review (Naigai Hyoron)*. In addition, a pamphlet on guerrilla warfare reportedly containing the basic policy for equipping and training partisans (believed to be a translation of the Chinese Communist Army Field Service Regulations) made its appearance in Japan during the same period.

Though the seriousness of intra-Party dissension and the effectiveness of government control must be carefully examined before any final estimate of the capabilities of the Communist underground in Japan can be made, the Party's potential should not be judged on the basis of its past performance.

CHAPTER XIX

Factionalism

THE NATURE OF PARTY UNITY

U NTIL the beginning of 1950 the Communist Party of Japan seemed to present a solid block united behind its leaders. There was little tangible evidence of personal rivalry among them, and the occurrence of schisms—so frequent in other Japanese political parties—appeared unlikely. Actually, ever since the revival of the Communist organization under Secretary General Tokuda, there had been symptoms of factional strife and personality clashes. If little of this reached the general public or even the lower-echelon Party member and if no serious splits or defections weakened the Party up to 1950, the reason must be sought in the nature of Communist organizations in general and in the unique character of the Japanese Communist Party in particular.

Within a Communist Party undoubtedly less room exists for serious disagreement on basic policy than in other political organizations. Every member subscribes to the principles of Marxism (as interpreted by Lenin and more recently by Stalin) and is guided by a common philosophy, that of dialectic materialism. The writings of Marx and Engels and those of Lenin and Stalin form a body of sacred literature which presumably contains the answers to all problems—economic, social, and political. Since these writings are treated with the respect ordinarily accorded only to religious texts, disagreements are confined to differences in interpretation. The basic premises underlying the Marxist classics are not challenged. Rivals for power as well as feuding theorists must back up their arguments by quotations from the Marxist canon, and victory is won by those whose conclusions are "correct" in terms of the prevailing Stalinist line. Because the general philosophy and ultimate goal of all Communists are identical, arguments—except for those stemming from personal rivalries—accordingly are narrowed down to disagreements over the application of Marxist theory or, in other words, to problems of strategy and tactics.

Another feature characteristic of Communist parties further reduces the danger of articulate opposition within the organization and produces conditions which permit greater uniformity of program and action than is possible in all but totalitarian parties. Communist organizations are built on the concept of "democratic centralism" (also called "Party democracy"). This concept, in theory, guarantees every Party member a voice in the determination of Party policy by permitting him to elect his representatives to the policy-making bodies (such as District Committees or the Party Congress). In practice, however, Communist parties have been ruled by self-perpetuating bodies of powerful leaders, generally members of the Politburo. Important decisions are made within this body which exercises absolute authority since the concept of "democratic centralism" entails absolute compliance by the Party member with decisions of the higher echelons. The pertinent clause in the Rules and Regulations of the Japanese Communist Party reads: "There shall be free discussion. Once a decision has been reached, however, it must be carried out immediately and to the letter. Lower echelons owe absolute obedience to the decisions of the higher echelons."[1] Noncompliance almost invariably results in expulsion. As a consequence of this state of affairs, Communist parties have exhibited a strongly autocratic character and a pronounced tendency toward "unanimous" decisions. Opposition elements have had the choice between absolute compliance with the Party line and expulsion. As the fate of purgees in the Russian as well as other Communist parties has shown, expulsion from the party organization means death—if not literally, at least politically—or at best, exile, isolation, and obscurity. Wholesale purges were unknown to the postwar Japanese Party until the crucial months following the Cominform censure. Even individual expulsions were few. There was little need for such extreme measures since the question of leadership had been settled in the first weeks following Japan's surrender and because of the minimum knowledge of Marxist theory requested of Party members during the period of "peaceful revolution."

Moreover, traces of "feudalistic remnants"—against which the Communists have been carrying on such a determined and protracted fight— are by no means absent from the Japanese Communist organization. To a larger extent than in revolutionary movements elsewhere, leadership within the Japanese Communist Party is determined by seniority. Newcomers, even those who proved themselves during the difficult war years, are not chosen for the top positions. The number of years spent in prison or exile rather than organizational drive or intellectual ability would seem to qualify a member for leadership.

Another trace of feudalism is noticeable in the Japanese Communist organization. The "boss system," long characteristic of Japanese unions, is not unknown to the Party. Younger members almost invariably attach themselves to one of the recognized leaders, expecting to advance gradually to positions of influence through the assistance of their individual sponsors. When Japanese political prisoners were released by SCAP in the fall of 1945, Tokuda assumed the rank of Secretary General in the new Communist organization. No one challenged him. He had been

among the founders of the first Communist group in Japan and had
spent eighteen years in prison, and, although he was out of direct touch
with the outside world during that period, his claim in 1945 to the
leading post in the Party was not contested. Shiga, the only other veteran
of so many years in prison, had led a somewhat shorter Party life. At
once he assumed the second-ranking position. Thus, from the outset, the
postwar Party was dominated by the Tokuda-Shiga combination, enlarged in 1946 to a triumvirate by the arrival of Nozaka, whose shorter
prison record was offset in the eyes of the Party by more than a decade
spent in working for the Japanese revolutionary movement with Stalin
and Mao. Direction of the Party, up to 1950, was firmly in the hands of
these three men, whose long personal acquaintance with each other and
whose specialization in different aspects of revolutionary activity greatly
reduced the likelihood of personal friction within the Politburo.

This is not meant to imply that the postwar Communist Party has
been homogeneous in character and united in every respect. It is a
matter of record that Central Committee members have at times not
hesitated to express opinions differing from those held by the acknowledged leaders. Some of them, especially those who had built up Communist groups during the war years when Tokuda and Shiga were in
prison and Nozaka abroad, were accustomed to independent action and
found it difficult to submit to the will of their superiors. But even among
this group there was none who would suggest removal of the triumvirate.
Not astonishing then is the fact that, although factions founded on personal friendship and past association did exist within the Central Committee, internal conflicts of a serious nature did not occur until 1950.

As is natural in a party which, like the Japanese Communist Party,
counts among its members an unusually large number of logicians,
interested rather in theory than in action, there have been numerous
debates on the finer points of Marxist theory. Such arguments were
generally settled without difficulty through the intervention of Party
authorities or by one side's acknowledging the superior reasoning of the
other. Only two cases merit attention: the Shiga-Kamiyama controversy
and the Ko Nakanishi case. These are significant because of the caliber
of the men involved and because of the importance of the issues raised.

THE SHIGA-KAMIYAMA CONTROVERSY

What is known in the Party annals as the "Shiga-Kamiyama controversy" was fought throughout 1947 in a number of high-level Party
meetings as well as in a series of articles written by the antagonists and
published for the most part in the fall of 1947 in official organs of the
Communist Party. At first glance it may appear as if the controversy,
centering around the respective merits of the 1927 and 1932 Theses and

the correct interpretation of the nature of authority in Japan, might be of interest only to the theorist. Both sides quoted abundantly from Marx, Engels, Lenin, and Stalin, backed their statements by an analysis of historical developments in Russia, Germany, and Japan, and reinforced their arguments by brief passages in German, Russian, and English. But as the discussion proceeded through successive issues of *Vanguard*, it became clear that Central Committee member Kamiyama was indirectly attacking the triumvirate and that his theories, if accepted by the Party, would necessitate a new strategy. In answering, Shiga injected into his refutations an element of personal invective. Beginning with the assertion that Kamiyama's theories showed "a lack of correct knowledge of Party history" and that the main fault in Kamiyama's reasoning consisted in his interpreting historical facts "to suit his own arbitrary conclusions,"[2] Shiga went on to point out that his opponent's brief Party life was probably responsible for this "faulty reasoning." With Kamiyama's rebuttal the following month (October 1947), it became obvious that the argument had transcended the realm of purely theoretical discussion and that Kamiyama—angered by Shiga's stinging rebukes—not only was now critical of the current strategy of the Japanese Communist Party but had begun to question publicly the principle on which leadership within the organization had been based. After pointing out that he, Kamiyama, and other Communists had been working for the Communist cause during the war years when, according to Shiga, there was hardly any revolutionary activity in Japan, Kamiyama challenged Shiga's position in the following words:

> As you have pointed out, my Party life is shorter than yours. This is quite true. But there are a number of things I would like to say about the way you treat this question . . . During your eighteen years in the penitentiary, I was sent twice to prison. Even so, I spent ten years outside fighting in the midst of the revolutionary movement a bitter and ceaseless battle. Is there an absolute guarantee that someone is right simply because he is older and has been longer with the Party? There are any number of examples in the history of the revolutionary movement throughout the world proving that this is not necessarily true. . .
>
> There is no need for you to point out what I gladly admit. I am a poor man's child, never got any systematic education, and my manners are a little crude. In theory and practice I have attempted to be true. When something seems unreasonable to me, I speak my opinion, as a Communist should and as Party regulations permit, until the day when the Party arrives at formal decision. Thus I submit this essay to you and other comrades for critical evaluation,

expecting objective criticism and kind instruction. With sincere wishes for your good health and a good fight [for the Communist cause], yours. . .[3]

Shiga hit back in a lengthy "Third Criticism of Comrade Kamiyama's Theories," published again in the Party organ, *Vanguard*. By this time there could be no doubt as to the core of the controversy and its implications for the Japanese Communist Party. Shiga specifically objected to Kamiyama's theory on the following grounds: Kamiyama did not make a clear distinction between social democracy and Communism. "He believes," Shiga asserted, "that new Communism is obtained by adding the two and simply dividing the result by two."[4] "Kamiyama," Shiga charged, "does not realize clearly that revolution is indivisible" and that whether it is carried out by peaceful methods or not "depends only on conditions prevailing at the time." Kamiyama's theory, Shiga stated, divides in a "formalistic way" revolutions into "violent revolutions" and "peaceful revolutions." "This has resulted," Shiga concluded, "in a mistaken notion of peaceful revolution perverting Party policy."[5]

The popularity of Kamiyama's position is evident from the fact that Shiga saw himself forced to mention that his opponent's theories had had "considerable impact" on the thinking of Party members and of pro-Communist intellectuals and that Kamiyama had already been hailed by some as the spiritual leader of the Party and by others as "Japan's Mao Tse-tung."

The Japanese Communist Party seemed threatened by a serious rift. A Kamiyama and a Shiga faction were forming, attacking each other with well-chosen Marxist terminological weapons, and here and there the ominous word "deviationist" was heard. But suddenly the excitement subsided. Kamiyama's reply to Shiga's "Third Criticism," announced by the *Vanguard* editors for the January edition of 1948, never appeared. The matter had been settled by the Party leaders, at least temporarily. Since the decisive debates took place behind closed doors, it is somewhat difficult to determine exactly what happened. Developments of the following months seemed to indicate that the argument had been ended by a truce between the contestants, with neither of them scoring a clear victory. Shiga maintained his leading position and continued to write on theory. Kamiyama, while not abandoning his views, apparently agreed to remain quiet and to abide by the Party's decisions. He was, however, not expelled, retained his membership in the Central Committee, and thus remained in a position to renew his attack at a more opportune moment. It seems likely that Nozaka played a role in preventing the expulsion of Kamiyama, whose views on strategy and peaceful revolution were akin to those held by the Party's policy maker. It was about this time that symptoms of a rift within the triumvirate appeared. Shiga's bitter attacks against Kamiyama's "deviations" did not receive the unqualified endorsement of Tokuda and Nozaka, who apparently had come to fear that Shiga's aggressive, doctrinaire attitude might jeopardize Party unity. Although the Shiga-Kamiyama controversy did not give rise to mass expulsions or even to the removal of the opposition leader, its importance should not be underestimated: for the first time since the revival of the Party, serious dissension had developed within the Central Committee.

THE KO NAKANISHI CASE

Ko Nakanishi, long-time resident of China and one of the key figures in the Sorge espionage case, had joined the Japanese Party in the postwar period, although his views on the character of revolution in Japan differed from those held by the Party leadership. Nakanishi, elected member of the House of Councilors in 1947, continued despite official Party censure to advocate a direct socialist revolution in preference to Nozaka's "go-slow approach." Although frequently warned that his strategy in its ultraleft radicalism would only alienate the masses and lead to the eventual destruction of the Party, Nakanishi volunteered his opinions whenever an opportunity presented itself. Party leaders perhaps felt that Nakanishi would be more dangerous outside than within the Party, where his following was small. Without a seat on the Politburo, Central Committee, or Control Commission, his opposition had hardly more than a nuisance value. The Central Committee at regular intervals took up the matter of "Comrade Nakanishi's deviations" and warned him to comply with Party policy. The last such warning, based on Shiga's recommendations, was unanimously adopted by the Seventeenth Plenum of the Central Committee in September 1949.[6]

The Cominform's attack on the Japanese Party's leadership presented Nakanishi with the opportunity he was seeking to expound his views in a more propitious atmosphere. At once he issued a statement to the non-Communist press asserting that the correctness of his views had now been proved by the Cominform and that it was time for the Communist leaders to give up their opposition to his strategy. In the midst of the consternation produced by the unexpected developments, the Party leaders decided to rid the organization at last of Nakanishi, who, under the changed circumstances, threatened to turn into the leader of an opposition faction. Nakanishi was expelled on January 10 before he could rally support. His expulsion failed to have any serious repercussions since it was overshadowed by evidence of the first major rift within the Party.

THE MAIN STREAM LEADERSHIP AND THE
INTERNATIONALISTS

Despite the incidents involving Kamiyama and Nakanishi, the Japanese Communist Party at the beginning of 1950 outwardly presented a united front. There were as yet no serious signs of dissension among the members of the policy-making bodies, the Politburo and the Central Committee. A few weeks later, the Party, thrown into confusion by the Cominform's severe attack against Nozaka's policy, faced an entirely new situation: for the first time members of the triumvirate found themselves in opposing camps.

On January 18, 1950 the Central Committee met to determine the Party's attitude toward the Cominform's blast against Communist strategy in Japan. In an earlier Politburo meeting Tokuda had attempted to placate the foreign Communists and to settle the incident by issuing a simple statement recognizing that there had been "certain inadequacies" in Nozaka's theories, but insisting that "all the defects" had "already been eliminated." He justified the Party's lack of aggressiveness by pointing out that "subjective and objective conditions in Japan" forced the Party to choose "zigzag actions and words" in order to achieve "a certain goal."[7] Shiga and Miyamoto had refused to endorse such a lukewarm attitude and Tokuda, in danger of being considered a Japanese Tito, had agreed to place the issue before an enlarged Central Committee session for final decision.

The atmosphere which prevailed at the eighteenth session of the Central Committee suggested that coöperation between the top leaders had come to an end. Shiga had gradually been drifting to the left since the days when he had accused Kamiyama of "opportunism." Nozaka's emphasis on the "incomplete character" of the bourgeois-democratic revolution in Japan, his wooing of the middle classes, and his cautious attitude toward the occupation authorities as well as his guarded statements on the question of neutrality in case of a U. S.–Soviet conflict, had, in Shiga's opinion, produced a situation where the Party was rapidly losing its revolutionary character. If this process continued unchecked, Shiga felt, there was serious danger of the Party's developing into a left-wing social-democratic group.* The Cominform's warning addressed to Nozaka only confirmed Shiga's misgivings.

When the Central Committee met at Party headquarters, they were handed a document entitled "Written Opinion." This document, drawn up by Shiga, was almost identical with one he had submitted to an

---

*In a New Year's message, entitled "The New Year and Proletarian Internationalism" and published in *Akahata* of January 1, 1950, Shiga in veiled language had given vent to such fears.

earlier Politburo meeting. It recommended the adoption of a new strategy emphasizing the proletarian character of a Communist revolution in Japan and stressed the need for closer coöperation with the international movement in view of the world situation. The new document, however, was couched in more conciliatory language, omitting, for instance, a comparison of Tokuda with the purged Secretary General of the Polish Communist Party, Gomulka, in an apparent attempt to win over those who disapproved equally of Nozaka's "soft" attitude and of his own dynamism. Shiga demanded that the Party seriously reconsider its past policy in the light of the "valid criticism" expressed by the Cominform. He further urged the Party to admit openly that "grave mistakes" had been made and to adopt certain corrective measures.[8]

Heated discussions ensued and an anti-Tokuda faction, led by Shiga and Politburo member Kenji Miyamoto, began to form.* Shiga, backed indirectly by the prestige of the Cominform, succeeded in forcing Tokuda and Nozaka to admit that mistakes had been made in the past and in extracing the promise that the Party would henceforth faithfully follow the line suggested by the Cominform. Although the majority of the Central Committee resolved to reject Shiga's "Written Opinion" in favor of Tokuda's general report, the unanimous resolution adopted by the Committee on Jaunary 19, indicated that Tokuda's victory had not been complete: "We will make every effort," it read, "to avoid the mistakes we have made in the past and we do pledge to live up to the expectations of the international proletariat."[9]

While surface unity had thus been preserved, subsequent developments attest to the fact that the struggle over the formulation of a new strategy was still going on and that factionalism was gradually spreading to regional and district agencies. Miyamoto, head of the powerful Control Commission and supporter of Shiga's views, was removed from his position. Miyamoto's place was taken by Etsuro Shiino, a loyal Tokuda man. In the meantime, copies of Shiga's "Written Opinion" appeared in Communist branch offices throughout Japan, although all copies had supposedly been seized by the Control Commission. Shiga's uncomplimentary remarks concerning the Secretary General had been reinserted and there were new passages condemning the Japanese Party's "completely Titoist attitude." Shiga, summoned to explain his stand before his colleagues of the Politburo, denied all knowledge of the affair.[10] Eventually, on April 15, Shiino, the new head of the Central Commission, took the unprecedented step of publishing an account of the whole

---

*Other important figures who backed Shiga were Shojiro Kasuga, Kozo Kameyama, and Satomi Hakamada. Shigeo Kamiyama is generally considered to have embraced in 1950 a considerably more "leftist" point of view than in 1947. He refused, however, to support fully either Tokuda or Shiga.

matter in the Party newspaper, accusing Shiga of a lack of coöperation with the Commission in its efforts to combat "factionalism" within the Party.

The Shiino commentary deserves closer examination, for it affords a better understanding of the issues involved than does the usual ambiguous Party statement. The Tokuda-Nozaka leadership, in command of the Party apparatus, was obviously facing a dilemma. Shiga's policy emphasizing the fight against "international capital" (that is, against the American position in Japan) and exhibiting a reckless disregard for what Tokuda preferred to call the "objective conditions" prevailing in American-occupied Japan as well as Shiga's advocacy of a direct fight against "foreign domination" would inevitably lead, Tokuda and Nozaka felt, to the outlawing and complete destruction of the Party. Shiga's strategy clearly involved unnecessary risks and promised little in return. Until the moment when Communist pressure on the Asian continent and in other parts of the world had reached the stage where an attempt to seize power in Japan could count on decisive aid from abroad, there was nothing to gain by untimely provocation—but much to lose. On the other hand, Tokuda did not go so far as to reject the Cominform's "advice."

Tokuda's attitude showed no signs of Titoism; it was governed rather by a realistic estimate of the situation. While accepting the recommendations of the Cominform and although willing to step up the fight against "international capital," Tokuda sought to preserve the legality of the Party as long as possible. Past experience, when the Japanese Communists had been forced into complete isolation by the repressive measures of the government, unquestionably had something to do with this decision. Tokuda—at least until the underground apparatus could be expanded and readied for action—had hoped to tread the narrow line between insurrection and maximum antigovernment activity within the limits permitted by the law. Shiino, spokesman of the Tokuda-Nozaka school of thought, professed to represent the "true internationalists" and branded Shiga's "self-styled internationalists" as "Trotskyist elements." Typical are the following passages of the commentary:

These elements are rallying around Comrade Shiga's "Written Opinion." They are organizing a fight against Tokuda and Nozaka. In this they are at one with the ruling class in attacking our leaders . . .

Their activities are obviously those of Trotskyist left-wing opportunists. Under the cloak of militant internationalism, they are assisting reactionary forces in Japan, which are a component of Japanese authority, by viewing internationalism apart from the interest of the Japanese people and by demanding that our fight be directed only against international monopolistic capital . . .

Under the pretense of basing their strategy on internationalism, they oppose the Party's demand for an over-all peace treaty for Japan and favor instead a separate peace treaty with the Soviet Union and China. Under the cloak of fighting international monopolistic capital, they incite the Party to riotous actions which isolate it from the masses.

The result of the three months' activity following the Eighteenth Plenum [January 1950] shows that wherever these [Trotskyist] elements have operated, the Party has become more and more isolated [from the masses] . . . and the struggle has been unsuccessful.

In areas, however, where the resolutions of the Eighteenth Plenum have been carried out, there emerges, contrary to Comrade Shiga's views, a broad united front . . . This united front aims at the independence of the people and at the protection of peace. It is achieved through daily struggles . . . In close connection with these victories, the regional struggles become the major foundation for the formation of a democratic people's front. Thus the hegemony of the worker is being established and the power of the Party is gradually increased . . .

We must learn from the experience of foreign parties and smash these new Trotskyist elements in Japan . . .[11]

The ominous term "Trotskyist" seemed to suggest that the anti-Shiga forces had decided to take action. A purge was generally expected; but only a few days after release of Shiino's commentary, the break, to all appearances, had been healed. Miyamoto, in a statement displayed prominently in the Communist press, denied the existence of a "Shiga-Miyamoto line" and warned against "anarchist tendencies within the Party."[12] A Central Committee meeting (the Nineteenth Plenum), convened toward the end of April to discuss the issue, found Shiga, Miyamoto, Kamiyama, and several others criticizing Tokuda's draft of the 1950 Thesis; but neither did the expected heated discussions develop nor was any concerted attempt made to oust opposition members. Together with Tokuda's report to this Plenum, emphasizing the need for carrying out a "nation-wide struggle spearheaded by regional fights," *Red Flag* was able to publish a statement by Shiga entitled "Let Us Stop Factional Strife and Establish Bolshevik Unity within Our Party."[13]

Two factors may account for this sudden about-face. On April 17 *Red Flag* triumphantly reported that *Pravda* had reprinted Tokuda's general report to the Eighteenth Plenum. This was generally taken as proof of Moscow support for Tokuda. At the same time mounting outside pressure, provoked by the increasing militancy of the Communist Party after January 1950, apparently had convinced the Party leaders that this was not the time to engage in factional strife. Secret reports concerning an imminent Communist unification drive in Korea may have contributed to the feeling that Party unity must by all means be preserved at a moment when circumstances might require unified and decisive action.

The purge of all Japanese Communist leaders by order of SCAP, about a month after the Central Committee meeting, placed the Party's legal apparatus in the hands of Shiino and his Interim Central Directorate, established, it will be recalled, on the very day of the purge and composed almost exclusively of Tokuda-Nozaka supporters, referred to in Party literature as the "Main Stream Group." While Shiga and Miyamoto were thus incapacitated, Shiino, probably with the support of Tokuda and pro-Tokuda leaders who had gone underground at about the time of the Korean war, began a concerted drive for the elimination of opposition elements.

There has been much speculation concerning the reasons which prompted Shiino to start a wholesale expulsion of deviationists at a moment when the Party was seriously threatened by disintegration because of pressure exerted by SCAP and by the Japanese government. All evidence points to the conclusion that even before the Comintern criticized the Japanese Party's temporizing tactics, there was, especially among students and young intellectuals, a strong undercurrent of dissatisfaction with the Tokuda-Nozaka leadership. Shiga was possibly the first to give it expression on the highest level, but the demand for radical action spurred on by the success of the Chinese Communists had always been there. The Party's revised strategy after January 1950 automatically encouraged the growth of an atmosphere of militancy which, in turn, contributed to a strengthening of that faction which demanded revolutionary action. Thus, indirectly and against its will, the Main Stream leadership was contributing to the strength of the Internationalist Faction. On the other hand, after the SCAP purge of the Party leadership, it had become even more imperative than before to retain as wide a field of "legal" antigovernment and antioccupation activity as possible. Although much of the Party apparatus and many of its previous leaders had been moved underground, there was no desire to give up the valuable sphere of legally recognized opportunity for mass propaganda. Members of the Internationalist Faction by their radical, but ineffective, actions were rapidly creating a situation which, it was feared, would prompt SCAP to outlaw the Party.

The expulsion of all Internationalists (reported to have constituted in certain areas up to one-third of the membership) was begun by Shiino almost immediately after he had officially become the director of the Party's—that is, the Main Stream leadership's—overt headquarters. On

June 18 the National Conference of Party Representatives* adopted a resolution against the "factionalists" and rebuked Shiga for "not having shown any concrete evidence of fighting schismatics."[14] This was the signal for a bitter struggle which lasted for several months. Only much later did a clear picture emerge from the confused reports of Party purges and counterpurges, accusations and counteraccusations, which took place in an atmosphere of government repression, arrests, and frantic police searches for the underground leaders. Thus, on August 28, 1950, a Japanese news service reported from Tottori in southwestern Japan that a Communist Diet member had been ousted by his Internationalist opponents, while the following day a Tokyo newspaper related the purge of Tomeji Tada, only pro-Internationalist on the Interim Central Directorate, together with that of Shigeharu Nakano, well-known author and Communist member of the House of Councilors; Toshiko Karazawa, woman Communist Diet member from Hokkaido; and Kikue Hakamada, wife of the purged Central Committee member Satomi Hakamada, reportedly a Shiga man.[15]

In an effort to disengage the Party from elements who were "provoking the occupation authorities unnecessarily," Shiino proceeded to dissolve numerous Party Cells dominated by the Internationalists and purged the leaders of the Communist-dominated National Federation of Self-governing Student Associations who, in violation of specific Party instructions, were engaging in illegal anti-American propaganda and violent demonstrations.

By the fall of 1950, the Internationalists had been decisively weakened as much by Shiino's action as by police measures directed against those who were found engaging in the distribution of anti-American literature. By crushing those elements who were endangering the legal status of the Party, the Tokuda-Nozaka group had thus succeeded in gaining precious time for building up its underground organization. At the same time the somewhat cautious attitude of Shiino toward the occupation authorities enabled the Party to continue a wide range of "legal" activities.

During the winter of 1950 there were strong indications that the rift within the Party was being successfully closed. There had never been any real obstacle to a reconciliation of the two factions. Both were agreed on the "correctness" of the Cominform's "advice." Both had come to the conclusion that a fight against "international capital," "threatening colonialization," and a determined effort to weaken the United States'

*This body was composed of the Interim Central Directorate (substituting for the purged Central Committee), the Central Committee alternates, the members of the Control Commission, and a number of regional representatives.

position in Asia were imperative in the light of international developments. As the area for "legal activities" was shrinking rapidly because of
SCAP's and the Japanese government's measures aimed at neutralizing
the Party through purges and various other kinds of pressure, the rival
groups, differing only in their degree of militancy, were drawing closer
through force of circumstances. The dismantlement of the legal Party
apparatus and the war on the continent impressed upon the whole Party
the need for unity. This trend was considerably strengthened by further
"advice" from abroad. An editorial published on September 3, 1950 in
the Peking *People's Daily (Jen-min jih-pao)*, reflecting the official views
of the Chinese Communist regime, undoubtedly hastened this process
of reconciliation. The significant passages of this appeal to the Japanese
Communists follow:

> Under American occupation, Japan is again becoming the center
> of imperialist aggression and fascist reaction in Asia. Because of this,
> the entire people of China and of the rest of the world cannot but
> rise up to oppose American imperialism, successor and patron of
> Japanese imperialism. They cannot but show the deepest concern
> over the situation in Japan and the struggle of the Japanese people. . .
> Two roads now lie before the Japanese people: one is indicated
> by the Japanese ruling class, the other is pointed out by the party
> of the Japanese working class—the Communist Party of Japan. . .
> Because of a lack of experience, the Party at one time made
> certain mistakes in matters involving principles; but during the
> period since last January it has corrected these mistakes. Thereafter
> its basic policy has been correct. . .
> At present the supreme task [of the Japanese Party] consists in
> achieving close unity within the Party. . . Some members of the
> Japanese Communist Party have recently expressed doubts about,
> or have refused to recognize, the correctness of the line of the Party
> leadership and have raised certain unsuitable slogans of an "ultra-
> left" adventurist nature. They demand that the Party, in the midst
> of the present situation, should stop what it is doing and engage
> in impracticable arguments with them and that it should adopt
> certain unsuitable organizational methods.
> That such ideas are incorrect is only too evident. These comrades
> should consider the present situation coolly, abandon their unsuit-
> able demands and slogans, and unite sincerely with the leading
> Party organs and the majority of the Party. Certain differences in
> opinion can be ironed out steadily on the basis of unity, and
> unanimity of opinion can gradually be reached through discussions
> as permitted by existing circumstances and by waiting and letting

develop'ments prove the truth. They should not . . . adopt undisciplined methods detrimental to the unity of the Party. Otherwise the situation will be exploited by the enemy. . .

On the other hand, the leading organ [Interim Central Directorate] of the Japanese Communist Party, with the utmost patience and consideration, must unite all sincere Party members holding divergent opinions and should not impatiently adopt crude organizational measures to deal with them. Ideological matters cannot be settled by crude methods. Otherwise disputes and quarrels within the Party would be intensified to the detriment of Party unity and would open the way to the enemy and *agents provocateurs*. . .

These are our sincere suggestions to our Japanese comrades. . .*

At this writing it is perhaps premature to assert that the Communist Party of Japan has fully recovered from its first serious internal dissension since the surrender. The bulk of evidence points to the conclusion that it has. A secret meeting of Party delegates (the Fourth National Consultative Conference) convened in February 1951 and adopted a more militant and internationally oriented set of Party Rules and Regulations together with a strong resolution against factionalism. This development plus the subsequent issuance of self-criticism by leaders of the opposing groups, Shiino and Shiga, suggest that the Japanese Communist organization—after having shed a considerable number of "moderates" and "fellow travelers," who had been attracted by the slogan "peaceful revolution," as well as a smaller number of overly impetuous revolutionists—is moving rapidly toward the time when unification of all Communist forces in Japan may have to be reckoned with. Writing from the underground, Shiga confirms this conclusion: "The conflict today is no longer one between two groups within the Party," he said; "the only question is whether or not the Party is on the correct path internationally—whether or not it has proper relations with the world."[16]

*"This Is the Time for Unity Among the Japanese People," *Jen-min jih-pao*, Sept. 3, 1950, reprinted in *Hsin Hua Yueh Pao*, Sept. 15, 1950. The tone of certain passages, it is interesting to note, is strongly reminiscent of the purged Nozaka's style. No confirmation of his participation in drafting the Chinese document has come to light. Shiino, a few days later, gratefully acknowledged the message. His reply was again reprinted in the major Chinese publications.

CHAPTER XX

International Relations

THE PARTY AND THE SOVIET UNION

Tʜᴇ first postwar convention of the Japanese Communist Party, in December 1945, was officially designated the Fourth Party Congress, indicating that the legal postwar Party was regarded as an extension of the illegal prewar organization. The current leaders of the movement are veterans of the twenties and thirties with extensive experience in Russia. Until 1950, the Japanese Party saw no need to replace or revise its basic policy (termed a "thesis") which had been drafted in Moscow in 1932. Thus, an unbroken thread of organization, leadership, and policy runs through the prewar history of the Party and into the postwar period.

Before considering specific evidence indicative of direct collaboration between the Japanese Communist Party and the Soviet Union during the postwar period, it may be useful to review briefly the stated position of the Party on foreign policy and relations with the Big Powers.

At the first postwar Party Congress, Secretary General Tokuda said: "Direct liaison with the Soviet Union will harm rather than assist our movement."[1] A few weeks later he stated: "At present we are aiming at the early establishment of a democracy in its real sense. In other words, democracy in the American way. What shall we do after attainment of this objective? It will be decided by the actual situation at that time both at home and abroad."[2] At the next Party Congress, in 1946, Tokuda made the point even more strongly: "At present," he said, "we have no ties whatsoever with the Soviet Union . . . I should like to state here that, in the future as well, our Party will never have relations with the Soviet Union."[3]

The Party clearly defined its position in a major foreign-policy statement, released to the press on April 4, 1946, as the following pertinent passages demonstrate:

> We will endeavor to maintain and strengthen friendly relations equally with all peace-loving and democratic foreign nations. . .
> The Party will reject such a policy as will plunge our nation into the turmoil of international strife. We absolutely oppose any kind of imperialistic war of aggression. We shall neither support such a war nor participate in it in any form whatsoever. . .
> Rumors are rife at present that there is a danger of war breaking

out between the United States and the Soviet Union. These rumors are nothing but vicious propaganda constituting an attempt on the part of militarists and reactionaries in this country to effect their own recovery or to expand their influence. As has been stated by the leaders of the United States and the Soviet Union, the governments and peoples of these two countries do not want a war—are actually trying to avert a war. . .

Other parties are spreading malicious propaganda which conveys the impression that our Party still has some connection with the Comintern, or Third International. As is well known, that organization was dissolved in June 1943. It is, therefore, evident that our Party today has no relation with any kind of international organization. We hereby declare that our Party is a party of the Japanese people and a party which devotes itself to the liberation of the working classes of this country.[4]

These official statements suggested an abrupt departure from the prewar policy of collaboration with the Soviet Union. A closer study of the period from 1945 through 1951 indicates, however, that this apparent break with the past was simply a shift in tactics. Emphasis on the "independent character" of the Party seemed to hold out greater possibilities for success in occupied Japan. Although, for the sake of expediency, the Party may have temporarily reduced its material ties with the Soviet Union, there is ample evidence that the basic relation remained unchanged. The Soviet Union continued to do its utmost to assist the growth of the Party in Japan, while the latter persisted in its praise of everything Russian and in its support of the Soviet position on every major issue. In short, there was little to suggest a "break" between the Party and the Soviet Union and every reason to assume continued Soviet direction of the movement in Japan. If the relation in question must be termed "cautious" during the period up to the beginning of 1950, it was, nonetheless, significant. Even after unconfirmed reports of Russian liaison with the Japanese Party and of numerous "secret Party instructions"[5] have been discounted, a substantial amount of evidence remains.

Practically all Japanese residents of non-Soviet areas had been repatriated by the end of 1946, but the Soviet authorities were clearly reluctant to release their hundreds of thousands of Japanese prisoners. Repatriation of Japanese nationals from Siberia and other Russian territories did not begin until December 19, 1946, after SCAP and the Soviet representative in Japan had reached an agreement on the issue. Even after this date, the Soviet authorities continued to procrastinate. Despite sharp notes addressed by SCAP to the Soviet member of the Allied Council for Japan, repatriation proceeded at a snail's pace and was at times even suspended for months on end because of "climatic and icing conditions," although SCAP offered to dispatch icebreakers to Soviet ports.[6]*

A Moscow broadcast of May 20, 1949, quoted in *Red Flag* of May 22, stated that at the time of the surrender a total of 594,000 Japanese prisoners of war had been in territories under Russian control. Of these, the same account asserted, 70,880 had been released on the spot during 1945. According to the official Moscow version, the remainder, with the exception of war criminals, were repatriated by the end of 1949. A Soviet Mission spokesman in Tokyo, on September 5, 1951, put the total number of Japanese "war criminals" in Soviet custody at 1,479. The Japanese government, on the other hand, estimated that 234,151 Japanese prisoners died in Soviet (or Chinese) camps between the end of the war and the summer of 1951 and listed 28,797 as "unaccounted for or missing." According to the same Japanese estimate, 17,637 still remain in Soviet hands.

The reason for Soviet unwillingness to repatriate Japanese prisoners speedily is apparent: each Japanese in Russian custody constituted a potential tool in the struggle for the determination of Japan's political future. The Soviet authorities believed that subjection of the prisoners to an intensive course of indoctrination before their return to Japan would have the effect of reinforcing the Japanese Communist Party. Whether preparations for such a propaganda operation had been made in advance of the Russian entry into the Pacific War is a moot question, but the speed with which a broad program of indoctrination was launched suggests the importance which the Soviet authorities attached to the matter. Some sort of direct liaison between the Russian repatriation agencies and the Japanese Communist Party's Repatriation Section, under Secretary General Tokuda, seems to have been established shortly after the return of the first group of prisoners early in 1947. Although the Japanese Communists consistently denied the existence of such liaison,[7] a Japanese Diet committee investigating the matter concluded, in the spring of 1950, that the Communist Party had, in fact, been in touch with Russian authorities and had obstructed the repatriation.[8] The United States member of the Allied Council for Japan referred, on May 10, 1950, to affidavits tending to link the Japanese Communist Party with the failure of the Russian government to observe the repatriation agreement.[9]

Russian indoctrination of Japanese prisoners was effected in close

*The Japanese Communist explanation for the Russian refusal to accept the SCAP offer was that the icebreakers were in bad condition and would have endangered the lives of crew and passengers. This statement appears in an official handbook of the Communist-controlled League for the Protection of Repatriates from the Soviet Union (Soren Kikansha Seikatsu Yogo Domei), *Shinjutsu wo uttaeru* (Telling the Truth). Tokyo, 1949, p. 46.

coöperation with the Japanese Communist Party. On September 15, 1945—thirteen days after the official surrender of Japan—the *Japanese Newspaper (Nippon Shimbun)*, "the Soviet Army's newspaper for Japanese prisoners," appeared in Khabarovsk.[10] This Japanese-language sheet, edited by several Japanese Communists,* was distributed throughout the hundreds of camps in Siberia† and formed virtually the only tie between the prisoners and the outside world.‡ Tass dispatches, speeches and policy statements by Japanese Communist leaders, and Russian accounts of events in Japan comprised the bulk of the newspaper.§ Direct attempts to guide the prisoners' thinking were made through gatherings organized by political commissars and propagandists assigned to the various camps.‖ Before boarding repatriation vessels, Japanese prisoners were asked to sign letters of appreciation addressed to Stalin, pledging friendship to the Soviet Union and expressing their desire to assist the establishment of a Communist order in Japan.[11]

There have been other indications of close programmatic conformity between the Japanese Communist Party and the Soviet Union. Radio broadcasts from Vladivostok, Khabarovsk, and Moscow to Japan have continued to stress the themes that Japan is ruled and exploited by imperialists and is in danger of becoming a fortress of aggressive American capitalism which threatens the peace of the Far East and of the world; the only recourse of the Japanese masses, the people of Japan are

*Among them was Haruki Aikawa, who, after his return to Japan, joined the editorial board of the Japanese Party organ, *Akahata*. He continued to concentrate on the repatriation issue and on Communist propaganda drives among repatriates before and after their induction into the Party. Aikawa was purged from his position by order of SCAP on June 7, 1950.

†Unofficial reports place the number of labor camps for Japanese prisoners in Soviet-controlled areas at 750, mostly in Siberia. Officers often were transferred to European Russia (Moscow area). See Kinichi Higuchi, *Uraru wo koete* (Crossing the Urals). Tokyo, 1949. Soren Kikansha Yogo Domei (League for the Protection of Repatriates from the Soviet Union), *Warera So-ren ni ikite* (We Lived in the Soviet Union). Tokyo, 1948, pp. 112-118.

‡The *Nippon Shimbun* was supplemented by wall newspapers which contained mainly camp news. In addition, prisoners were supplied with revolutionary literature, including selected Japanese fiction by members of the Proletarian School of writing. Another newspaper, the *Minshu Tsushin (Democratic News)*, was published "by the Soviet Army for Japanese residents of Dairen"; the following headline illustrates its editorial policy: "Where Do the Confiscated [Zaibatsu] Shares Go? To Wall Street?" (Nov. 26, 1947).

§Such as O. Kurganov's report on his visit to Japan (which appeared later in book form). Characteristic of the tenor of these accounts is this excerpt: "A tragic fate is apparently being prepared for the Japanese people—that of slaves to the American masters." O. Kurganov, *Amerikantsi v Yaponii* (The Americans in Japan). Leningrad, 1947, p. 208.

‖Two Russian-sponsored organizations of "progressive" prisoners, the *Tomo no Kai* (Association of Friends) and its successor, the *Minshushugi Domei* (Democratic League), produced a number of potential Party members. Japanese Communist leaders were honorary committee members of the latter organization.

told, is to support all movements that work for peace and national independence. The only political party which follows such a policy, the broadcasts conclude, is the Communist.* An identical line runs through numerous articles and press releases which Tass has supplied the Japanese Communist press.† The same theme, emphasized repeatedly by the Soviet representative on the Allied Council for Japan, has received conspicuous treatment in the Japanese Communist press.‡

In the absence of SCAP reports or Japanese government statements, it is difficult to ascertain how far Russian assistance to the Japanese Communist Party through indoctrination of prisoners, press and broadcast services, and political support in Tokyo and Washington has been supplemented by use of the physical facilities of the Russian Mission in Japan; but it is likely that some such collaboration has been afforded. The Russian Mission, which at peak strength was at least five times as large as any other, included many news analysts and interpreters with valuable Japanese Communist contacts.§ Moreover, at the end of 1949 the Communist press confirmed rumors of direct contact between the Mission and the Party in reporting that Yoshio Shiga, of the Politburo, had visited the chief of the Mission with whom he had "discussed various matters."‖

The Japanese Communist Party's acceptance, early in 1950, of the Cominform's criticism of Nozaka's policy and the Party's active support of Communist aggression on the Asian continent during the summer and autumn of the same year have further clarified the nature of the relation between the Communist Party of Japan and the international Communist movement, led by the Soviet Union.

*The same theme has been stressed by Russian writers. "General MacArthur, Premier Yoshida, and all Japanese-American reaction have long cherished the hope of outlawing the Japanese Communist Party. After all, it is the only mass party in Japan which, by its activities, paralyzes the attempts of American Imperialists to convert the country into a military arsenal and base in the Far East." H. Eidus, "General MacArthur's Campaign Against the Japanese Working Class," *Trud,* Nov. 12, 1949, as translated in *Soviet Press Translations,* Feb. 1, 1950.

†Important Soviet government and Cominform reports and policy statements have appeared in *Zen-ei,* the Japanese Party's monthly organ.

‡For example, on December 22, 1949, *Akahata* gave prominence to the text of a letter from the Soviet representative in Japan to General MacArthur, entitling it "The Yoshida Cabinet's Police Government—a Return of Fascism."

§Such as Misago Iwata, daughter of former Communist Party leader Yoshimichi Iwata. Miss Iwata returned to Japan after the surrender. She is Russian-educated and has been a close friend and protégée of Sanzo Nozaka's wife since the early thirties.

‖*Akahata,* Dec. 22, 1949. Official contact between the Russian and Japanese Communist Parties had been shown by a telegram sent on July 20, 1948 by a Politburo member, G. Malenkov, to Secretary General Tokuda after an attempt on the latter's life. *Akahata,* July 23, 1948.

THE PARTY AND CHINA

"Japan and China are inseparably linked together by strong cultural and economic ties," Sanzo Nozaka said in 1948. "In order to grow, Japan must cultivate an intimate and brotherly relation with the People's China,"* he concluded.

Brotherly ties have marked the relation between the Communist movements of China and Japan since the day when the Chinese Communist Chang T'ai-lei visited Tokyo in 1921 to bring about the crystallization of the left-wing movement. The traditional Sino-Japanese antagonism has never been allowed to affect coöperation between the two parties. Throughout the years, Japanese and Chinese Communists have worked together in Russia, China, and Japan.

The victory of the Chinese Communist armies and the establishment in 1949 of a People's Republic under Mao Tse-tung have brought about a change in the relative position of the Japanese and Chinese Communist parties. What was once a relation between equals has developed in the postwar period into one of master and disciple. Although the Soviet Union still determines the over-all Communist policy in Japan, the Japanese Communists seem to be turning more and more for aid and advice to Communist China.† Even without Nozaka's personal attachment to Mao Tse-tung, the strong cultural affinity between the two nations and the proximity and sheer size of the new power center on the continent might have compelled such a development. The Japanese Communist leaders do not hesitate to bare their admiration and respect for the accomplishments of their continental counterpart. "We are learning," Nozaka stated, "valuable theoretical and political lessons from the great Mao Tse-tung and from other Chinese Communist leaders."‡

*Sanzo Nozaka, *Senryaku, senjutsu no shomondai* (Strategy and Tactics). Tokyo, 1949, p. 282. Nozaka's Chinese background and his acquaintance with the men who control Communist China make him the Party's spokesman on Chinese affairs. The Japanese leader worked with Li Li-san and other Chinese Communists during his nine years in Moscow. In Yenan (1940-1945) he was in constant touch with Mao Tse-tung, Chu Teh, and other members of the Chinese Communist staff.

†The Japanese Communist Party is also reported to be a member of the controversial "Far Eastern Cominform." Although there have been numerous newspaper reports concerning this coördinating agency for the Asian Communist movements (allegedly formed in 1947), the existence of such an organization has so far not been documented. Another organization, the Peiping Bureau of the (Communist-dominated) World Federation of Trade Unions, is frequently referred to by the Japanese press as the "Far Eastern Cominform." This is probably because the Peiping Bureau at present plays a role similar in some respects to that of the Cominform. Persistent Japanese reports referring to a "Committee for the Preparation of Revolution in Japan," as part of the Peiping Bureau, have not been substantiated.

‡*Akahata*, Mar. 25, 1949. The first issue of *Zen-ei* carried the program of the Chinese Communist Party. In subsequent issues Mao Tse-tung's "New Democracy" was discussed in detail. "We Can Learn from the Spirit of the Chinese Communist Party," the title

Advice—and at times criticism—have been offered by the Chinese Party. The official Chinese statement on the Cominform criticism of the Nozaka strategy is indicative of the intensity of Chinese Communist interest in Communist Japan, and the spirit in which the Japanese Communists accepted the advice is illustrative of the weight Chinese Communist opinion carries in Japanese Party circles. The editorial which had originally appeared in the Peking *People's Daily* of January 17, 1950 under the title "The Road Toward the Liberation of the Japanese People" was republished by the Japanese Party for the information of its members. It said in part:

> The Japanese and Chinese people are friends. The peoples of Japan and China have common enemies, that is, Japanese imperialism and the American imperialists who support it. The people of the two countries have common friends. They are the Soviet Union and the people's democracies as well as the proletariat and oppressed peoples of the whole world who are carrying on the fight against imperialism. The Chinese people are greatly concerned with the liberation of the Japanese people. . .
>
> The courage which the Japanese Communist Party has exhibited in fighting the enemy has won for it the admiration of the Chinese as well as of the Japanese people. As comrades we sincerely hope that the Japanese Communist Party will show the same courage in accepting the Cominform criticism and in correcting Nozaka's mistakes. Only in this way, we believe, can the Japanese Communists live up to the expectations of the Japanese people and of the Chinese Communists, and only in this way can they avoid the traps set by the imperialists.[12]

Collaboration and coöperation between the Communist Party organizations of China and Japan are not limited to questions of strategy. The special relation between the two Parties is also evident in another field. Judging by Communist reports from both countries, there appears to be already some sort of understanding concerning the future trade relations between the two nations. Nozaka reports having discussed the matter in detail with Mao Tse-tung before returning to Japan in 1946 and again, three years later, when the issue of trade with Communist China was widely discussed in Japan. Nozaka stated: "Intimate economic relations between China and Japan not only are an absolute necessity in order to overcome the present serious economic crisis in Japan but are also important for Japan from a hundred-year point of view."[13]

of an article which appeared in *Zen-ei* of June 1, 1947, characterizes the relation between the two Communist parties.

The Communist view of the issue may be summarized as follows: Japan will assist the industrialization of China by furnishing machine tools, transportation equipment, agricultural machinery, chemicals, and electrical equipment. In exchange, Japan would receive from China the basic raw materials which it lacks: iron ore, coking coal, salt, and soy beans. The economies of the two countries would in this way supplement each other by an exchange of raw materials against industrial machinery.[14]

The desire of Japanese businessmen to see a free and profitable flow of goods between the two nations has not been materially affected by the advent of Communism in China. Japan's economy, if not supported by American subsidies, is to a large extent dependent on an exchange of goods with other areas of Asia.* Even the conservative and otherwise anti-Communist Prime Minister Shigeru Yoshida told an American journalist in 1949: "Japan is not in a position to neglect any market . . . China is a natural market, whether it is Communist or not."[15] This is perhaps the one point on which the Japanese Communists and their political opponents are in some agreement. It has also served as the Communist Party's entree to the Japanese business world.

During the early part of 1949, Nozaka conferred with prominent business and labor leaders throughout Japan. Japanese newspapers reported the enthusiasm with which the business world responded to the Communist appeal for the revival of trade with China. Attracted by the lure of immediate profit, many Japanese bankers, industrialists, exporters, and importers put aside their conflicting political views and joined the Communist-sponsored "Association for the Advancement of Trade Between Japan and China." By the end of 1949 the Association had established branches in the major cities of Japan. The Japanese Communists reported in September of the same year that a Chinese counterpart of the Association had been formed in Shanghai.[16]

The Japanese Communist leaders are confident that closer relations with Communist China will not only hasten Japan's economic recovery but contribute substantially to a Communist victory in Japan. To what extent active support may be forthcoming from the continent is a matter of conjecture, but the mere existence of a Communist China has its unmistakable implications for Japan. The Japanese Party's interpretation of the significance of the Chinese Communist success is nowhere more clearly expressed than in Nozaka's work "The New China and Japan":

> The victory of the Chinese Communists has a deep spiritual and ideological influence upon the Japanese working classes.
> The working people have by their own strength gained a great

*The following statistics illustrate China's role in Japan's foreign trade: in 1939 trade with China (including Manchuria and the Kwantung area, but not Hongkong) accounted for 23.4 percent of Japan's imports and for 48.8 percent of its exports.

victory in China—a country which was more reactionary, more feudalistic, and more of a colony than Japan. This has given unbounded encouragement to our workers and has inspired them with confidence in victory. Our workers had looked on people's democracy and on socialism as something in far-away Europe, but now it has happened in China, only an ocean away, in the country with which we have had the oldest and closest relations. If such was possible in China, why should it not now be possible in Japan?[17]

THE PARTY AND KOREA

The war in Korea, which began Sunday, June 25, 1950 with an attack by North Korean forces at a number of points along the 38th parallel, represented a new phase of Communist strategy which opened with the establishment of the Chinese People's Republic. A more militant line was discernible in Japan during the early months of 1950 and especially in the weeks immediately preceding the Korean war.

It can only be surmised how closely this new aggressive Communist policy was geared to the projected Korean venture. Japanese Communist postwar policy on Korea and the Party's close ties with the Communist movement in both North and South Korea point to the likelihood of coördinated planning and action. From the outset, Korea had received special attention from the Japanese Communist Party. The Program of Action adopted at the Sixth Party Congress in December 1946 demanded "complete independence for Korea."[18] Korea was the only foreign country to which the document referred specifically.

The question of the "liberation" of Korea received constant stress in the Japanese Communist press. The initial issue of *Vanguard* included two substantial articles on the Korean problem, in addition to the text of the program of the Korean Communist Party. Pak Heun Yung,* Secretary General of the Communist Party of South Korea, and other Korean Communists wrote special articles for the same publication. A representative sampling of the two-page daily *Red Flag* showed a monthly average of twelve items on Korea.[19] The basic theme of these discussions was—as is to be expected—the "deplorable state of things" in United States-dominated South Korea and the "rapid progress" in Soviet-sponsored North Korea.

---

*Pak Heun Yung is one of the founders of the Korean Communist Party, which was established in 1925. He went to Moscow in 1927 to attend Lenin University. Three years later Pak became Secretary General of the Communist Party of South Korea. He escaped at the time of the arrests of left-wing elements in 1946 and fled to North Korea, where he became, with Kim Il Sung and Kim Doo Bong, one of the "Big Three" of Communist Korea. Pak and Kim Il Sung led the Korean delegation which visited Moscow in the spring of 1949. At the time of the outbreak of war in Korea, Pak occupied the position of Foreign Minister of the North Korean Communist regime.

These informational and educational activities were supported at the organizational and planning levels. At the first postwar plenary session of the Central Committee of the Japanese Party in May 1946, Kim Chôn Hae, its Korean member, reported in detail on developments in Korea. He revealed that the Korean Communist Party maintained a liaison section staffed by Japanese Communists and indicated that prospects for unification under the Russian-trained partisan leader Kim Il Sung were bright.[20] In Japan, a school for the training of Korean revolutionists was maintained jointly by the Japanese Party and several Korean organizations.* The existence of such a school and the presence of a Korean within the Japanese Politburo suggest that the prewar unity of action between the two movements had been carried into the postwar period.

Kim Chôn Hae served with the Japanese Party in a dual capacity from 1945 to the autumn of 1949. In addition to his activities in connection with Korea, he was responsible for enlisting the support of the 600,000 Korean residents in Japan for the North Korean government and for the Communist Program of Action for Japan, mainly through the medium of the Korean League, a militant left-wing organization. At the time of its dissolution for "disturbance of public order" on September 8, 1949, the League had 360,000 members and, although not officially affiliated with the Japanese or Korean Communist Parties, provided an effective propaganda weapon against the Republic of Korea. It also assisted the Japanese Communist Party in its illegal exchange of information and individuals with the Korean peninsula, an exchange which generally went undetected.

Only rarely was the Japanese press able to publish data on Japanese Communist liaison with the continent. The following two cases were reported in the *Tokyo Nichi Nichi Shimbun* of July 25, 1950: On December 16, 1948 a 42-ton merchant vessel, en route to North Korea, was seized by Japanese authorities in a small port on the Japan Sea. Investigation of the cargo (consisting principally of automobile spare parts) uncovered several documents highly critical of the occupation and traceable to the Korean League. In October 1949, a 93-ton vessel arrived in the North Korean port of Wonson in order, it was said, to deliver eight million yen worth of Japanese electrical equipment to a Chinese Communist trade organization there. Implicated in the case were two men, members of the Central Committee of the Japanese Communist Party in the late 1920's, who were reported to have made at least five illegal trips to North Korea during 1948 and 1949 and to have brought back information to Nozaka.

The discovery by Allied counterintelligence in Japan of a sizable

---

*The first group of sixty-five Koreans was reported to have graduated on June 3, 1946. *Nippon Times,* June 5, 1946.

Japanese Communist-North Korean spy ring which had been successful in securing vital data on the large-scale United Nations landings at Inchon (near Seoul) on September 15, 1950 confirms in part the substance of numerous reports and rumors on Japanese Communist Party intelligence-gathering activities.

It is difficult to determine how early the Japanese Communists knew of the projected North Korean offensive, but information regarding the scheduled attack seems to have reached Party headquarters at least ten weeks before the event. Leaders of the suppressed Korean League and of other left-wing organizations are reported to have gathered secretly somewhere in Chiba Prefecture early in April to prepare for the expected developments. One account, published in the news bulletin of a non-Communist Tokyo research organization four days prior to the Communist invasion of South Korea reprinted the resolutions reportedly adopted at the "Chiba Conference":

> In view of the present situation, a strong fight for the overthrow of the Yoshida and Syngman Rhee governments seems indicated. This fight must be coördinated with the guerrilla activities of our South Korean comrades and with the activities of the Japanese Communists. . .
>
> The North Korean armies will carry out the southern campaign for the unification of the country at the beginning of the rainy season. They will be assisted by the Chinese Communist forces. To facilitate the achievement of this objective, we will engage in guerrilla activities directed at the destruction of imperialist industry. Our operations are scheduled, until further notice, for August.[21]*

The Japanese Communist Party was quick to support the attack launched by the North Korean Communists on June 25. Risking almost certain suppression, *Red Flag* on the following day declared that the North Koreans had been attacked from the south and had been forced to retaliate.† On June 27 *Red Flag* published a large photograph of the

*Two weeks before the invasion, usually well-informed correspondents were apparently unaware of preparations in Korea and Japan. The Far East correspondent for the *Chicago Tribune*, for example, reported: "Fears of an invasion have subsided. News gets across the border pretty fast, in both directions. There now is little apprehension about open war between the two halves of the dismembered country." *Nippon Times,* June 10, 1950.

†The Japanese Communist Party, in coöperation with its North Korean counterpart, had conducted a long-term campaign to prepare public opinion in Japan for this interpretation of the incident. Numerous dispatches from North Korea published in *Akahata* had been designed to emphasize the "aggressive character" of the South Korean government. Thus, on August 2, 1949, *Akahata* reported that "specialized units" from South Korea had crossed the 38th parallel to create disturbances and had been repulsed by North Korean troops and civilians. The newspaper added editorially that these "specialized units" had been in training for such an operation since 1947 (when South Korea was still under United States Military Government).

North Korean leader Kim Il Sung and the text of his radio address from Pyongyang calling on the population of South Korea to give active support to the Korean People's Republic in its struggle against "foreign imperialism." As a result, the Japanese government, acting on orders from SCAP, suspended publication of the newspaper.

Less than two weeks after the North Korean invasion began, the first signs of Communist sabotage in Japan were reported by the press. Following a statement by the Attorney General that antiwar campaigns and sabotage in transportation facilities were occurring frequently in connection with the Korean war, the Chief of the National Rural Police on July 7 alerted his men to possible destructive action by the Communists.* By the end of 1950 the new line had become clear. The Japanese Communist party would support the Soviet Union and assist the North Korean forces by strikes and sabotage. At the same time it would make final preparations for the "coming revolution in Japan."

The relation of this revolution to developments on the continent, as well as the Japanese Communist Party's defiant confidence in ultimate victory, is evident from Nozaka's statement published a year before the commencement of hostilities in Korea:

> Should all of Korea follow the example of China, the influence on Japan would be extremely great. The islands of Japan instead of being surrounded on three sides by capitalism and reaction would be surrounded by people's democracies and socialism. The same waters which wash the docks of Shanghai, Pusan, and Vladivostok beat also against the shores of Japan. There is absolutely no barrier which can stem this tide.[22]

*On July 28, 1950 an editorial in the *Nippon Times* noted: "It is a fact that cases of deliberate sabotage of essential communications and transportation facilities are increasing."

CHAPTER XXI

Anti-Communist Action and Problems of Internal Security

Partly as a result of increasing Japanese Communist activity and partly because of anxiety produced in Tokyo and Washington by the worsening international situation, pressure on the Japanese Communist movement was intensified and Japan's security forces were expanded following the outbreak of hostilities in Korea. Although the Security Pact concluded between Japan and the United States in September 1951 is designed primarily to protect the islands against aggression from abroad, Premier Yoshida suggested to the House of Councilors shortly before ratification of the agreement that provisions of the Pact might be invoked should the maintenance of internal security, for any reason, prove beyond the power of the Japanese government. "The Security Pact was concluded with the United States," he said, "after taking into account the possibility that maintenance of internal peace may get beyond our control."[1] Previously, it had been made clear by John Foster Dulles, chief United States negotiator of the Japanese Peace Treaty, that Japan would be expected to handle her own problems of internal security. Indeed, from action taken and plans under way prior to the signing of both the Treaty and the Pact, it is evident that Prime Minister Yoshida envisages calling upon the United States for military assistance in matters of internal security only as a last resort. Specific measures against the Japanese Communist Party have included those initiated by the occupying authorities (under General MacArthur and his successor, General Matthew B. Ridgway) and implemented vigorously by the Japanese government, as well as the private purges of Communists and their sympathizers from business and industry, purges with which the government has not officially associated itself.

PURGES OF PARTY LEADERS

As noted earlier, the first blow was struck by the Japanese government—on the recommendation of General MacArthur—in June 1950 when the twenty-four members of the Central Committee were removed from further participation in public life. Although the Party leaders immediately set up an Interim Central Directorate to serve as overt Communist headquarters, the organization's effectiveness in the legal realm was seriously impaired by the government's action. On September 8, 1951, in a second move against Communist Party leadership in Japan, the government purged members of the Shiino Directorate for activity inimical to the occupation, thereby further disrupting "legal" Communist operations.

BAN ON COMMUNIST PUBLICATIONS

On June 26, 1950, the day after Kim Il Sung's forces launched their attack against the Republic of Korea, *Red Flag* came out strongly in support of the North Korean Communists. As a result, General Mac-Arthur addressed a letter to Premier Yoshida, stating in part: "The paper gives evidence of the fact that it is not the legitimate organ of a Japanese political party but rather an instrument of foreign subversion used to disseminate among the people of Japan, and in this case particularly its large Korean minority, malicious, false, and inflammatory propaganda aimed at subverting the public mind to the prejudice of the public peace and welfare. Seditious acts of this nature cannot be tolerated in a peaceful and democratic society." The letter then called upon the Japanese government to suspend publication of the paper for thirty days. The last issue of *Red Flag* appeared the following day, carrying on the front page a large photograph of Kim Il Sung and the text of his appeal to the Korean people.

The demise of *Red Flag* on June 27 by no means marked the end of the Party's use of the press for revolutionary and anti-American propaganda. On the very next day, in place of the traditional central organ, another paper bearing the name *Flag of Peace (Heiwa no hata)* made its initial nation-wide appearance. In layout, news coverage, and editorial policy, the new central organ, formerly a regional publication, was indistinguishable from its defunct predecessor. Moreover, for the ensuing several weeks, despite suspension of a number of the most radically inclined Communist publications, many of the Party's regional, district, and Cell papers, showing little inclination to modify their outspoken stand on Korea, continued to level vicious attacks against the occupation forces and to call upon the Communists of Japan to rally in support of the Cause. This situation prompted General MacArthur to address an even stronger letter to the Japanese Prime Minister. The document, dated July 18, 1950, is included here in its entirety as it clarifies the new position taken by SCAP on the issue of Communism in Japan:

> Since my letter to you of June 26th designed to curb the dissemi-nation of false, inflammatory and subversive Communist propaganda, the international forces with which the Japan Communist Party is publicly affiliated have assumed an even more sinister threat to the preservation of peace and supremacy of the rule of law in democratic society, giving clear warning to free peoples everywhere of their

purpose by violence to suppress freedom. In these circumstances, it becomes obvious that the free and unrestricted use of the media of public information for the dissemination of propaganda to such ends by a minority so dedicated in Japan would be a travesty upon the concept of press freedom, to be permitted only at hazard to the vast proportion of the free Japanese press faithful to its public responsibility, and jeopardy to the general welfare.

In the great struggle which is now engaging the forces of the free world all segments must accept and faithfully fulfill their share of the attendant responsibility. That share as to none is greater than such as falls upon the media of public information. For there rests the full responsibility of insuring dissemination of the truth, and based upon the truth the development of an informed and enlightened public opinion. History records no instance where a free press failed in the discharge of this responsibility without inviting its own doom.

I am not concerned over any destructive influence Communist propaganda may have upon the great mass of Japan's responsible citizenry, for it has already given ample evidence of its devotion to the cause of right and justice and its ability to penetrate the mask of Communist hypocrisy. But passing events warn of distinct danger in the use by Communism of the media of public information to propagate its tenets of subversion and violence as a means of inciting the irresponsible and lawless minority elements of society to oppose law, disturb order, and subvert the general welfare. Therefore so long as Communism in Japan continues in the abuse of freedom of expression through incitation of such lawlessness, its free use of the media of public information must be denied in the public interest.

Accordingly, I direct that your government vigorously continue the measures being taken in the implementation of my aforesaid letter, and maintain indefinitely the suspensions heretofore imposed upon publication of *Akahata* and its successors and affiliates employed in the dissemination in Japan of inflammatory Communist propaganda.

In response to the General's first letter, the Japanese Attorney General's Office had suspended 113 of the more than one thousand official Communist Party publications registered with that office. The new SCAP letter stimulated the government's efforts. Another 180 propaganda sheets were immediately added to the black list. Simultaneously the Japanese police broadened and intensified the nation-wide drive against official and unofficial Communist publications. Throughout the remainder of 1950, police raids on Communist print shops, the seizure of bundles of banned literature, and the arrest of scores of publishers and distributors continued. Several hundred more Communist newspapers were suppressed for having violated Ordinance 325 which prohibited statements inimical to the policies of the Allied occupation.

During 1951 government action against Japanese Communist publications was reported almost daily in the non-Communist press from the northern island of Hokkaido to the southern tip of Kyushu. The frequency and intensity of raids increased with the rapid expansion of the Communist underground apparatus, the appearance of each new successor to the outlawed *Red Flag* calling for a new wave of police searches. In a week-long drive, late in March 1951, against a single publication—the *People's Newspaper (Jimmin Shimbun)*—the National Rural Police raided 250 print shops and distribution centers throughout Japan, arrested sixty persons, and seized more than 150,000 copies of that newspaper.[2] By the end of the year close to two thousand different Party publications had been banned and millions of copies of Communist literature confiscated, but the underground Communist presses continued to roll.

ANTI-COMMUNIST LABOR OFFENSIVE

On the industrial labor front, pressure against the Communist Party was exerted from two directions—by the government's dissolution of the pro-Communist National Liaison Council of Japanese Trade Unions and by the unofficial purge from business and industry of Communists and their sympathizers.

The government dissolved the Liaison Council on August 30, 1950 and purged its twelve leading executives. The official statement explaining the action pointed out that the organization had recognized and encouraged antioccupation activities and violence.[3] By suppressing this affiliate of the World Federation of Trade Unions the Japanese government had severed a link between the Japanese Communist Party and its international sponsors. Apart from the remnants of the once-powerful Communist-dominated NCIU (only about one hundred thousand members in 1951), most of organized labor had by the end of 1951 been combined in the National Council of Japanese Labor Unions *(Sohyo)*, founded in 1950, which was strongly anti-Communist.

A series of private purges conducted by business and industry further reduced the Communist Party's strength on the industrial labor front. These dismissals were carried out by the individual companies or industries concerned and, at least officially, had no direct connection with either SCAP or the Japanese government. Affected by the sweeping layoff of personnel were the press and radio, electric, motion-picture, mining, petroleum, rolling-stock, shipbuilding, iron and steel, automobile, printing and publishing, chemical, electrical engineering, machinery, electric-wire, food, and textile industries, as well as private railways and banks.

As a non-governmental operation, the "purges" lacked coördination and a fair, uniform standard by which to determine who should or should not be discharged. The yardstick applied by the Mitsui Mining Company, for example (which appears to have been typical), was so designed as to invite the most flagrant abuse of its presumed purpose. Consider the categories of individuals designated as "undesirable":

(1) Communists
   (a) Party members
   (b) Secret Party members
   (c) Former Party members
(2) Fellow travelers
   (a) Those whose actions can be linked to the Communist movement. Into this category fall: calling at district committees or other Party organ offices; persuading others to attend Party-sponsored lecture meetings; distributing leaflets or putting up posters persuading people to attend Party-sponsored lecture meetings; distributing or putting up leaflets or other printed materials published by district committees or cells; taking part in organizing "anti-taxation" or "give us rice" struggles; joining or persuading others to join the League for the Protection of Democracy, League of Repatriates from the Soviet Union, Democratic Scientists' League, Youth Fatherland Front, Industry Defense Congress, Japan-China Friendship Association, Japan-Soviet Friendship Association, Labor-Farmer Relief Association, and other organizations under direct Party leadership; playing or having played leading roles in various "circles" in working posts; taking part in demonstrations for aiding arrested Party members; collecting funds for relief of family dependents of Party members; contributing or having contributed to the Party treasury as so-called sympathizers; giving assistance to Party candidates in national, prefectural, or municipal elections.
   (b) Those who have taken part in labor-union activities or obstructed the company's business in the interest of the Communist movement or those who should be regarded as having done such.
   (c) Those who act or are likely to act in the manner described above.[4]

While the general attitude of the Party as well as the specific performance of Communists and Communist sympathizers in many factories and companies posed a legitimate question as to the advisability of their continued employment, the procedure used in purging individuals from business and industry admittedly gave no assurance that grave injustices would not occur. Nevertheless, it should be noted that nothing like the total number of employees vulnerable under the Mitsui-type stipulations was actually purged. In the program begun in July 1950 and almost completed by November of the same year, 10,869 "Communists and their sympathizers" were removed from Japanese business firms and key industries.[5]

CHECKS ON COMMUNIST INFLUENCE IN EDUCATIONAL INSTITUTIONS

With the beginning of the fall semester of 1950, student agitators, belonging in the majority to the Communist Party's radical "Internationalist Faction," took up the issue of the possible disqualification from teaching posts of professors sympathetic to the Communist cause* and started a nation-wide campaign of picketing campuses, boycotting examinations, and holding rallies and demonstrations in defiance of school and governmental authority. Radicalism centered in the left-wing National Federation of Self-governing Student Associations. This organization in 1950 claimed an aggregate membership of a quarter of a million students belonging to 380 self-government associations. "Student struggles" became so intense that President Shigeru Nambara of Tokyo University on October 5, 1950 sought police assistance to quell disorders on the campus as two thousand students gathered at a noisy rally and refused to heed the request of university authorities that they return to their classrooms. Similar demonstrations, accompanied by varying degrees of violence, interrupted normal educational activities throughout Japan. Radicalism reached its peak on October 17, 1950 when six hundred students from several Tokyo universities and colleges marched into the main building on the Waseda campus, surrounded the president's room where a meeting of the school authorities was being held, and demanded an "end to the red purge." Police, several hundred strong, arrived and finally succeeded in quieting the disturbance, but only after fourteen students and four policemen had been injured. One hundred forty-three students were arrested during the demonstration, which the Japanese press labeled "the worst scandal in the history of the student movement."[6] Education Minister Teiyu Amano blamed Communists and stated that dissolution of the Student Federation was "now an historical necessity."[7] President Koichi Shimada of Waseda expressed his regrets

*As early as 1949 Dr. Walter C. Eells, SCAP adviser on education, speaking at various universities on the principles of democratic education, had suggested that Communist professors be purged from Japanese educational institutions. This had brought forth a violent reaction from left-wing students in his audience, whose shouts and boos drowned out the American official. For a time during 1950 the battle cry of Japanese left-wing students was, "No more Eells."

over the campus flare-up and voiced the hope that students would reject the rule of violent force, cherish peace and autonomy, and respect the campus as a place to search for truth. He declared, however, that he would not stand idly by while a small number of students obstructed the process of education.[8] Eiichi Tanaka, Chief of the Metropolitan Police Board, called for immediate dissolution of the Student Federation.[9]

Thus, despite a desire to preserve academic freedom and despite some uncertainty and disagreement on how to reconcile this principle with the evident need for stricter control of Communists on Japan's campuses, by the fall of 1950 government and university authorities alike had come to the conclusion that some sort of control legislation might be necessary if law and order were to be preserved within the educational institutions of Japan. That local measures employed during 1950 and 1951 (such as the expulsion of Communist student agitators and the imposition of restrictions on campus student organizations) may in the future prove inadequate to cope with the potentially explosive situation was suggested in the fall of the year when the National Federation of Self-governing Student Associations opened a nation-wide protest campaign calling upon 170,000 students to rally against ratification of the Japanese Peace Treaty and the United States–Japanese Security Pact.*

THE SCREENING OF JAPANESE GOVERNMENT EMPLOYEES

Perhaps the most critical sphere of Communist activity is the government office, for there the Party member considers himself literally within the enemy camp. With the growing radicalization of the Japanese Communist Party and the mounting international tension, the necessity for removing Communists and active sympathizers from positions of public trust was deemed immediate. Accordingly, in the fall of 1950, the Japanese government decided to take action.

The Japanese Attorney General's Office estimated that about two thousand employees would be effected by the purge. There was a wide area of agreement on the need for such a measure. Chief Cabinet Secretary Katsuo Okazaki stated in August 1950 that Allied headquarters supported in principle action against Communists and Communist

---

*Student demonstrations against conclusion of a peace treaty excluding the Soviet Union and the Chinese People's Republic and in opposition to the United States–Japan Security Pact were reported from campuses throughout Japan. A large rally in Tokyo toward the end of October, for instance, was attended by seven thousand students from several colleges and universities. How radical the students had become by the end of 1951 may be judged from two incidents which occurred in Kyoto in November of that year. On November 7, two hundred leftist students attacked the car of an American missionary and the same day stoned the home of a right-wing Socialist. Five days later, more than a thousand students crowded around the Emperor in his limousine and sang the Communist International.

sympathizers within the government, adding that there was no conflict of opinion among cabinet members on the purge itself.[10] The first and major obstacle encountered by the government in carrying out its purge was the question of the legal basis for dismissing Communists in public service. So long as the Communist Party of Japan retained its legal status, it was argued, membership in that organization alone could not be construed as just cause for disqualifying an individual from a position with the government. After much discussion, government attorneys agreed that Clause 3, Article 78 of the National Public Service Law might be applied. It states that personnel may be dismissed if "they lack the necessary qualifications for a position with the government."[11]

On this basis the government proceeded, and by the end of 1950 more than one thousand "undesirables" had been removed from positions of public trust.[12] The screening process continued during 1951.

COMMUNIST CONTROL LEGISLATION

The question of whether or not it would be wise to outlaw the Japanese Communist Party has been a thorny one for the postwar Japanese government, anxious to avoid action which might call forth memories of Imperial Japan's Thought Police. Moreover, it is by no means certain that outlawing the Communist Party would accomplish the desired result. While pondering the problem, the Japanese authorities, in addition to receiving guidance from SCAP, have looked for inspiration to Australia and the United States. In Australia, consideration of the same question culminated in a hot political fight during the summer of 1951; it was put to a referendum, and the bill to outlaw the Party was defeated. The controversial Mundt-Nixon Bill in the United States is well known.

At least until early in 1950, the Japanese government's position on the matter remained fairly consistent: rather than declare the Party, as such, illegal, the Japanese authorities preferred to follow the example of their Pacific neighbors to the south and east and to judge each instance of Communist subversive activity on the evidence of the particular case. In March 1951, Chief Cabinet Secretary Okazaki confirmed that the government did not intend to outlaw the Communist Party immediately but acknowledged that the question was under active consideration. When, the same month, Agriculture-Forestry Minister Kozen Hirokawa proposed presentation to the Diet then in session of a Communist-control bill, to be sponsored jointly by the Liberal and the People's Democratic Parties, a heated controversy ensued. Views expressed during the resulting debate reflect the diversity of public opinion —or at least the Parties' strategy—on this important issue.

The Secretary General of Yoshida's Liberal Party told reporters that his organization had not decided on any measure to outlaw the Communist Party. The People's Democratic Party immediately criticized the Liberals for their refusal to join in submitting a bill concerned with what was termed the "crucial problem of the day." The objection of the Party most concerned took the form of a denunciation by the Communist Dietmen's group, who attacked the government and the Liberal Party for attempting to make political hay in the projected local elections by raising the problem of outlawing the Communist Party. The Socialist Party expressed strong opposition to the move. What appears to have been a premature announcement that Communist-control legislation was under consideration proved embarrassing for all concerned, especially the Yoshida government. Again the Prime Minister felt impelled to assure the press that he had no intention of outlawing the Communist Party immediately. On the eve of the elections, Attorney General Ohashi sought to placate public opinion by commenting upon the pros and cons of such a move. He declared that on the positive side outlawry would mean: destruction of the Communist Party as an organization of the masses; removal of legal protection from the Communists; disintegration of the Communist camp as a result of increasing feud between the Main Stream Group and the Internationalist Faction; and an all-out red purge. On the negative side, he said that the measure might: force the Communists further underground; increase the possibility of violence; and create a situation where civil rights might be violated in the attempt to intensify measures against the Communists.

By the fall of 1951, the study of Communist-control legislation had progressed to the extent that the Attorney General was able to inform the press that the government intended to submit a National Security Law to the Diet. This law, as proposed, would include provisions for banning general strikes, for controlling assembly and demonstrations, and a stringent press code. It was rumored that in its final form the new legislation would also embody sections of the once-feared Peace Preservation Law.

JAPANESE SECURITY AGENCIES

The two special agencies responsible for Japan's internal security are the Special Investigation Bureau of the Attorney General's Office and the National Police Reserve.

The Special Investigation Bureau was established in February 1948 to supervise purged militarists, nationalists, and other individuals deemed harmful to the development of democracy in Japan. With the establishment of the Yoshida Cabinet in the fall of 1948, the Bureau's jurisdiction was extended to include all subversive elements, and in June 1949 a special division devoted to Communists and other left-wing radicals was created within the Bureau. This division was to assume an increasingly active role; by 1951 the investigation of Communist organizations and activities in Japan had come to constitute the agency's principal task.

Considerable criticism—much of it unjustified—has been leveled from time to time against what has been referred to as the Japanese postwar counterpart of the U. S. Federal Bureau of Investigation. The contradictory nature of this criticism suggests that much of it must be regarded as unwarranted: the Bureau was too small; it was overstaffed. It was a fascist organization; it was inefficient and ineffective. Personnel were not sufficiently trained or experienced; former militarists and old-line police agents dominated the organization. These and a score of other accusations have plagued the work of the Bureau and rendered operations difficult.

Until the beginning of the Korean war—and, in fact, throughout 1950—the Bureau remained very small and ineffective. With half of its eight hundred personnel in Tokyo, only a few representatives in each of Japan's forty-six Prefectures, and about twenty in each of the major cities, the agency has been forced to depend on coöperation from the National Rural Police and local police units. When one remembers that the Bureau's work has not been confined to the Communist problem and that the Communist Party alone had in the spring of 1950 more than one hundred thousand registered members, it is not surprising that the Bureau's record during 1949 and 1950 may have fallen short of Japan's needs.

The most striking failure of the Bureau was its widely publicized inability, after months of intensive search, to apprehend any but one (Shoichi Kasuga) of the ten Communist leaders who disappeared about the time hostilities began in Korea. From the Russian sector of Berlin came the editorial comment: "The Japanese and American bloodhounds have worn blisters on their feet searching for these loyal sons of the Japanese people."[13]

On August 18, 1950 the Japanese government promulgated a special ordinance for the expansion of the Bureau. This ordinance increased the staff from six hundred to twelve hundred and provided for a complete reorganization. The Director of the Bureau, Mitsusada Yoshikawa,* remained to head the new, vastly expanded organization.

"The Korean War is not a fire across the river," Premier Yoshida declared on August 4, 1950. "Communist elements in this country are

---

*Yoshikawa (born in 1907) is an able and experienced administrator who made a name for himself as procurator in the Sorge spy case in 1941-42. He is perhaps better known in the United States for his testimony, during the summer of 1951, before the Senate Subcommittee on Internal Security, headed by Senator Pat McCarran, in the course of its investigation of the activities and influence of the Institute of Pacific Relations.

conspicuously baring their characteristics of fifth columnists as well as their traitorous plots. Accordingly, we are determined," he concluded, "to take vigorous steps to prevent red disturbances."[14] As an outgrowth of the concern within Japan over the matter of security, early in August 1950, upon SCAP recommendation, the Japanese government decreed the formation of a National Police Reserve of seventy thousand men to augment the existing law-enforcement agencies. Article 16 of the decree reads: "The National Police Reserve shall be established as an organ of the Prime Minister's Office. The National Police Reserve shall be the organ which is established to supplement the strength of the National Rural Police Forces to maintain peace and order within the country and to guarantee the public welfare." The Japanese Attorney General on August 14 further stated that the National Police Reserve was to "coördinate actions to clamp down on radical ideologies."[15] Two weeks later, Prime Minister Yoshida replied on the floor of the House of Councillors to a Labor-Farmer Party member, who charged that Japan had turned fascist since the outbreak of hostilities in Korea, that the sole purpose of the National Police Reserve was to protect public order against the dangers of Communism.

If the National Police Reserve is not a military organization, it is more than a police force. Organized into four principal units with head-quarters in Tokyo, Sendai, Osaka, and Fukuoka, its members must sign up for at least two years' service. They are all volunteers (many of them depurged former Japanese officers) and range in age from twenty to thirty-five. In contrast to the rural and metropolitan police, the reservists do not live at home but are given paramilitary training in camps through-out Japan—training intended to produce a highly mobile security force.

Necessary as these anti-Communist measures and the strengthening of Japan's security forces have been, for the Japanese government to attempt to rely upon them exclusively in dealing with the Communist issue is to invite disaster. The history of Communism in Imperial Japan offers convincing proof that force alone can, at best, only temporarily solve the problem—and then at the cost of freedom and at the risk of producing latent revolutionary pressures. In an unstable Far East where Communist aggression threatens the remaining free nations, such pressures, if allowed to accumulate, could prove beyond control. Whether Communism will be victorious in Japan will hinge in some measure on international developments, but above all it will depend on the extent to which the future government of Japan will show itself superior to its prewar predecessors in solving the pressing social and economic problems of the nation.

REFERENCES

Chapter II   BIRTH OF THE PARTY

1. Lenin in conversation with Katsuji Fuse, Japanese press correspondent, as quoted in *Lenin i Vostok*. Moscow, 1925, p. 63.
2. *Zhizn Natsionalnostei*, Moscow, Feb. 16, 1919.
3. *Pravda*, Jan. 24, 1919. *Pervyi Kongress Kominterna*, Moscow, 1933, pp. 165-166.
4. Lenin, *Sochinenya* (Works). Moscow, 1932, XXIV, pp. 542-51. (Reprinted from *Izvestiya*, Dec. 20, 1919.)
5. *Der Zweite Kongress der Kommunistischen Internationale*. Vienna, 1920, pp. 31-32. A written report was forwarded from Japan. It was published in the Congress proceedings under the initials Ya. K., which are assumed to be those of the socialist Hitoshi (Kin) Yamakawa. Ya. K., *Kommunisticheskii Internatsional*. Moscow, Oct. 1920, pp. 2843-46.
6. *Die Kommunistische Internationale*. Moscow-Petrograd, 1921, p. 149.
7. Jokichi Kazama, *Mosko to tsunagaru Nippon kyosanto no rekishi* (A History of the Moscow-linked Japanese Communist Party). Tokyo, 1951, I, pp. 39-40.
8. Kanson Arahata, *Kyosanto wo meguru hitobito* (Men Around the Communist Party). Tokyo, 1950, p. 8.
9. Naimusho (Japanese Home Ministry), *Nippon kyosanto undo gaikyo* (Outline of the Japanese Communist Movement). Marked "Confidential." [1935], p. 1.
10. Eizo Kondo, *Komintern no misshi* (Secret Emissary of the Comintern). Tokyo, 1949, pp. 128-31. Arahata, *Kyosanto wo meguru hitobito*, pp. 6, 9.
11. Kondo, p. 159.
12. *Proceedings of the First Congress of the Toilers of the Far East*. Petrograd, 1922, p. 3.
13. Kyuichi Tokuda and Yoshio Shiga, *Gokuchu juhachi-nen* (Eighteen Years in Prison). Tokyo, 1947, p. 32.
14. *Proceedings of the First Congress of the Toilers of the Far East*, pp. 32-33.
15. Takaaki Tateyama, *Nippon kyosanto kenkyo hishi* (Secret History of Arrests of Japanese Communists). Tokyo, 1929, p. 68.
16. Kondo, p. 157.
17. Nippon Kyosanto Chuoiinkai Ajipurobu (Propaganda and Agitation Section of the Central Committee of the JPC). [Official history of the JCP]. No title. [Tokyo], 1932, p. 23.
18. Yoshio Shiga, *Sekai to Nippon* (The World and Japan). Tokyo, 1948, p. 168. Tokuda and Shiga, *Gokuchu juhachi-nen*, p. 32.

Chapter III   DEATH AND RESURRECTION

1. Kyuichi Tokuda and Yoshio Shiga, *Gokuchu juhachi-nen* (Eighteen Years in Prison). Tokyo, 1947, p. 33.
2. Sadachika Nabeyama, *Watakushi wa kyosanto wo suteta* (I Discarded the Communist Party). Tokyo, 1949, p. 58.
3. *Fourth Congress of the Communist International*. Abridged report. Moscow, 1923, pp. 13-26.
4. Nabeyama, *Watakushi wa kyosanto wo suteta*, p. 62.
5. Jokichi Uchida, *Nippon shihonshugi ronso* (Debate on Japanese Capitalism). Tokyo, 1949, p. 47.
6. Kanson Arahata, *Sa no menmen* (Faces on the Left). Tokyo, 1951, p. 123.
7. Naimusho Keihokyoku Hoanka Gaijikakari (Foreign Nationals Section, Peace

Preservation Bureau, Police Division, Japanese Home Ministry), "The Time for the Proletarian Youth to Arise Is at Hand," *Sekka senden kenkyu-shiryo* (Research Materials on Red Propaganda). Marked "Confidential." Mimeographed. No date.

8. *Saikin no shakai undo* (Contemporary Social Movements). Tokyo, 1929, p. 622.

9. *Asahi Shimbun,* June 6, 1923.

10. *Ve Congrès de l'Internationale Communiste.* Compte rendu. Moscow, 1924, p. 223.

11. Nippon Kyosanto Chuoiinkai Ajipurobu (Propaganda and Agitation Section of the Central Committee of the JCP). No title. [Official History of the JCP]. [Tokyo], 1932, p. 46.

12. Tadao Kikugawa, *Gakusei shakai undo-shi* (History of Social Movements Among Students). Tokyo, 1947, p. 352.

13. *Inprecorr,* July 12, 1929.

14. *Saikin no shakai undo,* p. 230.

15. *Asahi Shimbun,* Sept. 23, 1925.

16. Musansha Shimbunsha, *Musansha Shimbun ronsetsu-shu* (A Collection of Editorials from the *Proletarian Newspaper*). Tokyo, 1929.

17. Letter from Manabu Sano, Dec. 30, 1949.

18. Sambo Hombu (Staff Headquarters), *Komintern narabi kore ni juzoku suru kakushu senden kikan no soshiki oyobi jigyo* (Organization and Tasks of the Comintern and Affiliated Propaganda Agencies). Marked "Confidential." 1928, p. 9. Keishicho (Metropolitan Police Board), *Rokoku yori kikan no hojin kyosantoin-cho* (Data on Japanese Communist Returnees from Russia). Mimeographed. 1925, p. 86.

19. Jokichi Kazama, *Mosko kyosandaigaku no omoide* (Memories of the Moscow Communist University). Tokyo, 1949, p. 87.

20. Takeharu Ayakawa, *Kyosanto undo no gaiaku* (The Evils of the Communist Movement). Tokyo, 1930, pp. 32-33.

21. [Official History of the JCP], p. 55.

22. *Inprecorr,* Jan. 5, 1928.

23. Appendix to *Marukusushugi,* Mar. 1, 1928. *Inprecorr,* Jan. 12, 1928.

Chapter IV   SYSTEMATIC SUPPRESSION

1. Nippon Kyosanto Chuoiinkai Ajipurobu (Propaganda and Agitation Section, Central Committee of the JCP). [Official History of the JCP]. No title. [Tokyo], 1932.

2. Sadachika Nabeyama, *Watakushi wa kyosanto wo suteta* (I Discarded the Communist Party). Tokyo, 1949, p. 118.

3. [Official History of the JCP], cited, p. 72.

4. *Ibid.,* p. 73.

5. Naimusho (Japanese Home Ministry), *Kyosanshugi dantai kikan-shi* (Organs of Communist Organizations). Marked "Secret." 1934, p. 1.

6. *Seiji Keizai Nenkan* (Politico-Economic Yearbook), 1920-1930. Tokyo, 1949, p. 50.

7. *Asahi Shimbun,* Apr. 11, 1928.

8. [Official History of the JCP], cited, p. 81.

9. Yoshitaka Komiya, *Nippon puroretaria nenshi* (Japanese Proletarian Chronology). Tokyo, 1932, p. 431.

10. Naimusho Keihokyoku Hoanka (Peace Preservation Bureau, Police Division, Japanese Home Ministry), *Tokko keisatsu reiki-shu* (A Collection of Special Higher Police Regulations). Marked "Secret." 1939, p. 100.

11. *La Correspondance Internationale.* Compte rendu sténographique du VIe Congrès de l'Internationale Communiste. Paris, July 26, 1928.

12. *Ibid.,* Aug. 16, 1928.

13. *Sekki,* May 20, 1928.

14. Sadachika Nabeyama and Manabu Sano, *Tenko jugo-nen* (Fifteen Years Since Our Change of Heart). Tokyo, 1950, p. 59.

15. Nabeyama, *Watakushi wa kyosanto wo suteta*, p. 124. Letter from Manabu Sano, Dec. 30, 1949.
16. Katsunosuke Yamamoto and Mitsuho Arita, *Nippon kyosanshugi undo-shi* (History of the Japanese Communist Movement). Tokyo, 1950, p. 176.
17. Nabeyama, *Watakushi wa kyosanto wo suteta*, p. 127.
18. Teikoku Zaigogunjikai Hombu (Headquarters of the Imperial Association of Reservists), *Sekai imbo to Nippon kyosanto* (World Plots and the Japanese Communist Party). Tokyo, 1933, p. 41. Takeharu Ayakawa, *Kyosanto undo no gaiaku* (The Evils of the Communist Movement). Tokyo, 1930, p. 56.

Chapter V   ARMED INTERLUDE

1. Seigen Tanaka, "The Era of the Armed Communist Party," *Bungei Shunju*, June 1950.
2. Naimusho (Japanese Home Ministry), *Nippon kyosanto undo gaikyo* (Outline of the Japanese Communist Movement). Marked "Confidential." [1935], p. 1.
3. Takeshi Suzuki, *Kyosanto choyaku no zembo* (A Complete Picture of Communist Activities). Tokyo, 1932, p. 70.
4. Katsunosuke Yamamoto and Mitsuho Arita, *Nippon kyosanshugi undo-shi* (History of the Japanese Communist Movement). Tokyo, 1950, p. 206.

Chapter VI   REORGANIZATION FROM MOSCOW

1. Jokichi Kazama, *Mosko kyosan-daigaku no omoide* (Memoirs of the Moscow Communist University). Tokyo, 1949, p. 280.
2. Sanzo Nozaka, *Bomei juroku-nen* (Sixteen Years in Exile). Tokyo, 1946, p. 16.
3. *Nippon mondai ni kan-suru ketsugi rombun-shu* (Resolutions and Theses Pertaining to the Japanese Problem). Moscow, 1934, p. 6.
4. *Ibid.*, pp. 26-27.
5. *Ibid.*, p. 49.
6. Naimusho Keihokyoku (Police Division, Japanese Home Ministry), *Shakai undo no jokyo* (The Social Movement). Marked "Confidential." 1931, pp. 92-93.
7. Sadachika Nabeyama, *Watakushi wa kyosanto wo suteta* (I Discarded the Communist Party). Tokyo, 1949, p. 138.
8. *Ibid.*, p. 139.
9. Naimusho Keihokyoku Hoanka (Peace Preservation Bureau, Police Division, Japanese Home Ministry), *Kaigai yori no sayoku senden insatsubutsu-shu* (A Collection of Printed Left-wing Propaganda Materials from Abroad). Marked "Confidential." 1937, p. 88. Excerpts from Ichikawa's testimony are contained also in revised form in Shoichi Ichikawa, *Nihon kyosanto toso shoshi* (A Short History of the Japanese Communist Party). Tokyo, 1946, pp. 202-214.
10. Nabeyama, *Watakushi wa kyosanto wo suteta*, p. 140.
11. Koji Yogo, *Nippon kyosanto no kohan ni tsuite* (On the Public Trial of the Communist Party of Japan). Tokyo, 1932, p. 7.
12. *Ibid.*, p. 27.
13. Okano (Sanzo Nozaka), "The War in the Far East and the Tasks of the Communists in the Struggle Against Imperialist War and Military Intervention" (Report of Comrade Okano at the XIIth Plenum of the Executive Committee of the Communist International). Moscow, [1932], pp. 8-10.
14. *Ibid.*, p. 52.
15. Naimusho (Japanese Home Ministry), *Kyosanshugi undo gaikan* (An Outline of the Communist Movement). Typewritten. [1934].
16. Naimusho (Japanese Home Ministry), *Gaikaku dantai no honshitsu* (On Communist Front Organizations). Typewritten. [1934].

17. Teikoku Zaigogunjinkai Hombu (Headquarters of the Imperial Association of Reservists), *Sekai imbo to Nippon kyosanto* (World Plots and the Japanese Communist Party). Tokyo, 1933.

18. Naimusho Keihokyoku, *Shakai undo no jokyo.* 1932, p. 71.

19. Naimusho Keihokyoku Hoanka (Peace Preservation Bureau, Police Division, Japanese Home Ministry), *Tokko geppo* (Monthly Report of the Special Higher Police). Marked "Confidential." Aug. 1932, pp. 7, 110; Sept. 1932, pp. 7, 134.

20. *Kyosanshugi dantai-kei kikanshi-cho* (Data on Official Publications of Organizations Having Communist Affiliations). From files of the Japanese Home Ministry. Marked "Secret." 1934, p. 1. "Some Experiences from the Activities of the Communist Party of Japan in the Army," *The Communist International,* July 20, 1934.

21. Okano, *The Revolutionary Struggle of the Toiling Masses of Japan.* (Speech Before the Executive Committee of the Communist International.) Moscow, 1933, p. 28.

22. Naimusho, *Kyosanshugi undo gaikan.*

23. *Zennozenkoku Kaigi* (All Japan Peasants' Conference). From files of the Japanese Home Ministry. [1934].

24. Naimusho, *Kyosanshugi undo gaikan,* Sec. II.

25. Manabu Sano and Sadachika Nabeyama, *Nippon kyosanto oyobi Komintan hihan* (Criticism of the Communist Party of Japan and of the Comintern). Tokyo, 1934, pp. 32, 60.

26. Yoshio Shiga, *Sekai to Nippon* (The World and Japan). Tokyo, 1948, p. 145.

27. Naimusho Keihokyoku Hoanka (Peace Preservation Bureau, Police Division, Japanese Home Ministry), *Tokko keisatsu reiki-shu* (A Collection of Special Higher Police Regulations). Marked "Secret." 1939, p. 16.

28. Shihosho Keijikyoku, *Sayoku zenrekisha no tenko mondai ni tsuite,* p. 3.

29. *Akahata,* Jan. 8, 1946.

30. Okano, "Against Provocateurs—Against Splitters," *The Communist International,* Sept. 5, 1934.

31. Naimusho (Japanese Home Ministry), *Chorakuki ni aru kyosanshugi undo ni taishite* (On the Declining Communist Movement), by Commissioner Nagano Wakamatsu. Handwritten. [1935], p. 28.

Chapter VII   TIES WITH AMERICA

1. Naimusho Keihokyoku (Police Division, Japanese Home Ministry), *Shakai undo no jokyo* (The Social Movement). Marked "Confidential." 1935, pp. 26-27.

2. Seigen Tanaka, "The Era of the Armed Communist Party," *Bungei Shunju,* June 1950.

3. Shihosho Keijikyoku (Criminal Affairs Division, Japanese Ministry of Justice), *Shiso kenkyu shiryo* (Material for the Study of Thought). Special issue No. 20, marked "Confidential." 1935, p. 510.

4. *Ibid.,* p. 509.

5. Naimusho Keihokyoku Hoanka (Peace Preservation Bureau, Police Division, Japanese Home Ministry), *Tokko keisatsu reiki-shu* (A Collection of Special Higher Police Regulations). Marked "Secret." 1939, p. 16.

6. *La Correspondance Internationale.* Compte rendu sténographique du VIe Congrès de l'Internationale Communiste. Paris, Aug. 16, 1928.

7. *Ibid.,* July 26, 1928.

8. *Inprecorr,* May 17, 1928, pp. 507-508.

9. Naimusho Keihokyoku (Police Division, Japanese Home Ministry), *Gaiji keisatsu gaikyo* (Summation of the [Activities] of the Foreign Affairs Police). Marked "Confidential." 1935, p. 131.

10. Los Angeles Police Department, Files Nos. 28121-M-2 and 29203-M-3.

11. Naimusho Keihokyoku, *Gaiji keisatsu gaikyo,* p. 130.

12. Naimusho Keihokyoku Hoanka (Peace Preservation Bureau, Police Division, Japanese Home Ministry), *Komintan shin hoshin no waga kuni ni okeru han-ei jokyo* (Impact of the Comintern's New Line on Japan). Marked "Secret." Mimeographed. 1937, p. 106.

13. Naimusho Keihokyoku, *Shakai undo no jokyo*, 1935, p. 127, and 1937, p. 149. Naimusho Keihokyoku (Police Division, Japanese Home Ministry), *Shuppan keisatsu gaikan* (Outline [of Activities] of the Publishing Police). Marked "Confidential." 1935, p. 511.

14. Copy of original contained in Naimusho Keihokyoku Hoanka (Peace Preservation Bureau, Police Division, Japanese Home Ministry), *Kaigai yori no sayoku senden insatsubutsu-shu* (A Collection of Printed Left-wing Propaganda Materials from Abroad). Marked "Confidential." 1937, pp. 51-53.

15. *Ibid.*, p. 342.

16. Naimusho Keihokyoku, *Shuppan keisatsu gaikan*, p. 516.

17. Naimusho Keihokyoku Hoanka, *Kaigai yori no sayoku senden insatsubutsu-shu*, p. 264. Italicized portion underlined in original.

18. Sanzo Nozaka, *Senryaku senjutsu no shomondai* (Strategy and Tactics). Tokyo, 1949, p. 2.

19. Naimusho Keihokyoku, *Shakai undo no jokyo*, 1936, p. 127.

20. Naimusho Keihokyoku (Police Division, Japanese Home Ministry), *Beikoku Kashu chiho kyosanshugisha ni kan-suru ken* (Concerning Japanese Communist Residents in California, U. S. A.). Marked "Confidential." 1938.

21. From the files of the Japanese Home Ministry. Typewritten. No title. [1939], 36 pp.

Chapter VIII   COMMUNISM IN WARTIME JAPAN

1. Susumu Okano (Sanzo Nozaka), "The War of Aggression Against China and the Japanese People," *The Communist International*, Nov. 1938.

2. Naimusho Keihokyoku (Police Division, Japanese Home Ministry), *Shakai undo no jokyo* (The Social Movement). 1942, pp. 1329-30.

3. Naimusho Keihokyoku Hoanka (Peace Preservation Bureau, Police Division, Japanese Home Ministry), *Tokko keisatsu reiki-shu* (A Collection of Special Higher Police Regulations). Marked "Secret." 1939, p. 7.

4. Sanzo Nozaka, "Letter to the Japanese Communists (Moscow, 1936)," *Nihon minshuka no tame ni* (Toward the Democratization of Japan). Tokyo, 1948, p. 10.

5. Shojiro Kasuga, "Braving the Storm," *Zen-ei*, Oct. 1947. Naimusho Keihokyoku, *Shakai undo no jokyo*, 1938, p. 85.

6. *To Kensetsusha; Arashi Wo Tsuite; Minshu No Koe.*

7. Naimusho Keihokyoku, *Shakai undo no jokyo*, 1938, p. 86.

8. Naimusho Keihokyoku Hoanka, *Tokko keisatsu reiki-shu*, p. 24.

9. Shihosho Keijikyoku (Criminal Affairs Division, Japanese Ministry of Justice), *Sayoku zenrekisha no tenko mondai ni tsuite* (On the Conversion of Individuals with Leftist Records). 1943, p. 211.

10. Shigeo Kamiyama, *Gekiryu ni koshite* (Defying the Torrent). Tokyo, 1949, p. 151.

11. The case is discussed in detail in a 54-page report by General Headquarters, Far East Command, entitled, "Sorge Spy Ring, A Case Study in International Espionage in the Far East," released by the U. S. Department of the Army, Feb. 10, 1949.

12. Shihosho Keijikyoku (Criminal Affairs Division, Japanese Ministry of Justice), *Shiso kenkyu shiro* (Material for the Study of Thought). Marked "Confidential." 1943, No. 94, p. 705.

13. Susumu Okano (Sanzo Nozaka), *Chien-she min-chu ti Jih-pen* (The Establishment of a Democratic Japan). Yenan, 1945, pp. 19-22.

Chapter IX   PREPARATIONS AT YENAN

1. Sanzo Nozaka, "The Era of Okano Susumu," *Rodo Hyoron*, July 1949.
2. *Ibid.*
3. *Ibid.*
4. Sanzo Nozaka, *Bomei juroku-nen* (Sixteen Years in Exile). Tokyo, 1946, p. 49.
5. Nozaka, "The Era of Okano Susumu."
6. .Sanzo Nozaka, *Nihon minshuka no tame ni* (Toward the Democratization of Japan). Tokyo, 1948, p. 29.
7. Nozaka, "The Era of Okano Susumu."
8. *Ibid.*
9. Sanzo Nozaka, *Heiwa e no tatakai* (A Fight for Peace). Tokyo, 1947, p. 86. The writers have tried to retain in their translation the flavor of the original.
10. *Ibid.*, p. 28.
11. Nozaka, *Nihon minshuka no tame ni*, p. 48.
12. *Hsin Hua Jih Pao*, Mar. 22, 1944.
13. *Japanese People's Emancipation League.* New York, 1945, p. 7.
14. U. S. Government, Office of War Information, China Division, Yenan Report No. 10, Sept. 8, 1944. The italicized portion is underlined in the original document.
15. Nozaka, *Bomei juroku-nen*, p. 76.
16. *Ibid.*, pp. 83-85.

Chapter X   RESURGENCE

1. Naimusho Keihokyoku Hoanka Daiichi-kakari (Section One, Peace Preservation Bureau, Police Division, Japanese Home Ministry), *On Trends Among Communist Elements, with Special Reference to the Conclusion of the War.* Handwritten. 1945.
2. *Ibid.*
3. Naimusho Keihokyoku Hoanka Daiichi-kakari (Section One, Peace Preservation Bureau, Police Division, Japanese Home Ministry), "Confidential Report from the Governor of Kanagawa Prefecture to the Home Minister." Typewritten. Sept. 27, 1945.
4. Kyuichi Tokuda and Yoshio Shiga, *Gokuchu juhachi-nen* (Eighteen Years in Prison). Tokyo, 1947, pp. 102 and 159.
5. For an English summary of Tokuda's speech, see *Nippon Times*, Oct. 21, 1945.
6. Kyuichi Tokuda, *Naigai josei to Nippon kyosanto no nimmu* (The Domestic and Foreign Situation and the Tasks of the JCP). Tokyo, 1949, pp. 280-281.

Chapter XI   PARTY ORGANIZATION AND ADMINISTRATION

1. *Nippon kyosanto kettei hokoku-shu* (Resolutions and Reports of the JCP). Fukuoka, 1949, p. 73.
2. Kyuichi Tokuda, *Naigai josei to Nippon kyosanto no nimmu* (The Foreign and Domestic Situation and the Tasks of the JCP). Tokyo, 1949, p. 276.
3. *Nippon kyosanto kettei hokoku-shu*, p. 76.
4. *Akahata*, Feb. 5, 1950.
5. Tsunesaburo Takenaka and Shoichi Kasuga, *Saibo katsudo hayawakari* (Cell Activities Made Easy). Tokyo, 1949, pp. 8-9.
6. Yojiro Konno, *To-Katsudo no benshoho* (Dialectics of Party Activities). Tokyo, 1949, pp. 11-12.
7. *Akahata*, July 18, 1948.
8. *Akahata*, Dec. 10, 1948.
9. *Akahata*, Apr. 22, 1948.
10. *Nippon kyosanto kettei hokoku-shu*, p. 95.

11. Tokuda, *Naigai josei to Nippon kyosanto no nimmu*, p. 266.

12. Some of the details appeared in the *New York Times*, Feb. 23, 1949.

13. *Kyodo News Service* Release, Oct. 5, 1950, and *Mainichi*, Oct. 7, 1950.

14. *Kyodo News Service* Release, Nov. 24, 1950.

15. Shojiro Kasuga and Shoichi Kasuga, *Kojo shimbun no tsukurikata* (The Factory Newssheet). Tokyo, 1948, p. 13.

16. *Ibid.*, p. 14.

Chapter XII   THE LEADERS

1. Kyuichi Tokuda and Yoshio Shiga, *Gokuchu juhachi-nen* (Eighteen Years in Prison). Tokyo, 1947, pp. 13-16.

2. *Ibid.*, p. 26.

3. Tokuda, *Waga omoide* (Memoirs). Tokyo, 1948, p. 74.

4. *Ibid.*, p. 32.

5. Tokuda and Shiga, *Gokuchu juhachi-nen*, p. 70.

6. Sanzo Nozaka, *Bomei juroku-nen* (Sixteen Years in Exile). Tokyo, 1946, pp. 1-3.

7. Shihosho Keijikyoku (Criminal Affairs Division, Japanese Ministry of Justice), *Sayoku zenrekisha no tenko mondai ni tsuite* (On the Conversion of Individuals with Leftist Records). Marked "Secret." 1943, p. 9.

8. Jokichi Kazama, *Mosko kyosandaigaku no omoide* (Memories of the Moscow Communist University). Tokyo, 1949, p. 288.

9. Tokuda and Shiga, *Gokuchu juhachi-nen*, p. 108.

10. *Ibid.*, p. 110.

11. *Ibid.*

12. Yoshio Shiga, *Nihon kakumei undo-shi no hitobito* (Men Who Made Japan's Revolutionary History). Tokyo, 1948, p. 94.

13. Tokuda and Shiga, *Gokuchu juhachi-nen*, pp. 125-126.

14. *Akahata*, Jan. 7, 1950.

Chapter XIII   THE COMMUNIST PROGRAM FOR JAPAN,

1946-1950

1. *Nippon kyosanto kettei hokoku-shu* (Resolutions and Reports of the JCP). Fukuoka, 1949, p. 73.

2. Eisaburo Kobayashi (ed.), *Kyosanshugi jiten* (A Dictionary of Communism). Tokyo, 1949, pp. 276-277.

3. Nippon Kyosanto (Communist Party of Japan), *Nippon kyosanto no susumu michi* (The Road Along Which the JCP Advances). Tokyo, 1948, pp. 15-16.

4. Sanzo Nozaka, *Nihon minshuka no tame ni* (Toward the Democratization of Japan). Tokyo, 1948, p. 189.

5. Nippon Kyosanto, *Nippon kyosanto no susumu michi*, pp. 63-64.

6. Nozaka, p. 63.

7. Sanzo Nozaka, *Chusho shokogyosha no ikiru michi* (The Road to Survival for Small and Medium Businessmen). Tokyo, 1948, p. 10.

8. Nippon Kyosanto, *Nippon kyosanto no susumu michi*, p. 65.

9. Ritsu Ito, "The Agrarian Problem," *Zen-ei*, Apr. 1-15, 1946.

10. Nippon Kyosanto (Communist Party of Japan), *Nihon no josei to kyosanto no nimmu* (The Situation in Japan and the Tasks of the Communist Party). Tokyo, 1946, p. 53.

11. Nippon Kyosanto, *Nippon kyosanto no susumu michi*, pp. 50-51.

12. Matsujiro Tanaka, "The Development of the Fishermen's Movement and the Present Tasks," *Zen-ei*, May 1948.

13. Nippon Kyosanto (Communist Party of Japan), *Kitaru-beki kakumei ni okeru Nippon kyosanto no kihonteki nimmu ni tsuite* (The Fundamental Tasks of the JCP in the Coming Revolution). Tokyo, 1950, p. 42.

14. *Nippon kyosanto kettei hokoku-shu*, p. 73.

Chapter XIV   THE STRATEGY AND TACTICS OF PEACEFUL
REVOLUTION

1. Sanzo Nozaka, "Do the Basic Work," *Zen-ei*, Oct. 1949.

2. Sanzo Nozaka, *Senryaku, senjutsu no shomondai* (Strategy and Tactics). Tokyo, 1949, p. 99.

3. Nozaka, "Do the Basic Work."

4. Nozaka, *Senryaku, senjutsu no shomondai*, pp. 229-230.

5. For a detailed treatment of Communist participation in Japanese parliamentarian politics, see Evelyn Colbert, *The Left Wing in Japanese Politics* (in press).

6. Kyuchi Tokuda, *Kokkai enzetsu-shu* (Speeches before the National Diet). Tokyo, 1949, p. 3.

7. See, for example, Kyuichi Tokuda and Sanzo Nozaka, *Gikai enzetsu-shu* (Speeches before the Diet). Tokyo, 1949, *passim. Akahata*, May 1, 1948; May 8, 1948; Apr. 19, 1949; Sept. 9, 1949.

Chapter XV   MOBILIZATION OF WORKERS AND PEASANTS

1. Supreme Commander for the Allied Powers, *Political Reorientation of Japan.* Washington, 1949, p. 741.

2. U. S. Department of State, *Activities of the Far Eastern Commission.* Washington, 1947, pp. 91-93.

3. *Ibid.*, pp. 49-58.

4. Figures from *Nippon rodo nenkan* (Japanese Labor Yearbook). Tokyo, 1949, pp. 104-105.

5. *Ibid.*

6. *Asahi nenkan* (Asahi Yearbook). Tokyo, 1951, p. 279.

7. *Ibid.*

8. U. S. Department of State, *Activities of the Far Eastern Commission*, p. 92.

9. General Headquarters, Supreme Commander for the Allied Powers, Civil Information and Education Section, Press Release, Oct. 21, 1948.

10. Katsumi Kikunami, *Rodo kumiai-ron* (On Labor Unions). Tokyo, 1948, p. 30.

11. Shoichi Kasuga, *Rodo kumiai no hanashi* (The Story of Labor Unions). Tokyo, 1948, p. 260 ff.

12. *Ibid.*, p. 260.

13. *Akahata*, Nov. 22, 1945.

14. Kasuga, *Rodo kumiai no hanashi*, pp. 126-127.

15. Kikunami, *Rodo kumiai-ron*, p. 88.

16. *Ibid.*

17. *Ibid.*, p. 90.

18. *Ibid.*, p. 91.

19. Kasuga, *Rodo kumiai no hanashi*, p. 272.

20. *Nippon kyosanto kettei hokoku-shu* (Resolutions and Reports of the Japanese Communist Party). Fukuoka, 1949, pp. 80-81. Italics ours.

21. *Ibid.*, p. 80.

22. Kikunami, *Rodo kumiai-ron*, p. 110.

23. See, for example, *Akahata*, Apr. 2, 1946; Apr. 12, 1946; Apr. 18, 1946.

24. *Akahata*, May 6, 1946.

25. *Akahata*, Aug. 24, 1946.

26. *Akahata*, Oct. 13, 1946.

27. *Akahata*, Oct. 31, 1946.

28. *Jiji nenkan* (Jiji Yearbook). Tokyo, 1948, p. 250.

29. *Akahata*, Jan. 1, 1947.

30. *Akahata*, Jan. 5, 1947.

31. Supreme Commander for the Allied Powers, *Political Reorientation of Japan*, p. 762.

32. *Akahata*, Feb. 4, 1947.

33. *Nihon tokei nenkan* (Statistical Yearbook of Japan). Tokyo, 1949, p. 639.

34. Supreme Commander for the Allied Powers, *Summation of Non-Military Activities in Japan*, cited, Apr. 1947, p. 52. Hereafter referred to as *Summations*.

35. *Ibid.*

36. *Nippon Times*, July 11 and 13, 1947. *Mainichi nenkan* (Mainichi Yearbook). Tokyo, 1948, p. 103.

37. *Jiji nenkan*, 1949, p. 250.

38. *Ibid.*

39. *Summations*, Feb. 1948, p. 28.

40. *Ibid.*, Aug. 1947, p. 203.

41. *Ibid.*, Jan. 1948, p. 209.

42. *Ibid.*

43. For details see *Summations* of the period.

44. *Summations*, May 1948, p. 273.

45. *Jiji nenkan*, cited, 1949, pp. 265-266.

46. *Summations*, May 1948.

47. *Nippon Times*, Dec. 30, 1948.

48. *Rodo nenkan* (Labor Yearbook). Tokyo, 1949, p. 91.

49. *Nippon Times*, Apr. 26, 1949.

50. *Nippon Times*, June 3, 1949.

51. *Nippon Times*, Mar. 27, 1949.

52. *Nippon Times*, Apr. 14 and 15, 1949.

53. *Asahi nenkan*, cited, p. 277.

54. See, for instance, O. H. P. King's article in *Nippon Times*, June 10, 1949.

55. Saneki Matsumoto, "On the Improvement of Our Agrarian Cells", *Zen-ei*, Oct. 1948.

56. *Ibid.*

57. *Ibid.* This report, in addition to an account of Communist achievements in Sakuragi, contains a considerable number of data on Communist activity in the countryside.

58. Yojiro Konno, "Our Party's Permeation of the Village," *Zen-ei*, Feb. 1949.

59. Nobuyuki Hiraashi, "The Education of Rural Activists and the Party's Program for the Village," *Zen-ei*, Nov. 1949.

60. *Ibid.*

61. Ritsu Ito, *Nomin toso* (The Peasant's Struggle). Tokyo, 1949, p. 59.

62. Kentaro Yamabe (ed.), *Zoku to-seikatsu* (Party Life II) Tokyo, 1950, p. 93.

63. Ito, pp. 68-69.

Chapter XVI   MOBILIZATION OF AUXILIARY FORCES

1. Kyuichi Tokuda, *Naigai josei to Nippon kyosanto no nimmu* (The Domestic and Foreign Situation and the Tasks of the JCP). Tokyo, 1949, p. 265.

2. *Nippon Times*, Feb. 15, 1949.

3. Supreme Commander for the Allied Powers, *Political Reorientation of Japan*. Washington, 1919, p. 321.

4. *Nippon kyosanto kettei hokoku-shu* (Resolutions and Reports of the JCP). Fukuoka, 1949, p. 176.

5. *Ibid.*, p. 175.

6. Ryo Nozaka, "On Party Work among Women," *Zen-ei*, Jan. 1949.

7. According to the national census of 1947, the 11,800,000 women who were gainfully employed represented 46.99 percent of all Japanese women between the ages of twelve and sixty years. Office of the Prime Minister, Bureau of Statistics, *Population Census of Japan.* Tokyo, 1949, p. 199.

8. For statistics concerning the wage-price relation in postwar Japan, see Jerome B. Cohen, *Japan's Economy in War and Reconstruction.* Minneapolis, 1949, pp. 459-60.

9. *Akahata*, June 5, 1949.

10. Ryo Nozaka, "On Party Work among Women."

11. *Nippon kyosanto kettei hokoku-shu*, p. 179.

12. *Akahata*, Mar. 10, 1949.

13. Tokuda, *Naigai josei to Nippon kyosanto no nimmu*, p. 36.

14. See, for example, Sanzo Nozaka, *Nihon minshuka no tame ni* (Toward the Democratization of Japan). Tokyo, 1948, p. 174.

15. *Nippon kyosanto kettei hokoku-shu*, p. 102.

16. Nobumasa Yoshioka, *Nippon kyosanto no kaibo* (An Analysis of the Japanese Communist Party). Tokyo, 1948, p. 188.

17. Tokuda, *Naigai josei to Nippon kyosanto no nimmu*, p. 265.

18. *Ibid.*

19. *Ibid.*, pp. 212-213.

20. *Nippon kyosanto kettei hokoku-shu,* p. 171.

21. *Ibid.*, p. 199.

22. *Ibid.*, p. 103.

23. *Ibid.*, p. 101.

24. *Ibid.*, p. 102.

25. In 1950 the *Nippon Seinendan*, organized loosely on a regional basis, was made up of 24,384 organizations with a total of 5,360,000 members between the ages of fourteen and twenty-four. *Asahi nenkan* (Asahi Yearbook). Tokyo, 1951, p. 274.

26. For details, see *Nippon Minshu Seinendan hayawakari* (A Brief Account of the Japanese Democratic Young Men's Association). Tokyo, 1949.

27. *Kodomo-kai no tsukurikata* (How to Set Up a Children's Club). Tokyo, 1949.

28. *Nippon kyosanto kettei hokoku-shu*, p. 249.

29. Kim Tu Yang, "The Korean Movement Is Changing Direction," *Zen-ei*, May 1, 1947.

30. Kim Tu Yang, "Toward the Correct Development of the Korean Movement," *Zen-ei*, May 1, 1947.

31. *New York Times*, Apr. 26 and 27, 1948.

32. *Ibid.*

33. *Ibid.*

Chapter XVIII   A NEW STAGE IN THE STRUGGLE FOR

POWER

1. *For a Lasting Peace; For a People's Democracy* (Organ of the Information Bureau of the Communist and Workers' Parties), Bucharest, Jan. 6, 1950.

2. "Reconsideration of the Democratic Revolution in Japan," *Chuo Koron.* Jan. 1949.

3. *Akahata*, Jan. 9, 1950.

4. Sanzo Nozaka, "My Self-criticism," *Zen-ei*, Mar. 1950.

5. *Ibid.*

6. *Daijuhachi-kai kakudai chuoiinkai hokoku kettei-shu* (Reports and Resolutions of the Eighteenth Plenum of the Central Committee). Tokyo, 1950, p. 2.

7. *Ibid.*, p. 41.

8. *Kitarubeki kakumei ni okeru Nippon kyosanto no kihonteki na nimmu ni tsuite* (On the Basic Tasks of the JCP in the Coming Revolution). Tokyo, 1950, p. 5. Italics ours.

9. *Ibid.*, p. 13.

10. *Ibid.*, p. 14.

11. *Ibid.*, p. 26.

12. *Akahata*, May 31, 1950.

13. *New York Times*, May 16, 1946.

14. *Kyodo News Service* Release, Oct. 21, 1951.

15. *Atarashii Sekai*, July 1951.

16. *Pravda*, Aug. 25, 1951. *Izvestiya*, Aug. 25, 1951.

17. Kinya Niizeki, *International Communism and Japan* [Japanese Foreign Office]. Mimeographed. Aug. 20, 1951.

18. The new Party Regulations were first published in *To-katsudo shishin* (Party Activities' Guide), Apr. 1951, and reprinted in *Zen-ei*, May 1951.

Chapter XIX   FACTIONALISM

1. *Nippon kyosanto kettei hokoku-shu* (Resolutions and Reports of the JCP). Fukuoka, 1949, pp. 74-75.

2. Yoshio Shiga, "A View of Party History", *Zen-ei*, Sept. 1947.

3. Shigeo Kamiyama, "A Reply to 'A View of Party History,' " *Zen-ei*, Oct. 1947.

4. *Zen-ei*, Nov. 1947.

5. *Ibid.*

6. *Akahata*, Sept. 30, 1949.

7. *Akahata*, Jan. 13, 1950.

8. *Akahata*, Apr. 15, 1950.

9. *Dai-juhachikai kakudai chuoiinkai hokoku kettei-shu* (Reports and Resolutions of the Eighteenth Plenum of the Central Committee of the JCP). Tokyo, 1950, p. 41.

10. *Akahata*, Apr. 15, 1950.

11. *Ibid.*

12. "For a Strengthening of Bolshevik Unity Within the Party," *Akahata*, Apr. 20, 1950.

13. *Akahata*, May 2, 1950.

14. *Zenkoku daihyosha-kaigi ni okeru Shiino gicho no ippan hokoku* (General Report of Chairman Shiino to the National Conference of Party Representatives). Tokyo, 1950, p. 19.

15. *Kyodo News Service* Release, Aug. 28, 1950. *Yomiuri*, Aug. 29, 1950.

16. *Jiji*, Aug. 29, 1951.

Chapter XX   INTERNATIONAL RELATIONS

1. Kyuichi Tokuda, *Naigai josei to Nippon kyosanto no nimmu* (The Domestic and Foreign Situation and the Tasks of the JCP). Tokyo, 1949, p. 247.

2. Exclusive interview with representative of Kyodo News Service in *Nippon Times*, Jan. 7, 1946.

3. Tokuda, p. 236.

4. *Akahata*, Apr. 7, 1946; reprinted in Sanzo Nozaka, *Nihon minshuka no tame ni* (Toward the Democratization of Japan). Tokyo, 1948, pp. 151-53.

5. The writers possess copies of numbered Party instructions marked "Secret" and having a direct bearing upon liaison work with Russian agencies. Use of these documents for scholarly purposes must await their verification and analysis.

6. See, for example, "SCAP Reminds Soviet of Repatriation Obligations," Press release, Public Information Office, Far East Command, GHQ, Tokyo, Sept. 8, 1948. "SCAP Makes Offer to USSR to Aid Winter Repatriation," same source, Oct. 25, 1948. Additional details are contained in the numerous statements of the United States representative on the Allied Council for Japan.

7. Tokuda's denial of the allegation is contained in an official Party publication, *Watakushi wa nani wo yosei shita ka* (What Did I Request?), Tokyo, 1950; and in a pamphlet published by the Party, *Hikiage seisaku wo abaku* (The Truth about the Repatriation Policy), Tokyo, 1949.

8. As quoted in "The Matter of Secretary General Tokuda's Request," *Nippon Kyosanto Kaibo*, June 1950.

9. The substance of his remarks appeared in the *Nippon Times*, May 11-14, 1950.

10. Haruki Aikawa, "Balance Sheet of the Democratic Movement in the Soviet Union", *Zen-ei*, Mar. 1950. As of November 7, 1949, 650 issues had appeared.

11. Toshi Futaba, *Shiberiya ni iru Nippon furyo no jitsujo* (The Truth about Japanese Prisoners in Siberia), Tokyo, 1948, p. 135; and numerous conversations with former prisoners of war.

12. *Dai-juhachikai kakudai chuoiinkai hokoku kettei-shu* (Reports and Resolutions of the Eighteenth Enlarged Plenum of the Central Committee of the Communist Party of Japan). Tokyo, 1950, pp. 47-50.

13. Sanzo Nozaka, *Atarashii Chukoku to Nihon* (The New China and Japan). Tokyo, 1949, p. 111.

14. Japanese Communist policy as regards trade relations with China has been taken up by Nozaka in numerous articles, speeches, and statements. A pamphlet by the same author and published by the Japanese Communist Party's Kanto District Committee, *Chu-Nichi boeki to Nihon no shorai* (Sino-Japanese Trade and the Future of Japan), Tokyo, 1949, contains the best summary of the Party's ideas on the subject.

15. Interview with the International News Service representative, reported by H. Handleman, INS Far Eastern manager, in *Nippon Times*, Feb. 4, 1949.

16. *Akahata*, Sept. 21, 1949.

17. Nozaka, *Atarashii Chukoku to Nihon*, p. 114.

18. *Nippon kyosanto kettei hokoku-shu* (Resolutions and Reports of the JCP). Fukuoka, 1949, p. 52.

19. Based on the period May-August 1949.

20. *Akahata*, May 28, 1946.

21. Kyokuto Jijo Kenkyukai, *Kyokuto Tsushin*, June 21, 1950.

22. Nozaka, *Atarashii Chukoku to Nihon*, p. 109.

Chapter XXI   ANTI-COMMUNIST ACTION AND PROBLEMS
OF INTERNAL SECURITY

1. *Jiji*, Oct. 15, 1951.

2. *Kyodo News Service* Release, Mar. 29 and Apr. 2, 1951.

3. *Mainichi Shimbun*, Aug. 31, 1950.

4. *Kyodo News Service* Release, Oct. 13, 1950.

5. *Kyodo News Service* Release, Nov. 22, 1950.

6. *Mainichi Shimbun*, Oct. 18, 1950.

7. *Asahi Shimbun*, Oct. 19, 1950.

8. *Kyodo News Service* Release, Oct. 16, 1950.

9. *Kyodo News Service* Release, Oct. 18, 1950.

10. *Kyodo News Service* Release, Aug. 31, 1950.

11. "Law No. 120, Oct. 21, 1947," *Roppo Zensho* (Compendium of Laws). Tokyo, 1949, (Section on Administrative Laws), p. 24.

12. *Kyodo News Service* Release, Nov. 17, 1950.

13. *Neue Welt*, Jan. 1951.

14. *Kyodo News Service* Release, Aug. 4, 1950.

15. *Kyodo News Service* Release, Fukushima, Aug. 14, 1950.

Index

Note: JCP is used throughout as abbreviation for Japanese Communist Party.

Communist Party, Soviet, Control of Comintern, 43; JCP modeled on, 90
"Communist Party of Japan," leaflet, 13
Communist Youth League, 40
Congress of Industrial Organizations (U. S.), 149, 204
Conservatives, Japanese, rural strength (1949), 167, 168
Constitution, Japanese, JCP program for, 126-127; women's rights, 171. *See also* Supreme Commander Allied Powers
Control Commission, JCP, 90, 93-95, 118
"Conversion of Individuals with Leftist Records" (Ministry of Justice), 114
Converts to JCP, case studies, 187-198
Cultural Association (Waseda campus), 18
Cultural offensive, JCP, 169-170

Daily Worker, 64
Dawn People's Communist Party, 1921 establishment by Kondo of, 12; failure, 13-14, 17; American ties with, 61
Democracy, JCP definition of, 124-126
"Democratic centralism," 216-217
"Democratic front" activity, 106, 154, 158
Democratic League of Korean Youths in Japan, 183
Democratic Party (Japan), 99, 100n, 208
"Democratic people's republic," JCP concept of, 124
Democratic revolution, 1950 Thesis on, 207
Democratic-Liberal Party (Yoshida), 168
Democratization Leagues, 159-162, 208
Diet, Japanese, 3, 4, 19; 1928 elections, 27, 29, 30; May Day demonstrations, 41; wartime strictness, 71; JCP members, 95, 110, 111, 115, 116, 126, 136, 227; JCP attacks on, 138-140; labor reform laws, 143; women members, 171; Segregated Communities' members, 185; repatriation of Japanese war prisoners, 232; Communist Control legislation, 249-250
Dimitrov, Georgi, Seventh Congress (Comintern), 68; aid to Nozaka, 74
District Committees, JCP, 96
Dobashi, Kazuyoshi, 147, 187-189
"Dodge Plan" (U.S.), success of, 161, 162
"Dollar diplomats," 49
Draft Thesis, 1931, 46
Draft Thesis, 1950, 132-133, 202-207
Drugs, JCP funds from, 103
Dulles, John Foster, 242

Economic demands, JCP (1946–1950), 127-132
Economic Stabilization Program ("Dodge Plan"), 161-162

Educational institutions, checks on Communist influence on, 247-248
Eells, Dr. Walter C., 247 n
Eighth Route Army, Chinese, 76, 82
Election-campaign funds, JCP, 100, 102
Elections, 1947 Communist influence, 157, 167; 1949 Socialist Party strategy, 167
Ely, Richard Theodore, 112
Emperor Hirohito, assassination plot, 112
Emperor institution, JCP program and attitude on, 16-17, 126; 1932 Thesis, 46, 47; Emancipation League, 80; SCAP directive, 88; tradition and wartime changes, 125-126, 135; 1950 Thesis, 205-206; demonstration by students against, 248 n
Engels, Friedrich, 108, 216, 219
Espionage, JCP funds for, 101
Eta. See Segregated Communities
Expansionist policy of Tanaka government, 34.
"Exploiting class," analysis in 1932 Thesis of, 46

Far Eastern Bureau, Shanghai, 35
"Far Eastern Cominform," 235 n
Far Eastern Commission (Allied), labor reforms sponsored, 143, 145
Far Eastern People's Congress (1922), 61, 109
Far Eastern Socialist Conference (1920), 10
Farmers, JCP work among, 53-54, 131, 148, 163-168
Federal Bureau of Investigation (U.S.), 66, 251
"Feudalistic remnants," 44, 206, 217
Finance, commerce, and industry, JCP program on, 127-130
Fishermen, JCP work among, 53-54, 132, 163, 164, 168
Food shortages, 173-174
Foreign and Domestic Review, 214
Formosa, nationalist movements studied by Peace Preservation Bureau, 32; capture of Watanabe, 35; Communists and JCP, 122
"Fractions," 150-154. *See also* Labor Unions
Front organizations, JCP support of, 100-101, 105-106
Fuchu Prison (near Tokyo), 88, 110
Fukumoto, Kazuo, career and influence on JCP, 25-26, 120-121; arrest (1928), 35 n; Stalin-Trotsky dispute (1927), 43; jail sentence, 49
Fukuoka, sale of drugs at, 103; Horizon Movement, 185; National Police Reserve headquarters at, 252

Unions. *See* Labor unions

United Nations landings, Inchon (Korea), 240

United Nations nationals, Korean-Japanese question, 181

United Press, on Cominform criticism, 201

United States, "dollar diplomacy," 49; influence on JCP from, 59; policy toward occupation of Japan, 88, 145; food for Japan, 158; economic stabilization program, 161; decline of prestige in Far East, 200; Memorial Day demonstration against soldiers, 207-208; occupation position on JCP, 209; JCP aims to weaken prestige in Asia, 227-228; aid to Japan on internal security matters, 242; position on communist control legislation, 249. *See also* Supreme Commander Allied Powers

United States–Japan Security Pact, attacks on, 212; provisions for internal security, 242; student rally against, 248

"United States Post-Surrender Policy," document quoted, 88

United States–Soviet conflict, Nozaka on possibility of, 222

Universal Manhood Suffrage Act (1925), 29, 67

University students and professors, JCP enrollment of, 170-171

Vancouver, B.C., JCP activity, 61, 62

Vanguard, 15, 17; description of contents, 104-105; on women's activity, 173-174; on Korean problem, 182, 238; Shiga-Kamiyama controversy, 219-220

Villages. *See* Farmers

Vladivostok, Arahata leaves Moscow for, 20; liaison, Russia and JCP, 23-24; Thought Police at, 33, 60

Voitinsky, Gregory, Comintern representative to Far Eastern Socialist Conference, 10; Shanghai Thesis Conference, 21 n

Wang Ching-wei, Japanese puppet at Nanking, 76

Wang Hsueh-wen, 76

Waseda University, 18; student agitation, 247-248

Watanabe, Masanosuke, leader in early "Communist Group," 22; Bukharin July Thesis (1927), 26; Nagoya riots, 34-35; Secretary General, JCP, 35; capture and death, 35-36

Wednesday Society, 12-13, 109

Woman Communist in Prison, A, 32 n

Women, JCP recruitment of, 171-175

Women's suffrage (1946), 171

Workers, JCP mobilization of, 148-149. *See also* Labor unions, Proletariat

World Federation of Trade Unions, 157, 162; 1950 Thesis on, 206; affiliation with National Liaison Council, 245

World Peace Congress, 1950 Thesis on, 206

World War I, effect on Japan of, 6, 9, 67

Yamakawa, Hitoshi, 10-13, 15 n, 27; arrest, 6; activity in founding of JCP, 14; quoted in *Vanguard*, 15; defection from JCP, 20; rejection by Bukharin July Thesis, 26

Yamamoto, Kenzo, union leader at Sixth Congress Comintern, 33, 34 n; evades arrest, 37; representative to Profintern, 37; disappearance, 59 n

Yamamoto, Masami, organizer (1933) captured, 56-57

Yanson, Jacob D., Soviet Embassy Trade representative, 26; head of Far Eastern Bureau, 35

Yasuda (family trust), 13

Yenan, Nozaka 1940 activity, 73-82; Seventh Congress, Chinese Communist Party, 128; Nozaka's antiwar work, 134

Yokahama, Tanaka activity at, 39, 40; JCP printing shop seized, 55; Okamoto incident (1937), 62-63

Yoshida, Shigeru, cabinets formed by, 126, 140; influence and power of, 136-137; JCP attacks on, 138, 166, 208-209, 240; strikes to overthrow, 155; efforts to break left-wing power, 160; demonstrations against, 162; rural strength of, 167-168; Korean problem, 181; SCAP orders to purge JCP and ban *Red Flag*, 210-211, 243; relations with Communist China, 237; U.S.–Japan Security Pact, 242; communist control legislation, 249-250, 251-252

Yoshihara, Taro, 9

Yoshikawa, Mitsusada, 251

Young people, enlistment of, 175-178

"Youth Action Corps," 177-178

Zaibatsu (big family trust), 128 n; Allied Occupation breakup of, 205

Zinoviev, Gregory, 11, 16, 20; President Second Congress of Comintern, 8; plans for Japan, 13